How to do just about everything you never thought you could -- and save money at the same time!

- Take the "squeak" out of a stairway
- Maintain an oil furnace
- Check dampness in your home
- Thaw out a frozen car lock
- Open jammed windows

Dozens and dozens or jobs, from plumbing and appliance repair to painting and hanging pictures, from outdoor gardening to indoor house cleaning—all included in this fabulous time and money-saving guide.

Charlotte Slater, whose fix-it advice column for the *Detroit News* now appears in over 150 newspapers in the United States and Canada, has put together an altogether marvelous handbook that no one should be without.

All the Things Your Mother Never Taught You

Charlotte Slater

Artwork by Detroit News *Staff artist*
Richard R. Rinke

BALLANTINE BOOKS • NEW YORK

Contents

PART I: Easy Repairs and Decorating Jobs

PART II: Electricity and Appliances

PART III: Common Problems in Plumbing, Heating and Cooling

Contents

PART IV: Working with Wood

PART V: Working on the Outside

PART VI: Taking Care of Your Car

PART VII: Odds and Ends

All the Things Your Mother Never Taught You

When Charlotte Clater began writing a fix-it advice column for the Detroit NEWS, she brought—in terms of mechanical experience—nothing to aid her.

In fact, she says "I was chosen to do this column because I know absolutely nothing about mechanical repairs. The idea was that I, a dummy in these matters, could explain basics to other dummies once I found out how to do a particular job.

"The result is that I started from scratch on each column, seeking advice from professionals in whatever field. If I don't feel I have a solid understanding of a project, I don't write it."

This collection of ALL THE THINGS . . . contains over 140 basic household and automotive repair jobs. From plumbing and appliance repair to painting and hanging pictures, this volume is a valuable aid to any person prepared to meet the challenge of doing-it-yourself and saving money.

It is a handbook to liberate women from the tyranny of waiting—for a husband to make repairs on the weekend between games on TV)—waiting for the plumber or electrician to come by sometime next week —waiting for the bill.

The Detroit NEWS created this how-to-fix-it service two years ago. The feature now appears in over 150 newspapers in the United States and Canada.

All the Things Your Mother Never Taught You

Part I:

Easy Repairs and Decorating Jbos

1 / How to make repairs around the house

There is one kit that no woman should be without. Not a make-up kit, not a set of heated curlers—it's a tool kit so you can make your own minor home repairs. And two general rules apply to a woman's tool kit:

First—never "save money" by buying the cheapest thing you can find. A poorly made hammer or screwdriver is not only a nuisance in the long run, but can actually be dangerous. Second—you should be able to lay hands on that kit at a moment's notice. That means "Hands Off, Kids!" (Maybe Dad, too.)

Drill—Drills come with several sized "bits" and there are many jobs that will require a drill. Electric models are not extremely expensive and sometimes double as sanders. But if the thought of an electric drill rather unnerves you, get a hand drill. It's not hard to turn.

Wrench—Start with an adjustable pipe wrench. Wrenches are used for turning square or hexagonal nuts and come in handy for things like plumbing. But all that comes later.

Hammer—Get a little tack hammer if you wish, for just that—tacks and similar lightweight fasteners. But the "old reliable" in your kit should be a good, solid claw hammer. That's the kind with the split end opposite the striking face of the head (claws are for pulling nails *out*). Make sure your claw hammer is well made.

Pliers—Pliers with a slip joint are good, since they will open a little wider than with a standard joint. Some pliers double as wire cutters—something I personally find very handy. But take a good look at what you have. Wirecutting pliers have a sharp scissor section that comes together between the joint and the toothed gripping portion. If you grip a nail with a wire cutter you will trim it in half.

Saws—You need a regular hand, or crosscut, saw for wood and a hack saw for metal. There are many kinds of special saws you'll have no need for, just ask for a small general purpose saw for wood.

Screwdrivers—You should have two sizes (large and small, naturally) of the regular flat blade type and two of the Phillips type. Phillips has a crossed blade that looks like an X on the end. It is possible to buy a "mix-and-match" set that has a handle and several kinds of blades which can be inserted—but they are more trouble than they're worth.

Level—A gismo that does exactly what its name implies; it shows you whether something is level or not.

Nails, screws, etc.—A hardware store can advise you on what common sizes would be best to keep on hand around the house. Suggestions, for starters, are 3-16 or ¼-inch bolts, washers and nuts; No. 6 or No. 8 wood screws 1 to 1¼ inches; 4 or 6-penny finishing nails (they don't have heads), and upholstery tacks.

Plunger—You may call it a "plumber's friend." It is the most common device for unstopping drains and toilets.

Incidentals—Other things that can be of help include a utility knife, extension cord, various grades of sandpaper, a cleanout auger (called a "snake;" it is run down drainpipes to break up obstructions), a stapling gun, extra electrical fuses (unless you have circuit breakers) and lubricating oil.

2 / A guide for picking the correct glue for the job

Buying a bottle of glue sounds like a simple chore—until you enter a large hardware store. Customers today have a choice of hundreds of different glue brands and compositions. And each one is designed for a specific job.

So here's a guide listing some glue types, sample brand names, and uses for which each type is best:

White vinyl glue (like Elmer's Glue-All, Ko-Rec, Dupont, Sears and Ward's white glues, Glu-Bird, Polyseamseal, Titebond and Evertite). Good for bonding wood, fabrics, paper, leather and cork. It's not, however, water- or weather-proof and cannot withstand high stress. Also among vinyl emulsions are specialties like Builders Adhesive and Concrete Adhesive, used for bonding furring strips to concrete or coating cured concrete, respectively.

Rubber cement (like Gripit, Ozite AP880, Scotch Grip 77, Brite Magic, High-Tack 975, Reliobond and many others simply named "rubber cement"). Most rubber cements can be used in the regular way or as "contact" cements. This means coating two objects with glue, letting the glue dry until "tacky" and then pressing the two pieces together. Good for nearly all general household chores, especially with paper products. But it cannot take great stress.

Contact cement (like Devcon Rubber, Pliobond, Craftsman Contact Weldwood, Fire-Safe, Duro and Duratite contacts). These behave somewhat the same way as rubber cement, but are a little stronger. Good for bonding plywood wall panels, veneers, plastic composition panels, nameplates, linoleum.

Mastic adhesive (like Webtex 200, DAP, Franklin and Ruscoe panel and tile adhesives). Mastics, like contact and rubber cements, retain a certain flexibility. Good for big-area jobs like bonding acoustical tile to plaster or concrete, paneling, repairing loose brick or slate.

Epoxy glue, clear, white or metallic finish (like Plastic Steel, Helor Quik-Set, Poxy Putty, and a long list of brands with the word "epoxy" included). Among the strongest glues on the market, with high resistance to weather and water. Involve two agents which must be mixed together to "create" the glue. Good for structural bonding of wood, metal, concrete, tile, glass, china and some plastics (not Teflon, polyethylene or polypropylene).

Formaldehyde adhesive (like Craftsman, Weldwood and Wilhold plastic resin glues). Good for structural bonding of wood, very strong, but are not weather resistant and should be used only on indoor furniture.

Resorcinol glue (most brands include the name "resorcinol"). A high strength, weather-proof agent especially good for outdoor wood furniture; also porous surfaces like cork, cardboard. Two ingredients must be mixed.

Silicone adhesive and sealant (like Duratite 48, Ward's vinyl repair kit and other brands with "silicone" in the name). Although it remains flexible, this glue is water resistant and can take temperatures up to 500 degrees (the high point for most glue is 120 degrees). Good for sticking things to bathroom tile, sealing breaks in dish racks, bonding pottery, glass, metals, also works on some plastics.

Plastic cement (like Duco, Liquid Solder, Scotch Super-Strength, Wilhold China & Glass, Duratite 65 and other brands with "plastic" or "model" in the name). Not particularly strong or weather resistant, but will bond glass, metal, wood and is suited to most types of plastic except polyethylene (garbage cans, laundry baskets, squeeze bottles), polypropylene heat-sterilizable bottles, plastic hinges) or Teflon. For these plastics, try silicone.

3 / If your door brake loses its whoosh

Pneumatic doors closers are those aluminum cylinders, usually about 10 inches long, that wheeze slightly and keep your storm or screen doors from slamming.

If the whoosh has gone out of yours, there may not be much you can do about it. Manufacturers have arranged it so the less expensive door closers can not be taken apart. You can replace the entire unit for about $4 (or more or less, depending on quality).

Most door closers contain a disc and spring attached to the rod that slides in and out of the back of the cylinder. The disc slides to the back of the cylinder as the door is opened.

As the door closes, the disc pushes its way back toward the front of the cylinder, compressing the air it meets along the way. This air resistance is what keeps the door from slamming.

The compressed air must naturally have an escape hole; and the speed with which it escapes determines the pressure or resistance.

If your door is slamming shut, one of two things is probably wrong. Either the disc inside the door closer is no longer functioning (which will necessitate a new unit)—or else the air-escape adjustment is wrong.

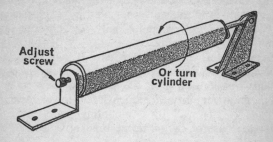

If the door takes forever to close, there are three possibilities. Either something is obstructing the action of the door itself (remove the closing device and try the door alone)—or the spring inside the door closer is shot (the unit will have to be replaced)—or, again, the air-flow adjustment is wrong.

Look for a small screw located at one end of the cylinder (either front or back) and turn it to adjust the air flow.

Some models have no adjustment screw. These models are often changed by turning the entire body of the cylinder forward or backward.

Cheaper door closers sometimes can't be adjusted at all. In such cases, the air-escape system may be just a tiny hole at one end of the cylinder. Keeping the hole free of paint and mud is about the only option.

4 / Help for a shaky towel rod

Does your bathroom towel rack wiggle on the wall? Or did it recently come crashing to the floor? Towel rack styles vary wildly and these directions might not fit your bracket.

But towel racks generally fall into four categories: Glued or stuck to the wall, cemented into tile, fastened with screws that show and, finally, the chrome racks with no screws showing.

We will deal with the latter here. If something goes wrong with the first three types the remedy is pretty obvious—either new glue, tile cement or new screws.

The great majority of hidden-screw towel racks are fastened to the wall by a mounting plate concealed under the base of each chrome bracket. (See sketch.)

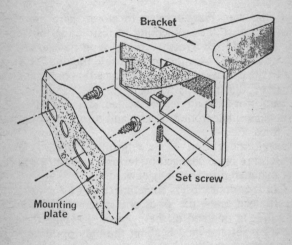

Bracket

Set screw

Mounting plate

Some brackets slip over a blade on the mounting plate; some cling to the mounting plate's turned-up "lip" with the aid of a set screw.

When a towel rack becomes loose, you need to take it off the mounting plate to determine the trouble. There are two general methods in removing the rack. One of them should work in most cases.

First, look at the bottom side of each bracket for a tiny hole that hides an equally tiny screw. If you find it, use a miniature screwdriver or perhaps the point of a nail file to unfasten the screw.

If you find no set screw, try simply lifting up on

the bracket. Most styles that slip on over the blade or screws do so in an up-and-down direction.

Now check the screws holding the mounting plate to the wall. Many towel rack "kits" provide screws that are too short. If the mounting plate screws seem to be coming out of the wall, you may need to make a quick trip to the hardware store for screws that are 1½ or 1¼ inches long.

The screw holes in the wall may have become enlarged. If so, fill them in with a substance like patching plaster or wood filler, let it dry and put the screws into the same holes. On a plaster or hollow wall you may need to buy some plastic "sleeves" that fit inside the screw holes and expand to a tight fit when the screw is inserted.

The sleeves are usually about a quarter of an inch in diameter. You will need to enlarge the screw hole to a quarter inch with a drill before inserting the sleeve.

If the mounting plate is firmly in place on the wall, the towel rack's problem is probably just a loose set screw (that little one on the bottom of the bracket).

Lost or stripped set screws can often be replaced by a plumbing supply house or a very well-stocked hardware store. But set screws come in many sizes. So take the towel rack bracket (or the old set screw) along for a match.

5 / Removing old tile is a chore

Planning to take up old linoleum, floor tile or rubber-backed carpeting? The best advice possible is: Don't.

Both tile and linoleum are pried and scraped up from the floor. Professionals often use a machine that acts like an air hammer working sideways. But if rental companies have the devices for the general public, the companies are few and far between. The best a do-it-yourselfer can hope for is a chisel, a large putty knife and a hammer.

Many fix-it books recommend heating each floor tile with a propane torch before removal. This helps soften the adhesive but it also presents the possibility of a scorched floor, a burned hand and various other catastrophes.

One alternative is to use the household iron turned to high heat. Place a damp rag between iron and tile to keep the iron plate clean. Heat does not affect all tiles, however.

Once the tile or linoleum is removed, the remaining glue must be scraped away to make a smooth surface for the new flooring. The adhesive is usually flexible, but paint thinner will often soften it even more. Another method is to let the exposed adhesive dry for a couple of days until hard and then sand it away with a rented floor sander.

Since removing old tile can be so difficult, the best way to recover that floor is to put new tile right over the old, if possible. Glue down any old tiles that are loose and fill in missing pieces with the cheapest tiles you can get. In short, make the old surface smooth and secure.

Remove the small wooden molding strip around the edge of the floor and the metal strips at the doorways. Be sure to remove all wax from the old tile floor, either with a solvent or by light sanding.

Some new tile is put down with spread-on adhesive, other types have a sticky back and can simply be pressed in place. No matter which you choose, install the new tile so the seams do not match the seams on the old floor. This will give the new flooring a more secure bond. (See sketch.)

Old indoor-outdoor carpeting is the next thing to

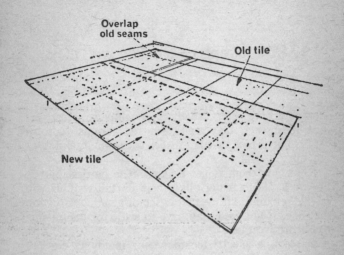

being permanent. If you must try taking it up, solicit sympathy cards in advance from your friends.

New rubber-backed carpeting can be had in tile-sized squares which pull up rather easily. But no one was thinking ahead when much of today's kitchen carpeting was installed several years ago.

There is no solvent that will loosen the carpet. It must be pulled up with the help of a putty knife and a 20-mule team. Much of the rubber backing will remain on the floor, stuck to the glue.

Unlike the adhesive for tiles, carpet glue usually "sets up" hard after installation and cannot be softened. It (and the foam rubber on top of it) must be sanded down until at least smooth and level—if not completely gone.

The area can then be covered with new "stick-and-stomp" tiles or carpet squares.

An installation tip: Use a rolling pin to press new squares flat and assure a complete bond.

6 / How to replace cracked bath tiles

The bathroom isn't usually a roughhouse area (although to each his own). But for various reasons, ceramic wall tiles or soap dishes occasionally crack or fall off the wall.

Replacing them is not difficult. The hardest part is finding a tile to match the others on the wall. If you have a few tiles left over from the original construction job, fine. If not, you may have to settle for contrasting or decorative tiles.

There is a special technique for removing cracked tiles or soap dishes from a wall. First scrape away the grout that white plaster-like substance) from around the edge of the tile. Use an old screwdriver or thin chisel.

Next, you must pry the old tile away from the wall. But do not pry from the edge. This puts pressure on the neighboring tile and may crack that one too. Instead, chisel a hole in the center of the damaged tile and pry or chip from there.

Scrape any remaining cement or mastic (glue) from

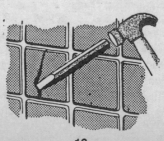

the wall where the removed tile was situated. What you're after is a nice flat surface for the new tile.

Spread or "butter" the back of the new tile liberally with mastic, a special adhesive for such jobs. When you buy mastic (at hardware or tile stores) be sure to tell the man what kind of tile you are using. Mastic for plastic and metal-backed tile is different from that used with ceramic tile.

Center the "buttered" new tile where you want it on the wall. You may want to crisscross it with long strips of masking tape after it is in place to hold the tile snugly against the wall while the mastic sets. Check package directions for length of setting time. Heavy soap dishes can be taped the same way; or you can prop them in place with a long stick braced against the opposite wall.

The last step is filling the border area of the tile with new grout (available the same place you buy your mastic). Mix the grout according to package directions. Press it into the seams around the new tile with your thumb.

Wipe excess grout away with a damp cloth; then let it dry for about 15 minutes. Check the tile every 15 minutes and keep wiping it clean until you are sure no film of grout is left on the tile. If you let it dry completely on the face of the tile, you'll have to remove the film with a razor blade or steel wool.

If you are replacing a half piece of tile, you will need to cut a full piece to size. Ceramic tile is best handled with a glass cutter, available inexpensively at hardware stores. Scribe the slick surface of the tile with the glass cutter. Then place a long nail under the tile beneath the scratch mark. Press down on both ends of the tile and it will break along the cut mark you have made.

7 / How to replace glass in a metal frame window

Replacing the glass in metal-frame windows is much the same as replacing it in wooden windows, with one exception—there are no glazier points.

Instead, you use what's called a spring clip, which looks something like a heavy bent hairpin, plus the usual prepackaged putty available in any hardware store.

The most common metal frames found in homes are in steel basement windows and aluminum storm and-or sliding windows.

One nice thing about basement windows—the putty is generally on the inside (they can also be taken off their hinges) so you don't have to crawl around outdoors.

First Step, remove remaining pieces of broken glass from the window (wear garden gloves). If glass is not broken out, but is cracked in several directions, try pasting a sheet of heavy paper over the glass with rubber glue. Then, when you knock the first piece out, the rest will not fall on you all at once.

Next, scrape the old putty away with a chisel or heavy screwdriver, removing the wire spring clips as encountered. Save them or buy new ones.

After the putty is removed, you should have a bare inset area with the rail or backstop exposed where the glass used to rest. (See sketch.)

Measure the width and length of the inset area, subtracting ⅛ inch from each figure. You now have the size of the new glass, which can be cut for you at a hardware, glass or lumber shop.

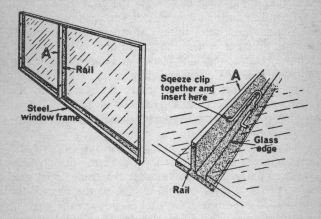

Before setting in the new glass, put a moderate layer of new putty on the rail where the glass will rest. This makes a cushion and weather seal. If the glass has a slight bulge to it, turn the convex side to the outdoors.

Now Comes the fun—putting in the spring clips. Looking at the clip itself, notice that one arm is straight and the other is wavy. At the end of each arm is a little "branch" bent at a 90-degree angle.

Along the sides of the steel window frame are several small holes (area A in sketches).

When the spring clip is in place, the wavy arm will be against the glass. (The curved part of the arm is beside the edge of the glass, pushing the glass sideways; the little branch at the end wraps itself OVER the edge of the glass, pushing the glass against the rail.)

This isn't as complicated as it sounds. Insert the branch end of the straight arm in one of the frame holes, letting the wavy arm rest flat against the glass. Now slide the wavy arm back along the glass toward the edge of the window frame, squeezing the clip together. When you reach the edge of the glass, the clip will snap into place. See sketches.

Roll Putty into fat "worms" and apply it all around the edge of the glass, covering the spring clips and extending a half inch or so onto the glass. Smooth the putty with a knife and paint it if you wish.

Aluminum-frame (sliding) storm windows come in several different styles and are usually very easy to remove, frame and all. They can be repaired within minutes at any window specialty shop. So it might be worth your time to simply carry the window to the shop and pay the labor charge ($4 or $5).

If you want to try it yourself, there are a few generalizations:

The glass rests against a rail (just like wooden and steel-frame windows), but is held there with glue instead of putty. You can simulate the commercial glue by applying a layer of rubber glue to the face of the rail PLUS a perimeter of rubber glue on the edge of the glass (about a half-inch wide). Let both surfaces dry, then press the glass into place. The two glued surfaces will stick together.

How To Get at the rail? Check the metal frame around the glass. There should be a rubber gasket or strip that runs around it, against the glass. If quite a bit of the gasket shows (about a quarter-inch), the strip simply pulls out (start it with a screwdriver). When you are through, it pushes back in place.

If you can barely see the edge of the gasket, the metal frame probably has to be knocked apart (although some are held together with screws). In either case, be very careful pushing either gasket or frame back together. Too much pressure will break your new glass.

8 / Fix leaded windows painlessly

Leaded windows are undeniably charming. But they are too expensive to repair, some home owners say.

The objection is valid, since many shops charge $15 an hour to repair such relics.

You must first determine whether the panes in your window are bounded by lead or by zinc.

Scratch the metal hard with your thumbnail. If the metal feels fairly smooth and you can see clear scars or scratches on it afterward, it is lead. Zinc will feel slightly rough and will not yield easily to pressure.

Pull the pieces of the broken pane entirely free of the leading. Wear work gloves; use pliers if you need to.

You should now be able to see the sunken channel in the leading where the glass used to rest. Clear any old putty or cement out of the channel with a screwdriver. Don't press any harder than you must, or you'll take some lead too.

Take the window off its hinges if possible, placing some kind of support under the glass section for the remainder of the work.

If the window is true lead, clip the four corners as shown in Sketch A with a pair of wirecutters or a linoleum knife.

Bend the four lead sides upward with your fingers or a pair of pliers. Take it easy. Old leading will sometimes crack if bent too far.

Now measure precisely to determine how large a piece of glass will fit into the opening you have created. Any glass shop will cut a piece to order for you.

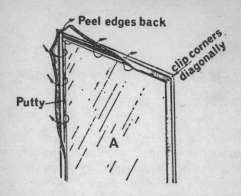

Lay the new glass into the cavity. Then pack the channel area beneath the turned-up leading with putty or glazing compound as in Sketch A.

Press the bent leading back down into place with a wooden spoon handle. Do this carefully or you will bend the entire leading network or break the pane you just installed.

This process will squeeze some of the putty out onto the glass but it can be scraped or wiped off later.

Solder the cracks where you clipped the corners. If the lead sides cracked during repair, they can also be soldered.

If your window is zinc, forget trying to bend it.

Measure precisely the top-to-bottom length of the hole to be filled, not counting the recessed channels.

Now measure precisely the width of the hole plus the depth of one channel (usually about an extra one-eighth of an inch). This will allow you to slip the glass into the cavity, side first, without disturbing the surrounding metal.

Fill the bottom channel with plaster of Paris mixed thin enough to pour. Let it harden while you go to the glass shop.

After slipping the new glass into the cavity, center it within the side channels (the top edge of the glass will not extend into its channel). See Sketch B.

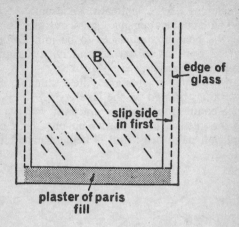

plaster of paris
fill

Now work putty or glazing compound in under the edge of the leading as well as you can with your fingers. Allow the putty to stiffen for a couple of days; then paint the white edges gray.

If you are replacing an odd piece of glass like a leaf or a flower, the measuring will be tricky. Tracing a paper pattern will help. The idea is to adjust the measurement (for zinc windows) so that about half the glass will come within the channels and half will rest on a plaster base.

9 / How to repair loose countertops

The plastic laminate on a countertop occasionally comes loose at the corner. When it does, it's nothing but an increasing annoyance. Sleeves catch on it. Food and water collect under it.

Refastening of the laminate can usually be accomplished with contact cement. Contact cement is the kind where you coat both surfaces to be joined, allow the two glued portions to dry separately, then smack the two surfaces together.

Many contact cements are quite flammable. So heed any warnings printed on the label.

Since countertop laminate cracks if you try to bend it too far, lift the loose corner up only far enough to slip a small paint brush full of cement under it.

Leave a blob of glue under the laminate. Then mash the countertop material down to spread the blob evenly. Lift the laminate up again and prop it with a pencil stub, an old fork or a putty knife to allow the two glue surfaces to dry. Make sure glue is extended clear to the edge of the counter and the laminate.

After the glue has dried for the time recommended on the label, press the laminate firmly back down, working from the center of the counter out toward the edge. A rolling pin can help you get firm, even pressure.

If your countertop problems are more severe— burns, buckling, warping—you may have to give up the idea of doing anything yourself.

Such problems usually mean replacement of an entire section of laminate. It's evidently the very devil to remove, coming off in bits and pieces with great difficulty.

10 / Solder—A handy talent to have around the house

Being able to solder may not sound like the most glamorous claim in the world.

But a rudimentary knowledge of soldering can come in very handy for lots of small repair chores around the house. You can often fix broken jewelry, fill a hole in a metal pail or fuse the stranded ends of an electrical wire with a drop of solder.

There are different kinds of solder and soldering irons. But the amateur repairman doesn't need to know about all of them.

Two general-purpose solders that are easy to use are acid-core solder and rosin-core solder. They both look like hefty wire and come wound on spools. Both contain a central core of material that acts as a "flux"—a cleaning and bonding agent. (Plain solder without a core requires application of a separate flux to the material being worked on.)

If you have to choose just one solder to keep around home, rosin core is probably your best choice. It can be used on both ferrous and nonferrous metals (either jewelry, wires or metal pails). Acid core works well on ferrous metals (those containing a portion of iron). But the work must be washed well after soldering or else the acid of the core will start corroding the metal. This makes acid core impractical for electrical connections and for some jewelry.

You can forget about trying to solder stainless steel, aluminum or chromium. They take special fluxes and solders and are too difficult for the novice.

Solder is made from tin and lead. Good quality solders that melt fast have a ratio of about 60 per cent tin to 40 per cent lead. The higher the lead content, the harder it is to melt the solder.

Home soldering irons are of two general types. One is the kind that looks like a fat screwdriver with a cord on the end of it. The other is a soldering gun, which looks like a pistol with a couple of sturdy wires in place of the barrel. It works with a trigger.

The rod irons are commonly available for home use from 30 watts to 100 watts in capacity. They all get hot enough for soldering. But the larger the iron, the larger its heat output and the larger the soldering job you can do.

Soldering guns have the advantage of heating up much faster than soldering irons. But many models continue to heat as long as you hold the trigger down, and you can melt the piece you are working on.

There are two basic rules for soldering.

First: the metal to be worked on must be free of paint and absolutely clean. Use a scouring soap pad on it, then rinse and dry. Or use steel wool and dry cleaning fluid. There can be no oil or dirt on the metal at all. That means keeping your fingers off the cleaned surface.

Second: The material to be repaired is your melting medium—not the soldering iron. This means that the iron is really used only to heat the material being worked on. The heated material then melts the solder. Solder applied to cold metal will not adhere.

Before beginning to solder, you must "tin" the end of your soldering iron. Tinning is simply coating the tapered point of the iron with solder. This makes the iron transfer heat more efficiently to the piece you're working on.

Don't try to tin the iron after it is red hot. The solder will just bead and make a big mess. Instead, hold a piece of wire solder against the end of the iron as the iron heats (see sketch A). When the solder begins to melt, spread it around over the whole tip of the iron. The iron has now reached the proper temperature for work.

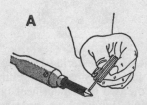

Put the piece of metal you're working on in some kind of vise. If you have a metal shop vise, fine. If not, put your clever brain to work. Wooden clothespins make good clamps for holding small objects.

Even if you have a metal vise available, it is a good idea to place thin pieces of wood or asbestos shingling between the vise edges and the metal you're working on. This keeps the heat from spreading out and being partially lost in the metal of the vise.

If you are mending a cracked piece of metal, place the two cracked edges as close together as possible. Then lay one tapered, tinned angle of the soldering iron on the crack to heat the working surface.

Touch the soldering wire to the heated crack, just in front of the iron's point. When the temperature of the working surface gets high enough, the solder will melt into and over the crack.

Move the soldering iron slowly on down the crack following it with the solder wire (see sketch B). At no time do you try to melt the solder onto your work by placing the wire under the end of the iron. Let the heated work surface do the melting job.

When dealing with something intricate like a cufflink or a piece of jewelry, you probably will not have a nice straight crack to work on.

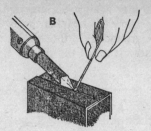

In cases where the soldering iron won't reach both surfaces to be joined, try "tinning" both surfaces.

Then place the two tinned surfaces face to face and use the soldering iron to heat the larger of the two pieces (or the easier to deal with). Keep the iron as close to the area to be joined as possible. As the larger piece reaches temperature, the two tinned surfaces should join satisfactorily.

Beginners shouldn't try soldering really valuable jewelry. And before you work on anything, try your skill on pieces of scrap metal.

11 / How to remove old wallpaper

Human nature being what it is, most people apply new wallpaper right over the old—which is fine, up to a point.

But there comes a time when accumulated layers on a wall must be removed. In an old house, you may discover as many as six layers of wallpaper in one room. What is worse, the paper layers may be interspersed with coats of paint.

If you don't like messy jobs, call a professional wallpaper remover. But if you are set on doing the job yourself, the time-honored method of steaming is still the best.

Wallpaper steamers can be rented by the day. Styles vary, but all heat water in a central container, then send steam up through a hollow plate with holes in it. Hold the steam plate against the wall for 30 seconds or so, then carefully scrape the wallpaper loose with a large putty knife (see sketch).

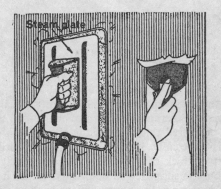

Work from the baseboards up. Steam rises and you will make your work easier this way.

Consider the ceiling. If it is papered and you don't want to remove its covering, leave the doors and windows of the room open during the steaming process (again, because the steam rises).

Steaming through layers of wallpaper is hard enough. But paint layers will make the job harder. Paint keeps the steam from penetrating to the bottom level of the wallpaper.

The remedy is to somehow pierce the accumulated layers, giving the steam entrance. Gadgets for scratching the wall surface are available in some hardware stores.

But if you don't want to buy anything, take a hefty block of wood and drive several nails through it until the nail points protrude just a fraction of an inch (see sketch). Then scrape this block up and down the wall to score the paint or wallpaper surface.

You don't want to scratch deeply enough to mar the actual wall underneath, so soak and chip away a small area of accumulated wallpaper first. Measure the thick-

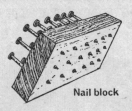

Nail block

ness of the built-up layers and make sure the nail points on your scraper block are just a hair shorter than the measured thickness of the layers.

This is especially important with wallboard walls (that sort of thick cardboardy substance).

Wallboard is supposed to be painted before it is ever papered. If it isn't, the paper will never come off and the wallboard is ruined. If your nail block pierces the protective paint layer on wallboard, the steam will soak into the wall and you will have a real mess.

A tip on making the nail block: If the wood is quite thick, try drilling holes where you want the nails to go; the nails will be easier to drive and will go in straighter. Just make sure the drilled holes are smaller in diameter than the actual nails. Otherwise, the nails will come right out.

You generally don't need anything like a nail block or steamer to remove just one or two layers of wallpaper. A rag soaked in hot water will often do the trick on a single layer. And some of the newer vinyl or fabric coated wallpapers are supposed to pull off without any water at all. Start with a corner and pull diagonally.

12 / Here's how to wallpaper your walls

Today's wallpapers are so imaginative and varied they can make plain painted walls seem like the dullard's way of decorating.

But is papering something you can handle yourself? How do you start?

In picking the wallpaper, go for the pattern that pleases you and the finish that will serve your purpose best. There are vinyls, combination cloth and vinyls, plain paper, flocked, unpasted, prepasted.

Have a good talk with your local wallpaper store manager and explain just what you want and what you'll do with it.

There are also different kinds of wallpaper paste. Ask him to recommend one that will work for the paper you pick out. Prepasted paper has a glue already applied to the back. But it isn't mess-free; you have to dip it in water. So if the paper you like is the regular kind without glue on the back, go ahead and get it. It won't be much messier than the newer variety.

Figure how much paper you will need by adding up the square footage of the walls you'll cover. Multiply the length of the wall by its height. A wall 20 feet long and 8 feet high will contain 160 square feet. Subtract from this the square footage of any doors and windows you'll be going around (width of the window times its height).

Different wallpapers come in different widths. But either the package or the store salesman should tell you how many square feet per roll you can expect from your chosen paper. (Most single rolls will cover 30 square feet.)

Even after the paper and paste is bought, you aren't nearly ready to start covering the walls.

You have to prepare the surface first. The walls must be: (a) reasonably clean; (b) smooth; (c) painted in some cases; and (d) sized.

Do not try to paper over a slick surface like old vinyl wall covering or enamel paint. Pull off any vinyl wallpaper; go over gloss enamel walls with medium sandpaper.

Scrape and sand any areas of peeling paint or plaster. If there are several layers of old wallpaper, consider removing them—especially if the old paper has begun to buckle or peel.

Remove the cover plates from wall switches. Turn off the electricity to the affected room before fooling with any wires. Then remove any wall light fixtures, disconnecting the wires from the fixtures.

Fill any gouges or nail holes with patching plaster or premixed compound. Allow the patches to dry, then sand smooth. Minor ripples and cracks in the wall can be taken care of with spackling compound, a plasterlike substance that you spread thinly on the wall with a flexible putty knife.

Most old walls will have been painted at one time or another so they don't need to be repainted. Just wash them well and rinse with a damp sponge.

But any new wall—especially dry-wall construction —should have a coat of oil-based primer for interior walls before papering. You can also use alcohol-based primer-sealer. Get your wallpaper man's recommendation.

Papering over a "dry wall" that has never been painted will make it almost impossible to remove the paper later without ruining the wall surface.

The last step is to apply a coat of what is called sizing. See the man you bought the paper and paste from.) Sizing is applied much like a paint—a roller will work fine. You can skip the primer paint on a fresh plaster wall or plaster patch if you wish. But it does need a coat of sizing.

Many people claim they have papered for years without using sizing. But sizing will make the papering job much easier for you. If not only makes a better bonding surface for the paste; you can also move the pastey paper around lots easier to correct minor alignment mistakes.

Decide where you are going to start. Behind a door is a good place. Measure the width of the paper—let's say it's 18 inches. Now hang a plumb line from the ceiling molding 18 inches (or slightly less) out from the edge of the door.

A plumb line is a simple device. Just cut a length of string the height of the wall. Tack one end firmly to the ceiling molding. Hang a heavy nail at the other end of it. Run chalk up and down the string. Then, holding the bottom of the string firmly against the wall, snap the string as you would pluck a guitar, to mark the wall. This is your paper guide.

Mix the wallpaper paste according to package directions and apply it with a wide paste brush to the back side of your first strip, spreading paste to all edges.

Now fold the paper gently into thirds (do not crease), as shown in the sketch, glue side to glue side. Let the paper sit this way for two or three minutes to "relax" and adjust itself to the wet paste.

Foil paper is best hung by applying paste to the wall rather than the paper. This lessens the chance of creasing the foil.

Unfold the top section of the pasted paper and place it on the wall, lined up with the chalk mark. Allow the paper to overlap baseboard and ceiling molding by about 3 inches. You'll trim it later with a razor blade.

Stroke the paper flat onto the wall with a dry "smoothing" or wall brush. Then unfold the bottom section of the paper and smooth it down the length of the wall.

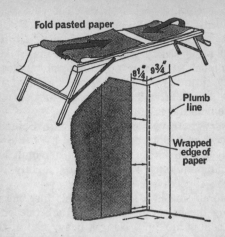

Go over the newly hung and trimmed strip with a sponge wrung out in clear water—the whole strip, not just the edges. This removes traces of paste and finger marks. Also wipe the molding clean.

The edge of the second strip of paper should abut (not overlap) the edge of the first strip. This is where previous "sizing" of the walls becomes important. Sizing makes the paper much easier to slide.

Paper right over any holes for electrical outlets, etc., then cut the hole out with a razor blade. Roll the seam or adjoining edges of each two strips of paper with an "oval" seam roller (a wooden wheel device). Do not roll the seams of flocked paper, Trim and wash each new strip as you go along.

Measure the distance from the last strip to the wall corner. Measure in three or four places, since corners are invariably a bit out of plumb. Use the widest measure you come up with—let's say 8 inches—add ¼ inch, and cut the paper to this width (see sketch).

Apply the strip to the wall, letting the extra ¼ inch wrap around the corner (the wrapped portion may be slightly uneven, but don't worry).

Now get out your plumb line again. The remaining

strip of cut paper is going to be (in this case) 9¾ inches wide. Make a chalk mark 9¾ inches out from the corner on the new wall. Then hang the left-over strip, lined up on the chalk mark.

Going around windows is something else again. The method depends on how much paper overlaps the window, etc. But it is quite acceptable to do something similar to the cornering, cutting a strip to fit the space between last strip and window, then patching in above and below the window with what is left of the strip.

13 / How to hang drapes evenly

My relationship with traverse rods has been such that I usually refer to them as travesty rods.

When putting up rods for draw drapes in a new apartment, everything looks fine until you hang the drapes, pull them closed and discover they are coming together somewhere off to the side instead of in the middle.

The remedy is amazingly simple. Describing it is the only hard part.

The two metal "carriers" that run back and forth on the rod when you pull the cords are called slides. When pulled together in a closed position, one overlaps the other slightly.

The one in front—the overlapper—is called the master slide. The one in back—the overlappee?—doesn't really have a name; but it's the important one when it comes to adjustments.

Things will be easier if curtains are taken down, although the rod can stay up.

Look at the back side of the secondary (no-name) slide. You should see a rope threaded over a little "bridge." Close by will be a metal or plastic prong around which the rope loops to keep the slide in place. (See sketch.)

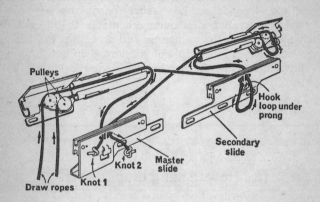

Pulleys

Hook loop under prong

Secondary slide

Knot 2

Master slide

Draw ropes   Knot 1

To center the slides, pull the draw ropes until the slides are as far "open" as they will go.

Unloop the rope from its prong on the secondary slide. Maintain moderate pressure on the draw ropes. If no one is there to help, you can even tie the ropes in a knot—anything to hold the slides in the open position.

With the rope unlooped from its prong, you can now simply push the secondary slide by hand as far toward the end of the rod as possible. Loop the rope back around the prong and you're ready to hang drapes.

If the ropes on your traverse rod have somehow been taken out, the sketch will give the best idea of how they should be installed.

Briefly, the shorter rope runs straight in over a pulley and attaches to the master slide. The longer rope enters at the same side, runs underneath the master slide, continues across the slot and bridge of the secondary slide, goes on to the opposite end of the rod and wraps around a pulley, then runs back the length of the rod, under the secondary slide and attaches to the master slide. (Follow the path of the rope in the sketch with a pencil as you re-read this paragraph and it won't be so confusing.)

14 / Wash draperies in your own home

You can wash draperies in your own home just like professionals do it in a shop. The only requirements are these:

You must know the fabric of your drapes, whether washable or not. And you need a sturdy clothesline, preferably outdoors.

Fabrics that must be dry cleaned should naturally not be washed. Also steer away from washing fabric-lined drapes (the lining may shrink) or pure cotton or antique satin drapes. They also will shrink unless guaranteed preshrunk at the time of purchase.

But synthetics usually wash well, as do sheers. If, after all precautions, your drapes do shrink, a professional cleaner can usually stretch them back again.

Dab some warm water and detergent on the back side of the drapery hem to test for color fastness. Blot the spot with a white cloth. If the color bleeds, better forget doing the drapes yourself.

Once you have determined that the wash job can be done, fill a smooth tub (the bathtub is good) with water and laundry detergent at about bath temperature —warm, not hot. Make the detergent mixture mild to moderate; a low sudsing detergent is best.

Remove the drapes from the traverse rod, but leave

the hooks on the drapes. You'll need them again soon and they won't get in your way during washing.

Wash drapes in pairs so that one curtain won't get any cleaner than its mate. Press the drapes down into the soapy water, putting the drapery-hook end of one curtain at the opposite end of the tub from the other. Do not scrub the drapes, but agitate them gently up and down in the water. A plunger or "plumber's helper" is a good prod and will save your back.

The whole point of this project is to be gentle. The sun often weakens drapery fabric. Machine washing and drying is harder on weak fabric than hand treatment is.

After about 15 minutes of soaking and agitating the drapes, it is time to rinse them. Do not wring the fabric out before rinsing.

Instead, lift the drapes up and let some of the soapy water drain out of them. Then transfer them straight to a sturdy clothesline or wire, hanging the drapes by their hooks just as they would hang at a window, spread fully.

The next step is to bring out the garden hose. This is why you need an outdoor clothesline or one over a basement floor drain. Spray the drapes with the hose to rinse.

Use a moderate spray (too hard may damage the fabric) and start at the top, giving special attention to the "header" or top hem. Work the spray on down the length of the drapes on both sides, making sure all soap is flushed away.

Let the drapes drip dry on the line, hang just as they are. You can help keep the permanent pleats in the header from losing their form. Fold the pleats into proper shape. Hold them at the top with one hand. With the other hand, strip the water out of them with a downward motion (see sketch A). Don't go past the header into the main portion of the drape. You can pin the header pleats to shape if you want. But this will slow down the drying process and may leave a crease.

When the drapes are dry, reinforce the header pleats with an iron heated to a temperature appropriate for the fabric; also touch up the rest of the drapery quickly if needed.

Most drapes are supposed to have easy, rounded pleats down the body. You can't get this effect with an iron.

After pressing the drapes, hang them by the hooks again—either on a line or at the window. Gather them into accordion pleats by hand and staple or tape wide strips of paper or cloth around the drapes at intervals

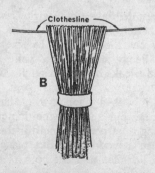

of a foot or two (see sketch B). Leave them that way for about a day.

Sheers should be washed the same way as regular drapes. But most sheers do not have drapery hooks.

So when it comes time to rinse, spread the sheers out full over two strands of clothesline.

Caution: If you wash fiberglass drapes, be sure to clean the tub out well afterward. These curtains leave a thin film of glass particles in the tub. The particles are irritating to skin, so wash your hands well too after doing the drapes.

15 / How to install Formica

Installing Formica over a whole kitchen counter is more than most amateurs could or should tackle. But you might want to try it on a smaller scale.

Formica is a brand name. The stuff is actually called something like laminated countertop material. But no one knows what you're talking about when you say that.

It really is best to have an electric saw—the finer the tooth, the better. If you don't have one, maybe a neighbor will cut the Formica to size for you. It won't cut with heavy shears or a knife. Formica is rather brittle and breaks off at odd angles unless you're careful.

You can cut it with a hack saw (a hand saw designed for metal), but support the material well at both ends, leaving a narrow channel for the saw blade. You can also use a wood saw. But place a piece of wood under the Formica and cut both pieces at once.

Turn the decorative face of the Formica down when using a circular saw, upward when using other saws. Cut the Formica $\frac{1}{16}$ too large on all sides, if possible. You can trim it back later, unless you're covering an inset or bordered area.

Sand any old finish off the wood you want to cover (or at least roughen the surface). Liberally spread contact cement with a paint brush onto the back of the Formica and the top of the old table (or counter, or . . .). Go all the way to the edges. Use a good strong contact glue—one designed for carpentry and home repairs. There are several on the market.

Read instructions carefully; some are flammable.

Let both glue faces dry until you can touch them without the glue sticking to your finger.

While you're waiting, collect enough waxed paper to cover the surface on which you're installing the Formica. It helps to collect a friend to help with the next step, too.

After the glue is touchable, line the Formica up on the surface you want to cover—with the paper between

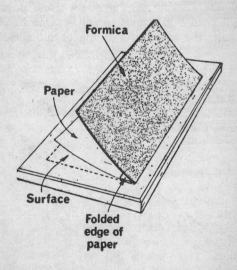

Formica

Paper

Surface

Folded edge of paper

the two glue faces (see sketch). The paper won't stick to the glue.

Pull back about half an inch of the paper at one end and press the end of the counter material onto the glued surface. Lift the loose end of the Formica just enough to pull more of the paper back. Smooth the Formica down by hand as each new area of paper is removed, until you finally secure the whole piece.

Now you need to "shock" the Formica to get rid of air bubbles and bond it really well. Smack it all over with a rubber mallet if you have one. No mallet? Then use a block of scrap wood and the sturdiest hammer you have.

Move the wood back from place to place over the Formica, covering all areas and giving the block a couple of good whacks with the hammer each time. Work from the middle of the piece outward.

To trim the edges of Formica, you'll need two metal files—one medium grade for shaping and one fine grade for finishing. Do the best you can to steady the piece you're working on. Put it in a vise if possible.

You'll need both hands for filing. One hand grips the handle; the other rests on top of and steadies the

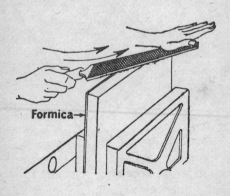

Formica→

far end of the file (see sketch). Use long strokes, going at an angle away from you. Lift the file at the end of each stroke, rather than rubbing the file both ways like an emery board.

16 / How to install mirror wall tiles

The person who dreamed up those mirror wall tiles did a great thing for cracked, ugly, lifeless walls. The squares are relatively easy to put up, too.

A sheet of directions usually comes in the package of tiles. The main points are that the wall surface has to be clean, dry and fairly smooth—and that you should rig a plumb line as a guide for your first row of tiles.

Minor wall surface bubbles usually don't cause much problem unless they fall right where you want to put one of the little stick-um pads that hold the mirrors to the wall. If one stick-um pad rides higher or lower than the other three supporting a mirror tile, it will make the tile sit like a table with one short leg.

The problem is, you usually don't discover this until the piece of mirror tile is already up. It is almost impossible to dislodge the tile from these little glue squares, although you can sometimes manage to scrape the one offending glue pad out from behind the mirror corner with a screwdriver.

You can then compensate at one of the two corners by using a blob of silicone adhesive (from any hardware store) in place of the glue pad. The silicone dries to a flexible but sturdy base. And it comes in a tube with a nozzle, so you can shoot it under the corner of a tile already in place.

To line tiles up correctly, drop a plumb line about ¼ inch inside the corner or edge you plan to start from. Fasten a string to the wall near the ceiling with a nail or tack. Tie a weight—like a heavy nail—to

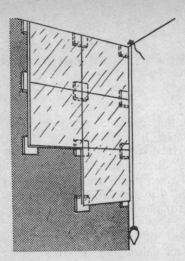

the end of the string and let it hang straight. Run chalk up and down the line. Then hold the bottom of the line secure against the wall and snap the string as you would pluck a guitar. This leaves a chalk mark —your lineup guide for the tiles.

A package of mirror tiles will rarely contain as many glue pads as you would need if you put one pad at each corner of each tile. But you can let neighboring tiles "share" pads . . . sometimes two corners to a pad; sometimes four.

As you near the end of the tiling job, you will invariably end up with a strip that is narrower than the precut tiles. (Measure first and it will be no surprise; but it will still be there anyway.)

This means cutting the last tiles to fit. Cutting glass is not a very hard job, but it does take a couple of tries to get the hang of it. Practice on a spare tile or an old piece of window glass.

Decent glass cutters cost about $1 to $1.50 at hardware stores. The cutter has a tiny cutting wheel in its nose. This wheel should be kept oiled so it will always turn freely.

Place any glass you are cutting on a sturdy flat surface. Place a folded section of newspaper under the glass. Use a wide ruler or yardstick as a guide and brace for the cutter.

Score the surface of the glass with the cutter (the face of the mirror; not the back). Bear down reasonably hard and run all the way to or off the edges of the glass. Try to do the job with just one stroke. It will give you a cleaner break.

After scoring the glass, place the tile over a pencil or table edge and press down, breaking the glass evenly along the cut mark.

If you have to go around odd shapes, like light switches or thermostats with the tiles, you can "chew" a rough circle or square into the edge of the glass tile. (Split a tile in half rather than trying to knock a chunk out of its middle.) This makes a real mess of glass powder and splinters; so wear gloves and goggles or glasses and work outdoors.

Mark the shape you want on the glass with a felt-tip pen.

The chewing is done with the slots or teeth along the edge of the glass cutter. Insert the edge of the glass into one of the slots (the one nearest the thickness of the glass) and use a "church key" can opener motion with the instrument.

17 / How to refinish hardware in older homes

Part of the charm of an older house is the hardware in it. But invariably, previous owners or renters have slopped one or more coats of paint over doorknobs, hinges and window fasteners.

Paint thinner won't touch the old paint and scraping is not practical. But you can get it off of most metals with paint and varnish remover—that gloop that you use to take the finish off of old furniture.

Paint remover may cause discoloration of some metals. But metal polish will usually bring the hardware back to its original color. Test a small or hidden spot on the metal to see what the reaction is.

Hinges and some metal fasteners can usually be removed by undoing the screws that hold them in place. Do remove hardware that you can. It makes things much easier.

Drop the hardware right down into the container of paint remover and let it soak for a few minutes. (Most brands of remover have directions that say how long it takes them to work.)

Arm yourself with rubber gloves, an old toothbrush and steel wool. Then retrieve the hardware from the gloop and scrub it well with the steel wool. Some paint removers are flammable, so read directions and heed any warnings.

After all the old paint has been loosened, wipe the hardware as clean as possible with a dry cloth. Then

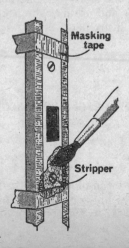

wash it with soap and water. The best paint removers will wash away well. Others leave a wax residue which must be removed with lighter or cleaning fluid.

If you can't take the hardware off of the door or window, you can still use paint remover. But the job is a little trickier, because one slip will take the paint off the woodwork too.

Protect the wood around the painted metal with wide borders of masking tape. Then carefully brush the paint remover onto the metal, allowing it the recommended time to work.

Wipe the metal clean with steel wool and a dry cloth. Several applications may be necessary.

18 / A fast brush-up in painting pointers

The two basic types of paint are oil base (thinned with turpentine) and water base (thinned with water and usually called latex).

Oil paints generally can be used anywhere—inside or out. Latex paints are most often used indoors. (There are exterior latexes on the market. But surfaces must be cleaned and deglossed very carefully according to instructions.)

Although professionals often stick to oil base products, amateurs are better off with latex paint for interior surfaces simply because of easy clean-up. Brushes and spills can be taken care of with mild soap and water before the paint dries. But it dries fast!

No matter which type you choose, it is best to buy a well-known brand. Cheap paint may seem like a bargain at first; but you will find that it doesn't cover as well.

Choice of brush or roller depends on the paint selected. The rule of thumb is synthetic to synthetic, natural to natural.

Translation: With latex paint, a synthetic or Orlon brush is usually recommended; with oil paint, a natural bristle brush.

There's a difference in rollers too. Those covered with Dacron or other synthetics are designed primarily for latex paint; oil base usually calls for a roller covered in natural lamb's wool, although this isn't a rigid rule.

It's smart to use a roller on large flat surfaces. But you'll need a brush too, for hard-to-reach crannies. (There are little corner rollers and flat spreaders on the market, but somehow one or two areas seem to crop up where nothing but a brush will do.)

Buy all the paint you'll need at one time. Like knitting yarn, paint shades sometimes differ slightly from lot to lot. This is especially true of custom-mixed colors.

Upon opening the paint can, take a hammer and nail and pound a couple of holes in the groove where the lid normally fits. Stretch a piece of heavy wire (a section of coat hanger is fine) from hole to hole as a handy place to scrape paint off of the brush. This avoids getting paint in the groove (see sketch). And when transferring paint to a roller pan, try using a soup ladle or a paper cup (for the same reason).

Putting the lid back on automatically covers and seals the nail holes, so there is no evaporation problem.

When the actual painting starts, do the brush work first—angles of walls, edges along woodwork, etc. Then whiz along with the roller, coming as close to the wall angles and woodwork as possible (brush and roller create different surfaces and you want the surface to be as uniform as possible).

Brushes should be dipped into the paint no more than one-third the bristle length. And don't "lean" on the brush while painting; forcing paint into the "heel"

Coat
Hanger
Wire

of the brush means paint will soon be running down over your hand.

If using a roller, don't carry too much paint on it and don't let the roller spin at the end of each stroke (unless you LIKE having blue freckles).

Extension handles—much like broomsticks—are available for rollers in case the paint job includes the ceiling.

Lining a roller pan can save clean-up time later. One paint dealer uses old newepapers to line his pans; he says the printer's ink doesn't streak the paint. Some people use aluminum foil. But a caution here: Aluminum will often cause latex paint to change color.

The normal order of painting? It's ceiling first, then walls, then woodwork.

One final note: There are some interesting specialty paints on the market. One is epoxy paint—a lacquer-like finish that can be used for such things as painting ceramic tile if you hate the color of your bathroom. Epoxies have two different compounds that are mixed together just before using.

Epoxy cannot be used on plastic tile. A regular oil base enamel with an undercoat is fine for plastic.

There is also a special super-tough enamel for wood or concrete floors. But be sure to remove all wax from the floor first or else the paint will stay "tacky" till doomsday.

The instructions on all paint cans should be read and followed to the letter.

19 / What to do before you tackle painting

Planning to put fresh new colors on the walls? There are a few things you should do before you start painting.

First, determine how many square feet of wall space must be covered. This really isn't hard to do: Measure the length and height of a wall and then multiply.

For instance, if a wall is 10 feet long and eight feet high, it contains 80 square feet. Each wall to be covered is measured this way (the ceiling too if you're going to paint it). The final figures are then added together to get the total square footage of the entire room.

A quart of paint usually covers about 100 square feet (a gallon 400 square feet). If you are making a drastic color change, two coats of paint may be needed, doubling your purchase.

Paint sticks best to clean, dry surfaces. So at least go over walls and ceiling with the vacuum cleaner. Since a certain amount of oil collects on walls after a couple of years, it is even better to wash the walls with a sponge and mild detergent solution—especially in the kitchen. Be sure to let the walls dry completely before painting.

The labels on some paints say no special preparation is necessary. But if you are painting over glossy enamel, it is smart to roughen the finish a bit; the new paint will adhere much better. Commercial gloss cutters are available for this; they brush on just like paint. For the really ambitious, there's sandpaper.

Buy or have on hand several large drop cloths and a big roll of masking tape. You can use old sheets as drop cloths, or disposable cloths are available in most paint and hardware stores. If using a plastic cover, remember the paint flecks may not stick to it; so fold the cover together carefully after the paint job is over.

Put masking tape wherever you want a straight, clean edge for the painted surface—where wooden molding meets the wall, on window glass next to the sash, and so on.

Remove the plates covering wall switches and electrical outlets. This goes for the thermostat too, but better tape a little plastic sack or piece of kitchen wrap over the exposed mechanism to protect it from paint splatters. If painting the ceiling, loosen ceiling light fixtures.

All lamps and other light objects should be moved to another room. Heavier furniture can be grouped, either in the middle of the room or at one end, and covered with a drop cloth.

The floor can be covered with newspapers. But since they tend to slide around, another drop cloth is even better.

Perhaps the most tedious job in preparing to paint is the repair of cracks and picture-hanger holes. It really should be done, though, for a professional-looking job.

Small cracks and holes in plaster walls are generally patched with spackling compound, available in any paint or hardware store. Follow package directions.

But before applying the compound, use a putty knife or beer can opener to scrape all crumbling plaster from the edge of the crack. It will probably grind you to make the crack wider with this scraping, but the patching job will look better for it.

After the patch has dried, it may need to be sanded smooth.

Hollow or dry wall construction requires a slightly different technique, since there is no backing for the patch to cling to.

For fairly large holes, take a piece of wire mesh (screening will do) slightly larger than the hole and fasten a string to the center of it. Fold the mesh just enough to stuff it through the hole.

Pull the mesh up snug against the back side of the wall by tying the string to a pencil placed across the front of the hole.

Apply a first layer of patching plaster against the mesh, bonding the mesh as well as possible to the back edge of the hole. Build layers of plaster gradually, finishing with spackling compound.

20 / How to repaint without "alligatoring"

People who do their own interior painting seem to run into an amazing number of problems.

One of them is referred to by professionals as "alligatoring." This term describes a phenomenon often encountered in old homes where there are several layers of paint—a situation where hairline cracks are present in the old paint surface. A new paint job seems to remedy the problem, until the new paint dries and there are the same old crack lines in the wall. (The word "alligatoring" depicts pretty well what the surface looks like—lines and cross lines in an uneven pattern.)

Alligatoring usually occurs when a second coat of paint is applied before the first coat is entirely dry. The top surface dries. Then, as the bottom layer of paint dries, it pulls the top surface apart slightly, giving the cracked effect.

(A first coat can feel dry to the touch without really being dry. If you can scratch or peel it by scraping your thumbnail up the wall, the paint is not yet dry.)

Once it happens, alligatoring plagues the house-keeper from then on, unless it is remedied. This is because any new paint—even if applied years later—will sink into the tiny cracks and simply perpetuate the flaws.

The solution is to fill the hairline cracks and build an entirely new surface on which to paint. It is an exasperating and time-consuming process. But it is the only option if those skinny, leafless trees and other odd shapes on your wall are driving you crazy.

First, the old paint must be sanded lightly to make a good gripping surface. You don't need to sand right down to the bare wall. Just roughen the surface slightly with medium-grade sandpaper. Then clean the wall of all the residue from sanding. Use the vacuum cleaner first; follow with a damp rag if necessary.

The next step is to apply spackling compound to the affected area or to the entire wall, depending on how severe the problem is. Spackling compound is a plaster-like substance that can be bought in either powdered form (which must be mixed with water) or in premixed form. The premixed containers are the easiest for do-it-yourselfers.

The spackling compound should be spread over the wall with a very flexible, broad putty knife. Too stiff a spreader will drag the spackling compound out of the cracks you are trying to fill. The blade on the kind of putty knife you want can be bent easily to almost a 90-degree angle. It is more expensive than a cheapo putty knife, but worth it for all the trouble you're going to.

In spreading the spackling compound, use light to moderate pressure on the putty knife. Just enough to give it a slight bend (see sketch). The compound

should then fill all the hairline cracks satisfactorily.

Allow the compound to dry at least the amount of time specified on the package. (In fact, ALWAYS read and follow directions on products used in a painting job.) Then sand the dried surface lightly to remove overlap marks and so on.

Believe it or not you're still not ready to paint. The dried spackling compound is very absorbent. It really needs a coat of primer-sealer before painting if you want a nice even, professional-looking job.

The primer-sealer spoken of is not simply a thin coat of whatever paint you plan on using. It is a special preparation. Ask your paint store for a pigmented, alcohol-based primer and sealer (also called a stain kill). It will accept either oil-based or latex paint as a finish coat.

There is one trick to working with an alcohol primer-sealer. It dries very fast—often within 45 minutes to an hour. So you need to cover your surface as fast as possible.

You can use a roller. But the cleanup after using this primer requires denatured alcohol (available at the paint store) and the roller will never really come clean.

You can clean a brush with denatured alcohol. But

if you decide on a brush, get a wide one that is natural bristle. Synthetic brushes don't work as well with alcohol primer-sealer.

Let the primer dry completely (check product directions).

Now, chief, you are ready to paint.

21 / How to keep a paint brush clean from job to job

No matter how well you clean a brush after painting, it always seems to be stiff when you go back to it. Either that or the bristles are bent at funny angles.

A really good paint brush can cost $20, so it's worthwhile to know the tricks of caring for it. Here are some tips from a veteran professional:

Let's say you're part way through a project with oil paint and you want to finish the work tomorrow. Wipe excess paint from the brush on the rim of the paint can. Then stand the brush in a container of mineral spirits deep enough to cover the bristles. (Mineral spirits are sold in paint stores and cost less than pure turpentine.)

But first, take a page of newspaper, folded in half, and wrap the bristle portion.

Wrap around the brush, crease the paper, then feel for the end of the bristles within the paper. Put your finger across the end of the bristles and fold the wrapped paper up. This gives about half an inch leeway at the end of the brush and prevents bending the bristles (see sketch). Tuck the top of the paper in if you have room. If the container is small there is no need.

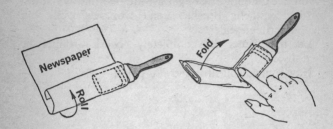

The paper will keep the bristles straight while the brush stands on end in the mineral spirits.

Another method used by some home handymen is to forget the mineral spirits and just put a plastic bag around a used brush, secured with a rubber band. This keeps the paint in the brush from drying out overnight. But don't try it with fast-drying paint.

When entirely through with the paint job, scrape excess paint out of the brush onto a newspaper with a table knife or anything dull and flat. Put a small amount of mineral spirits in a can and swish the brush around in it.

Wipe the bristles as clean as possible on the edge of the can and pour the used mineral spirits into another container (preferably a throw-away). Start with fresh mineral spirits and repeat the first cleaning process three or four times, emptying the used cleaner each time.

But the last time, take the brush handle in one hand, the bristles in the other and wring, as you would with a cloth. This will take the last of the paint out of the brush heel. Now use water and bar laundry soap to clean the brush of mineral spirits.

Shake the water out, smooth the bristles and wrap the bristles in a single sheet of newspaper. Let the brush dry in the paper for at least two or three days before putting it into oil paint again.

Let the mineral spirits you used sit in the discard container for a few hours until the paint settles to the bottom. Then pour off the clean cleaner on top to use again. Do not pour the left-over paint and cleaner down household drains.

For anyone who does much painting, there is a very handy gismo called a spinner, sold in well-stocked paint stores in a domestic size for about $5. It is a metal shaft with a clip on one end and a plunger at the other. A brush handle slips into the clip. The brush spins rapidly when you push the plunger, sending paint and cleaner flying out of the bristles by centrifugal force. The clip will also hold a roller.

This step takes the place of scraping the brush on the side of the cleaning can. You can approximate the action by twirling a brush handle between the palms of your hands.

The process for cleaning a paint roller is basically the same as for a brush. But the roller should be stood on end to dry after washing and should not be wrapped in newspaper.

Cleaning a brush or roller of latex paint is much easier. Just use water and bar laundry soap at the basement wash tub. Let the water run for a while to get all the paint out of the brush and the drain. Do wrap the brush in paper afterward to keep the bristles straight as they dry.

22 / Clustering pictures? Pattern them first

Hanging a cluster of different-sized pictures, or a "picture wall," can be a lot easier with the use of pencil, scissors and the Sunday newspaper.

It takes a talented octopus to juggle a half dozen frames on a wall until just the right balance is achieved. So turn each framed picture face down on a sheet of paper, trace around it and cut out an easy-to-handle pattern the exact size as the picture.

Once you have all the patterns cut, make a small hole in each piece of paper to mark where the top of the hanging wire or the hook is on the back of the frame. This involves a bit of measuring, since the frames have been traced face down.

Assuming the hook is centered on the frame, measure the width of the paper pattern, divide that number by two and you'll know how many inches from the side edge the hole should be. But you still don't know how far down from the top.

So scoot a table up as close as you can to a wall, turn the picture frame face down on the table and run the top edge of the frame up flush against the wall.

Measure the distance from the wall to the hook (see sketch). Keep the ruler nice and straight to make a 90-degree angle with the wall.

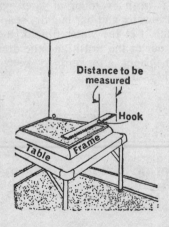

(The reason for all this hokus pokus? The paper pattern includes the flaring front edge of the frame and you can't be accurate measuring around that curve on the back side of the frame.)

Take the measurement from the wall to the frame

hook and measure the same distance down from the top of the paper pattern. Poke a little pencil hole in the pattern where the hook should be. (If there are two hooks on the frame, not centered, you can pull this wall trick from both the top and the side.)

Now spread all the patterns out on the floor and slide them around until you get the balanced combination you want.

The patterns can then be transferred, in the same combination, to the wall. Hang them with small pieces of masking tape (which doesn't stick to paint as badly as clear tape).

Once the patterns are correctly placed on the wall, make marks through the little pencil holes to show where each nail or stick-um hanger should go. If you are using stick-um tabs, remember the dot indicates where the hook—*not* the top of the tab—should be.

Paper
Patterns

23 / Hanging pictures? A tricky business

Ever drive a nail into an apartment wall only to have the nail wiggle around or droop like a tulip caught in a late spring freeze?

Hanging pictures or wall fixtures can be tricky business without the right kind of hanger. So here is a run-down of the various types to be found in a large hardware store.

By far the most common today is the tab type stick-um hanger. Landlords who foam at the mouth over holes in their walls have boosted the popularity of these hangers.

Stick-ums are usually moistened and then applied to the wall. But some are like convention name tags—you peel off the backing to expose a gummy surface.

A few drawbacks: Anything heavy (like a mirror) or valuable (like a custom frame) should not be trusted to the stick-ums. If the paint job on the wall has been done improperly, the glued tab can pull the paint right off as it drops the picture to the floor. The tab will also come loose if you place it directly over any heated pipes running inside the wall.

A fairly new member of the stick-um family is wide, double faced gummed tape that can be applied around the whole perimeter of the picture frame. The frame is then clapped onto the wall, where it stays (with the above reservations). One woman who has used the tape says, however, that it is very hard to remove.

The directions on one package seem to bear this out. They read, "To remove, insert knife blade between picture wall and pry frame loose. Then rub remaining tape firmly with thumb and scrape carefully with thumbnail."

Still among the most reliable hangers are the good old hooks with the little nails running through them at an angle. (See sketch A.)

To keep from chipping the wall while driving the nail, place a small square of tape over the spot where the nail will enter. If you have trouble getting the nail started, remove it from the hanger, drive it a fraction of an inch into the wall at approximately the correct angle, pull it back out and combine it with the hanger.

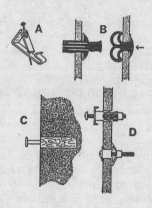

Rooms with wallboard or hollow-wall construction (and that includes most modern apartments) require the special kind of bolt (which can be combined with a separate little hook or whatever you want).

For the best holding power, expansion type "toggle" or "Molly" bolts should be used. These fit into holes drilled beforehand in the wall (package directions tell what size hole), and expanding wings or ribs spread out on the back side of the wall as the screw is tightened (sketch D).

Some newer types now on the market are plastic and are hammered into the drilled hole just like nails. The hammer blow causes the back side of the "nail" to bulge and turn back on itself. (See sketch B) for lighter weight pictures.

Solid masonry walls are among the most difficult to deal with. Again, a hole must be drilled—with a special masonry drill bit.

You can buy a wide variety of "sleeved" screws or nails for masonry walls. The sleeves are made of lead, plastic or fiber (looks sort of like pressed tobacco). Again, the packages tell how large a hole to drill.

The sleeves are put into the drilled hole; they then expand when the nail or screw is inserted, wedging the fastener firmly in the wall. (Sketch C.)

24 / Hung up on pictures? Try this

Every picture hanging method has its drawbacks. The stick-on tabs sometimes don't hold well. Either that or they stick too well to the wall and you take part of the paint off, too, when you remove the sticker.

Metal hangers with the slanted nails are good— and often the only choice with fairly heavy frames. But it takes some fancy measuring to get them in just the right place on the wall. (You usually end up trying to hold your hand behind the picture to see just where the top of the hanging wire will come.)

There's an alternative for light to medium-weight pictures in wooden frames. It's simple, fast; and all you need is a drill, a pair of pliers with a wire cutting section and a good eye.

Select a couple of lightweight finishing nails (the kind with little or no head) and drive them into either side of the frame about a third of the way down the side.

But first, drill "pilot holes" into the frame where the nails will go. Pilot holes make driving the nail much easier and keep the wood from splitting.

Use a drill bit that is *smaller* than the diameter of the nail. This is where your "good eye" is needed. I tried the process with fairly small nails. The smallest drill bit I had was $\frac{1}{16}$ inch, which was pretty close to the diameter of the nail. It worked fine; but I should have had a slightly smaller bit or a fatter nail.

Drill from the back side of the frame and don't go so far that the drill bit pops out the front side of the frame.

Drive the nails into the frame. Then trim off the small nail head with the wire cutting pliers.

Press the prepared frame against the chosen wall at exactly the place and angle you wish. The protruding nails will mark the face of the wall. Balance a small "level" on top of the frame as you position it, if you want the picture absolutely straight.

Drill two holes in the wall where the nails have made their marks. Use a drill bit the same diameter as the nails. Then just press the picture into place. It will lie flat against the wall. If slight adjustment is needed, one nail can sometimes be bent a fraction.

(I did not have any wire cutters handy, so I left the head on the nail. This worked all right on dry wall construction, although I had to give the picture a smack to drive the nail into its hole. The nail head also slightly roughened and enlarged the hole, but not badly.)

The nail method works with both plaster and dry wall construction. Very thin paneling or a hard surface like brick might pose problems. Advantages are exact placement, ease of patching or repainting and ease of cleaning the walls.

25 / How to display a rug on the wall

Some area rugs are too pretty to walk on. They can, however, be a striking accent when hung on a wall.

There are a number of methods for hanging a rug but two seemingly contradictory things should be kept in mind:

1. The heavier the rug, the more support it will need to keep from stretching the nail or tack holes you put in it.

2. The fewer holes you have to make in the wall, the better.

A small lightweight rug is most often nailed to the wall at the four corners of the rug or across the top. Small nails or carpet tacks work best.

But a heavier rug will require several tacks across the top edge to avoid putting too much strain on each tack. And you don't want that many holes in your wall.

One remedy is to buy a strip of wood about 1-by-2 inches (or 2-by-2 at the largest) nearly the length of the top edge of the rug. Tack the rug to this wooden strip (as in sketch). Then insert a couple of eye hooks in the wooden strip and hang the whole affair from wire or decorative chain like a picture.

Or drill a hole near each end of the wooden strip. Insert a couple of sturdy screws into the wall, allowing the screw heads to stick out from the wall a bit. Then just fit the drilled holes in the wooden strip over the screw heads.

Another possibility is to whip-stitch a band of sturdy muslin or similar material across the back of

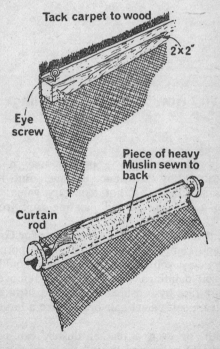

Tack carpet to wood

2 x 2"

Eye
screw

Piece of heavy
Muslin sewn to
back

Curtain
rod

the rug's top edge. Leave each end of the band open (see sketch) and run a decorative curtain rod through it. Then hang the curtain rod from matching supports or from wire or chain.

Some people build an entire frame of wooden strips to back up a rug before hanging it. This is particularly helpful if the rug edges end to curl or the whole structure of the rug is a little unstable.

If a rug is thin and carpet tacks show too much on the front side of it, there is the option of securing it to its strips of wood with broad, double-faced tape available in hardware stores. The tape could also work as a bonding agent to the bare wall.

But keep in mind that removing the tape and rug from the wall later on could be a sticky business that might ruin the wall's paint job.

26 / How to clean oil paintings

The only oil painting you possess may be a too-blue seascape by great-aunt Minnie. But it probably has sentimental if not monetary value. So why not take a few tips on oil painting care from professionals.

Edward R. Gilbert, chief conservator for Greenfield Village and Henry Ford Museum in Dearborn, Michigan, says do-it-yourself cleaning agents should not be used on oil paintings. Dust should be removed from the picture face by brushing the painted surface lightly with a clean, soft camel hair brush (like a large watercolor brush.)

A cloth, or even a feather duster, can catch on little flecks of paint and "chip" them off the surface. Using a cloth also requires enough pressure to flex the canvas, causing cracks in the paint.

To help keep oils clean, hang paintings at a slight

angle (about five degrees) so it will be harder for dust to settle on the surface (see sketch).

If a painting is in good condition, the back of it can be cleaned carefully with the vacuum cleaner using reduced pressure.

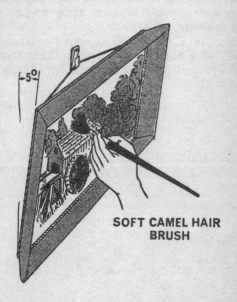

SOFT CAMEL HAIR BRUSH

Dust often settles against the back of a canvas where it meets the stretcher (the wooden support structure to which the painting is tacked). Dust can retain moisture, which causes damage, so it is smart to install a dust cover over the back of a painting.

The cover can be a simple sheet of cardboard fastened to either the back of the frame or the stretcher (whichever is handy). A good material to use is a light foam substance encased in paper and available at some art stores.

Attach the dust cover with screws; nails or staple guns jar an old or delicate painting too much on insertion. Cardboard expands and contracts with moisture, so make the holes in the cardboard a bit larger than needed for the size screw used.

Do not expose oil paints to extreme temperature or humidity changes. Also keep them away from heaters and sunlight.

Never carry a frame by its top edge; support the entire structure. The same thing applies to unframed paintings.

In case of a tear, medical adhesive tape can be applied to the back of the canvas to keep torn fibers in position until the painting can be restored by a professional.

Part II:

Electricity and Appliances

27 / How to cut appliance repair costs

Major appliances are formidable when they go on the blink. They sit there brooding and refusing to work right—great hulking metal boxes that defy you to begin tampering with their intricate innards.

But you don't have to tamper much to run a few basic checks. You may spot the trouble yourself and save an expensive service call.

Ovens with automatic timers, for instance, are responsible for a huge number of pointless service calls.

You put the oven on automatic bake, set the time you want it to start and the time you want it to stop.

When the baking is through, you forget to turn the automatic switch back to manual. The next time you try to start the oven, it won't heat.

Sounds simple-minded. But repairmen say it happens all the time—especially when the auto timer isn't used very often.

Sometimes a guest in the house has turned the automatic switch by mistake, and you don't even know about it. So check that device first, if you have one and the oven isn't heating.

There are a couple of things to keep in mind about refrigerators.

Every now and then, a zealous housekeeper will accidently pull the plug on a refrigerator while sweeping behind it. If you ever do this while the refrigerator is running, wait three or four minutes before plugging it back in.

If you don't wait, the refrigerator's condenser will

alternately click and hum at you and the refrigerator won't start again. What's worse, the condenser may burn itself out trying vainly to restart.

(There's something about pressure build-up in the condenser. If stopped in midcycle, the condenser needs time to equalize its pressure before restarting.)

If your refrigerator just plain isn't running, check the most obvious things first.

Open the door. If the interior light comes on, you know there's no problem with the electrical wall outlet. If there is no light, or it isn't burning, test the electrical outlet by unplugging the refrigerator and plugging a lamp into the outlet. (An outlet that doesn't work can also mean a blown household fuse.)

Assuming the outlet is all right, make sure the refrigerator's cold control or temperature knob has not been changed or turned off by accident.

Self-defrost refrigerators occasionally deposit a puddle on the floor. This is usually because the evaporator pan (where the water runs) is slightly ajar or the tube leading into the pan is either out of place or cracked.

A self-defrost with a static condenser (all those little fins on the back of the refrigerator) usually has a drain pan that has to be emptied manually. So you know about it already (or else your kitchen is a swamp).

But another kind of self-defrost has an air-cooled condenser, usually located under the refrigerator behind a removable front panel. On top of the air-cooled condenser is where you'll find the evaporation pan. The air and heat from the condenser are supposed to get rid of the drain water without much worry on your part.

One thing you really must do, however, is clean that evaporation pan every now and then. It will get pretty rank after a few months, if you don't.

28 / The fuse: how to change it

Before tackling any kind of electrical problem, it is essential to know what a fuse is and how to change it.

Fuses and circuit breakers are the safety values in a household electrical system.

If your house has circuit breakers—and many modern homes do—life is that much simpler for you.

When a short circuit or an overload causes more current to flow than the electrical wires can safely handle, the circuit breaker which looks much like a normal light switch) simply flips itself over to "off."

Replacing it is just a matter of flipping it back to "on." But read further. Some of the advice for changing fuses applies to circuit breakers too.

Most older homes have fuses instead of circuit breakers. A metal strip inside the fuse has a lower melting point than the copper household wiring. Fuses are rated according to the amount of current they can carry, 15 amperes being the most common size (or sometimes 20 amps for the kitchen). When the current exceeds 15 amps, the fuse melts or "blows," breaking the circuit.

Screw-in fuse

Normal 15-amp fuses screw in like a light bulb and have a clear top, so you can see if they are blown. If so, they will be slightly discolored inside and melted together.

Never replace a blown fuse with a penny or a piece of aluminum foil. Don't even put a larger amp fuse in. To do so cancels the safety that a fuse is designed to provide. A house fire could result.

Stand on a dry surface while changing fuses and don't hang on to anything metallic with your free hand.

If the same fuse blows frequently because of sudden power surges to certain appliances, try buying slow-blow fuses. They are commonly available and absorb some of the "shock" when an appliance starts up. They are commonly called "fusetrons."

But putting a new one in isn't going to accomplish much unless you determine what blew the fuse to begin with. The same applies for circuit breakers.

If you are fairly sure the problem was a simple overload, the obvious answer is to turn off some of the lights and appliances being used on the affected circuit.

If you suspect a defective appliance or light caused the blackout, but are not sure whch one is the culprit, try this: Unplug or turn off everything on that circuit. Then turn each appliance and light back on again separately. When you hit the defective one, the new fuse will blow again.

If the new fuse blows while everything is still unplugged, there is something wrong with the household wiring and an electrician should be called in.

There are other, larger fuses in a home—sometimes in a separate fuse box. They control the entire system and-or large appliances like ovens. These are usually cartridge-type fuses that snap in and out. Find out what kind of cartridges you have and keep a supply on hand.

But fuse box styles for the cartridges vary according to age and some are safer to handle than others. So it might be wise to ask someone experienced in home

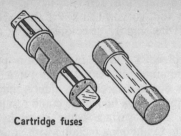

Cartridge fuses

repairs to show you how to change the cartridge fuses in your home.

Getting back to the normal 15-amp fuses—locate all the fuse boxes in your house before the need arises. they are usually in the basement or utility room. On the inside of the fuse box door should be pasted a chart telling which fuse controls what. If the chart isn't filled in, experiment by unscrewing each fuse to see which lights go out; then make a note. Everything in one room is generally *not* on the same circuit.

29 / How to install electrical plugs

An electric plug doesn't have to be stepped on or otherwise crunched before it needs replacing. After long use, the prongs can become badly bent, corroded, or loose.

If the wiring insulation (covering) where it joins the plug is badly frayed or cracked or the wire has broken off at the terminal screws, you may not need a new plug, but will need to re-set the old plug.

Many plugs on today's appliances are solid rubber.

That means there is no way to take them apart. So if they are out of order, you'll have to just cut them off, throw them away, and buy a new plug.

To install a new plug or re-set an old one:

1. Cut the electrical cord in two about an inch before it joins the plug (after you have unplugged the appliance from the outlet, naturally). If you have pliers that double as wire cutters, use them. If not, use a sharp knife and your kitchen cutting board.

2. Electric cords are made up of two wires, each covered (insulated) individually, plus an outer wrapping or insulation. Remove about two inches of this outer covering by slitting it lengthwise with a knife and then peeling it off. Be very careful not to cut too deep; otherwise you will damage the wire beneath.

Some cords are not round; they are sort of flat, with what looks like a seam running the length of them (seen often on hair dryers, radios, etc.) In this case, don't remove anything yet. Just slice down the center seam for about two inches—this separates the two wires.

3. Checking to make sure you have not damaged the inner insulation of the two wires, use the paring knife to strip about a half-inch of insulation from the end of each wire. (This step applies to the flat style of cork

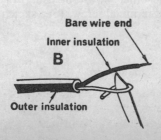

Bare wire end

Inner insulation

B

Outer insulation

too.) Again, be careful with the knife or you will damage the strands of the actual wire.

4. Push the little cardboard-like covering off the prong end of the plug. Inside the plug, you will see a screw at the base of each prong. These are terminal screws; if they are not already loosened, loosen them (they don't come out all the way).

5. Feed the prepared cord end through the back of the plug. Then tie a knot with the two pieces of wire, called an underwriter's knot. (See sketch.) Tighten the knot and pull it down into the cavity of the plug.

6. Straighten the bare strands and then twist the strands of each separate wire, much as you would a piece of thread before threading a needle. This keeps the strands from bristling out, touching the other wire and causing a short.

7. Bring the end of one wire around the back of one prong and wind the exposed wire end around the terminal screw of that prong. Wind the wire in the same direction the screw will turn when it is tightened. That way you aren't working against the wire strands when you tighten the screw. Follow the same procedure with the other wire, but using, of course, the other prong and terminal screw. (See sketch.)

Terminal screw

8. Avoid getting the insulated portion of the wire under the terminal screw; you want a good firm connection. Also make sure there are not any loose strands of wire sticking out at odd angles to make trouble.

9. Tighten the terminal screws. Put the little fiber disk cover back over the prongs and you're in business.

Note: *If the wire is the flat kind, there are handy plugs for sale which do not require all the cutting and stripping described here. You simply insert the wire in the plug, and close a little clamp device which pushes metal prongs into the wire, making the connection.*

30 / How to cope when electrical power fails

Severe thunderstorms and flooding seem to make themselves right at home every now and then—your home, that is.

There are a few things you should do when these unwelcome guests arrive.

If you suddenly lose all electrical power in your house, check to see if your neighbors have the same problem. If they don't, you have undoubtedly blown a main fuse and should call the electrical company.

If several houses or the whole area is in darkness, there may be a line down somewhere and you should still call the company.

Whichever the case, your next step should be to unplug all motor-driven appliances that normally run constantly. This means the refrigerator, the freezer, air conditioning units and anything else you can think of that might turn on automatically when the power returns.

There are two reasons for this. First, it takes more energy to start a motor than to keep it running. If all motors in your house start at one time when the electricity returns, you are likely to blow a fuse.

Second, power occasionally does not come back on at full voltage. Motors that run—or try to run—on reduced voltage soon burn themselves out.

Do leave a couple of light switches on so you can tell when you have electricity again.

The rule about unplugging motor-driven appliances also holds during "brown-outs" when the electric company reduces its voltage or the voltage lowers for some other reason.

Signs of lowered voltage are dimming light bulbs, a flopping and shrinking television picture, motors that hum but won't start (turn them off right away), or fluorescent lights that start blinking turn them off too).

If your basement is flooded, do not step into the water if the water is in contact with any electrically energized appliance—this means anything that is running or might start running on its own. To do so is to risk your life.

This rule also applies when the water level reaches electrical outlets (they are themselves energized) or plugged-in extension cords. And it makes no difference whether the power is off in your neighborhood. You never know when it will come back on.

Don't touch fuses or circuit breakers while standing in water.

If your basement floods regularly, put your appliances up on risers permanently. Once an appliance has been soaked, wait about a week before using it to give it time to dry out completely.

31 / How to check for proper electrical grounding

Many of today's hand-held tools and major appliances come equipped with three-prong plugs. Hedge clippers, portable dishwashers and garbage disposal units are examples.

The third prong is a "grounding" device. This means that in case of a short in the appliance, the "ground" is designed to direct wandering electrical impulses away from you and back into the electrical outlet box.

In houses built within the past six or eight years, all electrical outlets are made to take three-prong plugs. This is a nationwide standard.

But with older houses, chances are you will have to trip off to the dime store for an adapter (see sketch A)

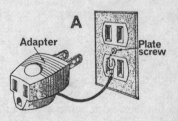

A
Adapter
Plate screw

before you can plug in a three-prong appliance.

These adapters cost under a dollar and plug right into your wall outlet. Branching off from the adapter is a short wire or "pigtail" with a metal hook on the end of it. The hook is to be fastened under the center screw of the outlet plate (as shown in sketch A). There are directions included with the adapter.

This procedure supposedly completes your grounding path. (The center screw on the outlet plate is connected to the outlet box, which is supposed to be grounded.)

But there's a catch.

Not all boxes for the old-fashioned, two-prong outlets are in fact grounded. And there's no way to tell by looking.

There is a simple test to find out. It requires an investment of under a dollar.

First, visit a hardware store and buy what is called a pigtail light socket. This is a simple light socket with two wires coming out the back of it instead of two prongs. (See sketch B.)

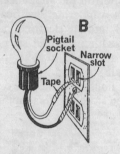

Screw a regular light bulb (25 watt is plenty) into the socket. Now examine the two wires. They should be covered with rubberized insulation except for about an inch of bare stranded wire at the ends.

Just above the bare wire, wrap a wad of electrician's tape around the insulation for a firmer hand-hold on the wire see sketch B).

When performing this test, do not hold onto anything metal and do not touch the bare strands of wire.

Look closely at the wall outlet you are preparing to test. On nearly every outlet manufactured during the last 50 years, one prong hole is shorter and skinnier than the other.

Stick one of the bare light socket wires into the short

skinny hole. Wriggle it around a bit to make good contact.

Touch the other bare wire to the center screw of the outlet plate.

The bulb will light up if your electrical box is grounded.

(You can run the same test on newer three-prong outlets, using the rounded grounding hole instead of the plate screw.)

But don't give up testing just yet. If the bulb does not light, change the one bare light bulb wire from the skinny prong hole to the fatter prong hole. (The other wire still touches the outlet screw.)

If the bulb lights this way, it is good news and bad news. The electrical box is grounded all right. But the "polarity" of your outlet is backward.

Reverse polarity is too complicated to explain here except to say that it is dangerous. If an appliance with a polarized plug is used on an outlet with reversed polarity, you have a good chance of electric shock.

One such outlet means all the outlets in the house should be checked. A few final words about grounding. A lack of it should be remedied by an experienced electrician—as should the problem of reversed polarity.

Some hand-held tools need no grounding because they are double insulated. They are usually marked with a statement on the name plate and/or an international symbol—a small square within a larger one.

Many other two-prong appliances, like toasters, are not double insulated and are not grounded. They should be disconnected when not in use. Plugging a two-prong adapter into a three-prong adapter does nothing to ground the appliance.

Never circumvent grounding devices or instructions when they are provided—especially on camper trailers or swimming pool pumps.

32 / How to replace light switches

Simple on-off light switches that control just one light are called single-pole switches. They can be replaced by the home owner if they stop working or start throwing out sparks.

Most hardware stores carry light switches. They are replaced as an entire unit, so there's not much taking apart or putting together involved.

The first step—and most important—is to turn off the electricity flowing to the affected switch. Throw the lever shutting off power for the entire house; or unscrew the fuse controlling the light switch's own line.

If the wiring in your house is aluminum rather than copper, ask your hardware man for a new switch on which the terminal screws are compatible with aluminum.

Unscrew the wall plate or cover of the switch (as shown in left sketch). You should now see the switch mechanism sitting inside an open-sided box inserted in the wall.

The switch is held in the box with screws (usually two). Unfasten there and pull the switch mechanism out of its wall cavity (see right sketch).

You will usually see two wires connected to the switch mechanism, the end of each wire being held firm under a small screw called a terminal. Loosen the screws (don't take them all the way out) and unhook the wires.

A word of caution here. If you remove the switch from its box and find more than two wires attached to it, or find some odd "octopus" arrangement, it is best

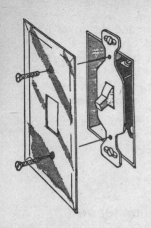

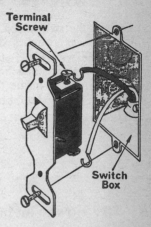

Terminal
Screw

Switch
Box

to seek the help of someone experienced in electrical repairs. If you insist on doing it yourself, be sure to hook up the new switch the same way you found the old one.

Getting back to a normal single-pole switch, you may find it attached to a black wire and a white wire; or it may be attached to two black wires. This varies from region to region across the country. It doesn't matter what you find; just use what was used before.

Examine the bare wire ends. If they look caked and corroded, you can try cleaning them with a bit of sandpaper or dry steel wool. Or you can cut them off with wire clippers, carefully pare away about half an inch of the insulation or wire covering to expose fresh new wire, and hook the new wire end as before to fit under the terminal screw.

A new switch may have terminal screws top and bottom (as in the sketch) or the terminals may be on either side. It doesn't make any difference.

Nor does it make much difference which wire is hooked to which terminal (except in the case of three or more wires).

Attach the wires to the new switch. Fold excess wire

neatly behind the switch as you push it into the wall cavity.

Replace the switch box screws and the cover plate.

Some newer switches do not use terminal screws. Instead, the wire feeds straight into the back of the switch through a small hole. It is held in place by a spring mechanism inside the switch. Directions on releasing the spring should be printed on the back of the switch.

33 / How to install a dimmer switch

Dimmer switches can allow you to create a lot of different effects in your home with lighting. And there's no special trick to installing the switches.

Dimmer switches work with regular light bulbs. But there are a couple of things to keep in mind before installing the switch.

The first is to buy one that has been tested and rated for watt capacity. The watt capacity of the dimmer switch must exceed the total wattage of the light bulb (or bulbs) to be used with it.

The second point is to make sure the light switch you are replacing does not control some appliance outlet as well as the light you have in mind.

Now to installation.

Begin by shutting off the electricity to the wall switch you'll be working on. Do this by removing the proper fuse in the household fusebox or by flipping the circuit breaker switch.

Unfasten the screws holding the wall plate or cover on the old light switch. You should now see the switch mechanism sitting in an open-sided box inserted in the wall.

The switch is usually held in place by two screws running into the front edge of the wall box. Undo these and pull the switch forward.

You should now see two wires connected to the switch. If there are more than two, you've got something more complicated than a single-pole switch and these instructions will not apply.

To remove the old switch, look for two screws on the switch body holding the ends of the wires. Loosen the screws and unhook the wires.

On some light switches, the wires don't run to screws. Instead, they feed into little holes in the back of the switch body. Internal clamps hold them secure. To release the clamps, look for a small hole with "Press Here" or something similar written above it. Inserting a miniature screwdriver into the hole will release the clamp.

The new dimmer switch, if it is a common type, will have two wires of its own running out the back of it. These are to be hooked to the two wall wires that were attached to the old switch.

It doesn't really matter which switch wire is attached to which wall wire. (One wall wire may be black and the other white; or both may be black. Just use whatever was used on the other switch.)

Included in the package with your dimmer switch, you will often find two little plastic things that resem-

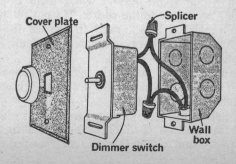

Cover plate — Splicer — Dimmer switch — Wall box

ble sewing thimbles. These are splicers and are to be used for connecting the wire ends together.

Hold the exposed end of one switch wire and the end of one wall wire together side by side. Then screw the splicer cap down over the two ends. Turn the splicer until it's secure, but don't overdo.

One important thing to watch: The bottom edge of the splicer cap should come down well over the insulated portion of the two wires. If there is exposed wire showing, unscrew the splicer and clip the wire ends to a length that will fit within the cap.

With both connections completed, stuff the spliced wires to the back of the wall box, slide the dimmer switch into place and secure it with screws.

34 / How to repair a pull chain on a light fixture

A light with a pull chain that won't work every time is enough to make you want to yank the fixture out whole.

A a matter of fact, that's just about what you'll end up doing to fix it—but not in blind rage.

When a pull chain doesn't work, there is usually something amiss inside the socket. It's not really possible to repair it. You'll need to replace it—a job that is not expensive or particularly difficult if you take it step by step.

Let's assume your pull-chain light is a hanging fixture. (If it's a table lamp just turn the accompanying sketch upside down.)

The light bulb screws into a socket which is covered by a metal shell. The shell, in turn, snaps into a half-round metal cap of the same color (see

Electrical wires

Cap

Socket switch

Shell

Bulb

sketch). The electrical wires from the ceiling feed down through a hole in the top of this cap.

The first thing you want to do is shut off the electricity to the light fixture you'll be working on. Do this by unscrewing the fuse or flipping the circuit breaker that controls electricity to that part of the house.

Unscrew the light bulb from its socket.

The next step is to separate the metallic shell from its cap. Most shells snap into place under the cap and have a spot on the body of the shell where the words "press here" are printed. (If you don't see this, the shell may be held to the cap by a band or ring that unscrews.)

The people who designed the snap-in shells never meant for anyone but Hercules to unfasten the devices. When you "press here," you will likely get no results. An easier way is to get a very thin screwdriver, slip it up under the edge of the cap and pry gently at several different points while pulling down on the shell. Start at the "press" sign.

This method risks bending the cap out of shape, so take it easy and don't rush.

As you pull the shell away, you will expose a small rectangular gismo with one screw on each side of it. This is the combination socket and switch. The screws are called terminal screws and the two electrical wires from the ceiling will be attached to them. Remove the wires by loosening the terminal screws.

Since you will not be replacing the metal cap of the light fixture, don't try to remove it. Just leave it where it is.

Take the metal shell and the faulty socket with you to a hardware or dime store and have them matched for size and type. You usually have to buy the new switch-socket with a new shell around it. They come as a unit. (Inside the new shell will be a cardboard liner. Don't throw it away. Leave it in there when installing the new socket.)

Back home again, take the new socket mechanism out of its shell and attach the electrical wires to the terminal screws. Use the same two wires that were attached to the old socket.

One terminal screw on the new socket will be brass colored; the other silver. If one of the electrical wires you are working with is white and the other black, run the white wire to the silver screw and the black wire to the brass screw. Light to light; dark to dark. (In fact if one of the wires has any identifying marks at all—like a colored thread in the covering—it should go to the white terminal screw.)

If both electrical wires are identical, it doesn't matter which one goes to which screw.

Make a three-quarter loop at the end of each wire and hook the end of the wire under its appropriate terminal screw. Turn the screw down tight. If the bare wire end is stranded, make sure there are no strands bristling out from under the terminal screw.

Once the wires are secured, slip the shell back up over the new socket and snap the shell firmly into the metal cap. It usually clicks twice.

Replace the light bulb, turn on the electricity to that part of the house and try your new light fixture.

35 / Fixing appliance plug isn't too difficult

Any housewife who uses electric appliances has to contend with "female" plugs—those found on coffee pots and waffle irons.

Electric fry-pan plugs are more complicated, usually include a thermostat and should be tackled by the electric company or a commercial repairman.

If a plastic female plug is cracked or damaged, it is easier in the long run to replace the whole plug instead of trying to glue the old one back together.

Cut the cord in half about an inch before the plug and take the old plug to a hardware store to have it matched for size. (Before cutting the cord, one assumes you have made sure the other end is not plugged in.)

When buying the new plug, make sure the one or two screws holding the two halves together are easily undone.

Take the plug apart. Inside you will see two little metal "sleeves" that hold the prongs when the appliance is plugged in. At the end of each sleeve is a small screw, called a terminal screw.

If the cord is perfectly round, it has an outer layer of insulation. Remove about two inches of this covering by slitting it lengthwise and around with a very sharp knife.

Be careful not to cut too deep or you will damage the inside layer of insulation. With the outer cover removed, you should see two separate wires, each

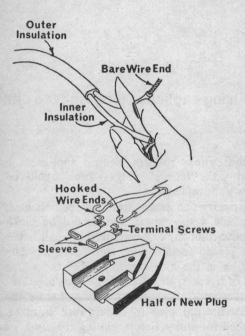

with its own wrapping. Remove about a half inch of this last insulation to reveal the bare copper strands of each wire. Again, take it easy.

If the cord is not round, but is rather flat with what looks like a seam running the length of it, you will have no outer insulation to remove. In this case simply slit the cord lengthwise down the seam for about two inches, then remove insulation from the end of each wire as previously described.

The plug sleeves, along with their terminal screws, lift out for easier handling. Loosen the screws if they are down tight, but don't take them all the way off.

Twist each wire's copper strands (the way you would prepare thread for a needle) and wrap each wire end around one of the terminal screws in the direction the screw will turn when you tighten it.

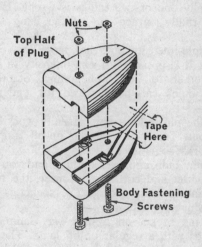

After securing the terminal screws, lay the sleeves and wire into place in the plug body. Check to make sure there are no loose wire strands touching the opposite wire.

To make sure the sliced insulation does not continue to split or unravel, wrap the cord where it joins the plug with plastic or electrician's tape. If possible, extend the tape slightly within the back edge of the plug to help protect the wire from wear.

Fasten the other half of the plug in place with the screws provided—and that's it.

36 / How to replace lightbulb socket

When a three-way lamp doesn't go three ways any-more, usually one of two things is wrong. Either the bulb is partially burned out or the lamp socket is defective.

A multiple-intensity bulb has more than one fila-ment in it. It is possible for one intensity to burn out and the other to keep functioning. Standard-size, three-way bulbs can be replaced for under a dol-lar.

But if the old bulb is still partially working, don't throw it out. Try it in a regular on-off lamp. Some-times it works; sometimes it doesn't.

If the new bulb improves nothing and you are sure the wall outlet and cord are in order, the trouble is probably in the lamp socket. The socket is the por-tion into which the bulb screws.

Fixing the socket on a three-way lamp is really the same as with a regular on-off lamp. The business that makes the bulb change intensity is inside the socket, which is replaceable for about 65 cents.

First unplug the lamp.

The socket is encased in a brass-colored shell which disassembles as shown in the sketch. Do not unscrew the cap of the shell if you can help it (the lamp will usually come apart in your hands if you do.) Most modern sockets are the same size so you should be able to leave it in place.

If you do have to remove the cap for some rea-son, note that it unscrews from the lamp in a counter-clockwise direction. But check first for a small set screw (see sketch) present on some models. It must be loosened first.

To remove the upper part of the shell, look just to the right of the on-off switch for the word "press" printed on the metal. Squeeze the shell at that point and pull up. This is easier described than done. You may need a pair of large pliers or a screwdriver.

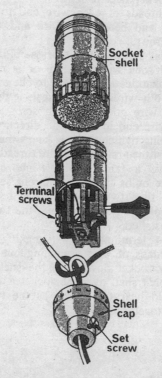

Pull the socket mechanism and attached cord up from the lamp, giving yourself leeway to work. You may have to remove the felt from the bottom of the lamp to allow cord movement.

There are only two wires attached to the socket of a normal three-way lamp. Each bare wire end is under a terminal screw on the socket. Loosen the two screws (they don't come all the way out) and unhook the wires.

If the wire ends look corroded or burned, clip them off, peel back the wire covering about an inch and expose new metal. Tie an "underwriter's knot" in the wiring if room allows (see sketch) before attaching it to the new socket mechanism.

Twist the threads of each wire end to keep them from bristling and bend each wire end to fit under the terminal screws.

One terminal screw will be brass-colored and the other silver. If one wire is white or is marked with any kind of identification, it goes to the silver terminal screw. If both wires are identical, it doesn't really matter which wire goes to which screw. But do try to bend the wire end in the same direction the screw turns when being tightened. This keeps the screw from working against the grain of the wire threads.

If you have a fancy multiple-intensity lamp in which separate bulbs light on different settings, there may be more than two wires running to the socket. Be sure to hook the new socket up the same way the old one was installed.

Tighten the terminal screws, making sure there aren't any threads of wire branching out from them. Push the new socket down into the shell cap. Slide the new (or old) shell over the socket and push firmly. You should hear two clicks as the two parts of the shell snap together.

37 / How to put ring back in doorbell

You say your local Avon lady is in tears because, when she comes to your house, she has to knock instead of ding-donging?

Repairing a doorbell can be a very simple chore. Of course, if the entire wiring system needs to be replaced, you may not want to get into that. But before you call an electrician, try these basic tests:

Unscrew the plate of the doorbell outside the house. Do not turn the electricity off, as you will need the current to test the bell and the voltage is not high enough to be dangerous. Check whether the area behind the plate is clean and dry; bugs sometimes build little nests behind the plate and foul up the connection.

There should be two lightweight electrical wires under the push buttons. The exposed end of each wire will be wrapped around a small screw (called a terminal screw). Make sure the screws are tight, holding the wires firmly in place.

The next step is to deliberately cause a "short", to see if the bell rings. To do this, place the blade of a clean screwdriver across both terminal screws at once. (Or, if you wish, the wires can be disconnected and the two stripped ends touched briefly together.)

If this procedure makes the doorbell ring, the problem is in the button itself and a new one can be bought very inexpensively.

If shorting the circuit does not make the bell ring, check the mechanism of the chime itself back inside the house.

The box covering it is not air tight and dirt collects easily inside it, causing moving parts to stick. Some chime covers are fastened with screws; some just lift off. Clean everything you can reach with a duster or the little brush attachment on the vacuum cleaner. You might even try a toothbrush.

Again, you wlil see two lightweight wires connected to terminal screws (perhaps three wires if you have a back door buzzer). Make sure the connections are firm.

Your next checkpoint is the transformer—a small box (usually hexagonal) which steps the high household current down to the low voltage used in the doorbell. The transformer is probably located either near your main fuse box or in the rafters of the basement ceiling. It will have two lightweight wires hooked to one side of it (just like the wires under the pushbutton) and a heavier wire coming out the other side of it.

Do not fool with the heavy wire; it is standard household current. But check the exposed connection where the doorbell wires join the device.

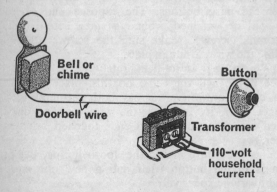

After making sure the connection is secure, test the transformer to see if it functions: Get a flashlight bulb; wrap a scrap piece of wire around the screw threads of the bulb base; touch the tip of the bulb base to one of the terminal screws where the doorbell wire joins the transformer; at the same time, touch the end of the piece of wire to the other terminal screw. The bulb should flicker. And don't worry about a shock—the voltage is too low.

Another test: While holding the blade of a clean screwdriver against one terminal screw, brush the shaft of the screwdriver across the second terminal screw. This should produce a few little sparks.

Notice: There may be more than one transformer in your basement; there is sometimes one for the furnace. To determine which is which, try tracing the wires from the transformer as far as possible. If the wires run to the furnace, the conclusion is obvious.

If it's impossible to trace them, and if the wires going into the transformer are not the same skinny kind you saw on the doorbell upstairs, just leave the transformer alone.

The last place to check is the fuse box. The transformer is usually on the same circuit with some of the household lights. If the fuse for that circuit has blown, replace it.

If the fuse blows again right away after being replaced, there is probably something wrong in the wiring itself and you may want to call an electrician or the power company.

38 / How to fix a toaster

Scraping charred crumbs off burned toast can't be anyone's idea of how to prepare breakfast.

If your automatic pop-up toaster won't pop up, there are two basic things that could be wrong: Either the timer is faulty or the latching mechanism isn't working properly. If it's the timer, there is not much you can do about it yourself.

But first you may want to try a few simple steps with the latching mechanism. Every brand uses a different system and even that may change from year to year. But two common types are shown here. One is a General Electric using a bimetal bar; the other is a proctor using a solenoid.

First, unplug the toaster.

Then take the toaster apart, exposing the end where the lever and lightness-darkness control are located. You'll have to explore a bit to see how the toaster comes apart. On some, the plastic end is fastened with screws in the front or on the bottom; the metal end panel may be pried off. On some, the metal shell of the toaster is an entire unit and must be unfastened both front and back.

In any case, you will need to pull the knob off the end of the carriage lever. Note which side of the knob is face up so you can put it on the same way again. After removing the knob you will probably find a little piece of bent metal threaded through a hole at the end of the lever. Don't lose it; replace it just as you found it before putting the knob back on.

Most toasters have a crumb tray on the bottom. Unfasten the tray and tap all bread particles out of the toaster. A chunk of bread may be all that is obstructing the toast rack as it slides up and down.

Run the carriage up and down several times with the lever, noting each part that moves and how the latch works. If there is an obvious hang-up because of a bent portion in the mechanism, straighten it with a pair of needle-nose pliers.

Obtain from the nearest hardware store a can of non-flammable cleaning fluid (some of these lubricate at the same time) and clean the track taken by the carriage supports and the lever. Use a small, stiff paintbrush to help if need be.

Lubricate sparingly all the moving joints or pivot

points that you observe while operating the lever. Use something light like sewing machine oil or the combination cleaner-lubricant.

On the GE toaster shown (Sketch A) it is impor-

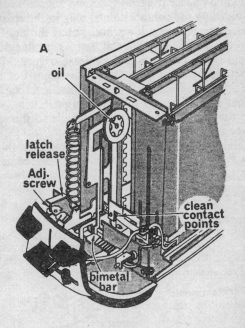

tant that the contact points—two little dots of copper —be free of dirt and oil. Otherwise the toaster doesn't get the message to shut itself off. Take an emery board and scrape the points gently to clean.

While the toaster is cold, the points should be apart about the thickness of a nail file. If they are not, try to separate them slightly with pliers; but easy does it.

There usually are also a couple of contact points in the back of a toaster where the cord attaches. If your appliance does not heat at all, these back contact points may need to be cleaned.

The catch on this particular GE is released by

the action of a bi-metal bar—a strip made of two separate metals that react differently to heat. As the toaster heats up, the bar bends one way; as it cools, it bends the other way, pressing an adjustment screw against a latch release trigger.

After cleaning the contact points, plug in the toaster, press the carriage lever down and watch through the sequence to see if the bimetal bar is pushing the adjustment screw clear up to the release trigger. Make sure the trigger is not bent. If it is straight but still isn't working, you can try raising the level of the adjustment screw just the merest fraction.

If the toaster still doesn't work, take it to the electric company or a repair shop.

The latch mechanism on the Proctor toaster shown (Sketch B) works with a solenoid instead of a bi-

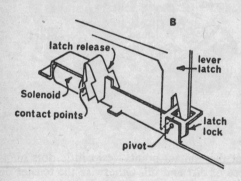

metal bar. The solenoid looks like a little spool of copper thread and becomes a magnet when activated.

Again, all moving parts, tracks and pivot points should be cleaned and lubricated lightly.

This particular model frees the carriage lever when the solenoid attracts or pulls back the latch release trigger, allowing the square latch lock and its extended arm to swing up, releasing the catch on the carriage lever.

The solenoid cannot attract the trigger if it is caked

with oil and dirt. So clean the contact area between the end of the solenoid and the face of the latch release trigger with a nail file or emery board if it appears dirty.

If the carriage lever on your toaster will not stay *down,* the checkpoints are essentially the same as have been outlined, with this exception: The carriage lever may have been bent down somehow (maybe the toaster was dropped). In this case it is hitting the bottom of its running slot (on the toaster shell) too soon. Try bending the lever back up. But carefully— carriage levers snap off easily.

39 / How to clean fan vent on kitchen range

The vent hood over a kitchen range often has a little metal plate that says "clean fan and filter frequently." If you still have the instruction booklet for your vent fan, great.

But if the booklet has disappeared, here are a few tips on what is at best a grubby job. Why do it at all? Because a caked fan will sometimes overheat and become a fire hazard. It is also a breeding ground for germs and, depending on location, can sling dirty grease back into the kitchen.

Most fans installed in hoods or down within the stove have a grease filter. This is a woven metal mesh that needs to be washed. It is usually easy to remove, being held in place with screw knobs or else sliding into place.

If the filter is all metal, you can put it in the automatic dishwasher. Otherwise, use a strong household cleaner on it (tub and tile spray foam is good) and swish it up and down in hot soapy water. Don't scrub the filter; you may break the metal strands.

If you are unfortunate enough to have an unvented fan, there is yet another filter to worry about. Unvented fans don't send the air outside at all. Instead, they send the "used" air back into the room after removing some of the grease and smoke from it.

To take care of the smoke, there is usually a dark panel filled with activated charcoal. These charcoal filters can't be washed; they must be replaced (every three months to a year depending on use).

Now comes the fan itself. But before you do anything to the fan, protect yourself by either flipping the circuit switch or unscrewing the fuse controlling electricity to the area of the house where the fan is located.

There are two general types of fans. One is the propeller style with blades like any old fan. The other is newer and called a squirrel cage. A squirrel cage fan looks like a round oatmeal box lined on the inside with blades.

If your vent fan is a squirrel cage, there isn't a lot you can do to it. To be cleaned properly, it must be taken apart at a shop. So just give the outside shell a swipe and let it go at that.

Propeller fans aren't quite so protected as squirrel cages and do need to be cleaned well. This is especially true if the fan is the old style, inserted in a wall or ceiling and has no grease filter.

First remove the protective grill (see sketch). Look for screws on the perimeter of the grill. If there

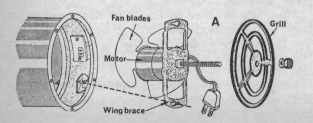

are none, the grill is probably attached with a center knob or screw.

You should now encounter either the small black motor of the fan or else the fan blades themselves, depending on how the device was installed.

If you are faced with the motor first, look for a cord coming out of it and ending in an ordinary electrical plug. Unplug the cord from the wall socket. Next, you need to remove the whole fan mechanism from its cubicle.

There is often a wing-like metal brace running across the back of the motor and extending out from either side of the motor (as in sketch). Look for a screw toward the end of each wing and unfasten the screws. You should now be able to lift the fan and motor out as one unit for cleaning.

Some fans have a three-pronged metal brace across the back of the motor instead of the wing brace described. Each brace arm may end with a little rubber gismo that looks like a tiny doughnut. A metal prong fits up through the hole of each doughnut. The braces simply snap onto and off of the metal prongs.

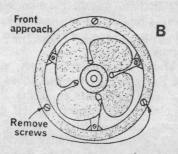

Upon removing the protective grill, you may be faced with the fan blades instead of the motor. Look for two to four screws along the frame edge of the fan and unfasten these. (See sketch B.) The fan, motor, plus the attached frame should now come out of the wall as one unit.

Unplug the electric cord at the back of the motor as the fan comes out.

Never soak a motor in water or get moisture inside it. Instead, clean the fan blades and the outside of the motor with a cloth soaked in strong household detergent or dry-cleaning type solvent.

Also clean out the cubicle where the fan was located, paying special attention to any damper or flap that opens when the fan starts running.

40 / How to replace vacuum cleaner belts

A busy housewife probably uses her vacuum cleaner as much or more than a businessman uses his car.

If you have an upright vacuum with a rotating brush on the bottom, one of the things you should do once a year is replace the belt that makes the brush whirl. Constant use makes the belt stretch and sometimes even break.

Different brands have different types and locations for the belt. But generally the belt looks like a big, thick rubber band and runs from the shaft of the motor to a point on the brush roller. (If your upright vacuum is not doing a good job, turn it on, turn it over and look at the brush roller. Don't stick your fingers in it. The roller should be going around. If not, you probably have a broken belt.)

The belt is usually simple to replace. Yet on some models where a particular twist in the belt is required, people continually put the thing on backward.

When installed backward, the belt makes the brush turn in the wrong direction. So instead of flipping dirt back toward the air intake of the vacuum, the brush scoots dirt away from and ahead of the vacuum.

Consult your owner's manual if you still have it. Otherwise, turn the vacuum over and look for a partial plate covering the bottom of the appliance. Naturally, unplug the vacuum before working on it.

Remove the partial plate. Sometimes it snaps off; sometimes screws must be unfastened. Still others have a couple of small metal arms called cam locks that pivot on a pin and operate much like the lock on a window.

The next step, on most upright models, is to remove the brush roller. It often just yanks straight out. If not, there are probably spring clips on the ends that must be pressed in while you pull.

If the belt is buried down on the side somewhere and looks like it will be hard to reach, take the vacuum to a shop. It won't cost much to have them do the job for you.

But if the belt is easily accessible, there's no reason you can't make the change yourself. Remove the belt from the brush roller and the shaft of the motor. Jot down the make and model of your vacuum and take the note and the old belt to the vacuum shop with you so the belt can be matched for size and style.

When installing the new belt, look on the bottom of the vacuum (near where the belt runs) for any

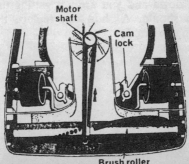

arrows or directions printed on the vacuum. Follow them to the letter. Some belts turn one way; some the other.

The Hoover upright shown in the sketch is an example of the type of arrangement that requires a twist in the belt, since the belt runs vertically around the brush roller and horizontally around the motor shaft.

Loop the new belt over the brush roller first. Then snap the roller back into place. At this point, the "bottom" leg of the belt will be closer to the body of the vacuum than the "top" leg of it is.

On the model shown in the sketch, the directions say this bottom portion of the belt should approach the motor shaft from the right (there is a little arrow to point the way). Stretch the belt up and loop it over the groove in the motor shaft. The finished job, with this particular upright model, should look like the sketch shown here.

Replace the protective plate. If you can't get the plate back on, or if the plate does not cover the newly installed belt, you may have put the brush roller in backward. With most models, the brush snaps in only one way. But on others it is possible to switch ends of the roller. The remedy is simple. Just take the roller out and put it back correctly.

One more thing to check. The bristles of the brush roller should stick out past the line of the protective plate on the bottom of the vacuum. If they don't, they have worn down and you are not getting the cleaning power you should. A shop can replace the brushes for a reasonable price.

41 / How to take the "stick" out of an iron

An iron that drags instead of slides over clothes can cause a dreadful buildup of steam—not in the iron, but in the woman doing the ironing.

A sticking iron is usually caused by material that has partially melted and stuck to the sole plate (ironing surface). If the accumulation is bad enough, no amount of bathroom cleanser will remove it. And scraping with a knife or razor blade is the worst possible move, since you can easily scratch the sole and create little "burrs" that snag clothing.

Your best bet is fine-grain sandpaper—for either "goop" or burrs. Sandpaper scratches the sole plate; but it does so evenly. With a succession of finer and finer abrasives the plate gradually regains a satin finish.

Wrap a piece of sandpaper around a small block of wood and sand the plate with an even, up-and-down stroke. Don't concentrate entirely on the sticky

areas; sand the entire plate to insure an even surface. Use a fresh piece of sandpaper occasionally.

After all burned-on residue is gone, change to fine steel wool. Polish with the same up-and-down motion until the sole plate takes on a dull, smooth gloss.

If you start this project with a medium-grain sandpaper, be sure to use fine-grain paper before going to the steel wool.

The last abrasive is bathroom cleansing powder used with a soft, damp cloth. Polish with the cleanser until you are satisfied with the finish. Wipe the plate clean with a damp cloth. Do not "dunk" the iron to rinse it.

On a steam iron, dust and damp cleanser will accumulate in the steam holes. Clear the steam holes as well as possible with a straight pin. Then put water in the iron, turn it to a steam setting and hold it in a horizontal, ironing position (but up off the board) for a minute or two, letting the steam clear out the last of the cleanser.

42 / How to replace fuse on a range

An electric frying pan and a toaster may be handy, but they can't replace your electric range when it goes on the blink.

Electric ranges and ovens are fairly complicated and operate on very high voltage so there aren't any major things you want to tackle in the way of repairs.

But fuses in a range don't control the burners or the oven (that's the job of one or two large cartridge fuses in the basement or utility room). Instead, they control the oven light, automatic timer and "convenience outlet" or electric plug-in usually found on the control panel.

The fuses are regular 15-amp, screw-in fuses (Edison base)—the kind you see in home circuit fuse boxes—and are easy to replace once you find them. Sometimes there is one fuse in the range; sometimes two. It depends on how fancy your range is.

The fuses blow or burn out when a defective appliance is plugged in to the convenience outlet or when the extra appliance draws more electricity than the circuit can handle. (The outlets shouldn't carry anything with more than 1700 watts for any length of time.)

Before replacing any fuses, disconnect the electric range somehow. Either pull it out and unplug it or shut down the circuit breaker or fuse box in the basement that controls the range.

Now comes the job of finding the 15-amp fuses. You're likely to need a flashlight, so start the search with one in hand.

Different manufacturers put their fuses in different places. Here is a list of the most common locations:

—Under one of the burners—usually either right rear or front left. Lift the burner and search the nooks and crannies near it. The fuses are often tucked back

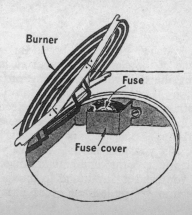

Burner

Fuse

Fuse cover

out of the way in a corner. They may be covered by a small metal protective plate held in place with screws or clips (see sketch).

—The face of the oven area, normally hidden from view by the edge of the drawer that holds pots and pans.

—Under the oven area. Remove the pots-and-pans drawer completely. Get down on the floor and shine the flashlight up toward the bottom of the oven.

Fuses are rarely located on the back side of a range. So you shouldn't have to move the appliance. They can be located behind a removable piece of the range's control panel. But most makers put them in one of the above spots.

Replace the ruined fuses with new ones of the same size (15 amps). Plug in the range again. If the convenience outlet still doesn't work (and the rest of the range does), you'll probably need a serviceman.

43 / How to replace range's defective burner

They say a watched pot never boils. But you may boil when one of the elements on your electric range quits working the day you're "cooking on all burners."

It is sometimes possible to replace a defective burner yourself. Electric ranges are cumbersome and complicated and any home repairs have to be fairly simple tasks. But you may be able to save yourself a service call, if you have the right kind of range.

The kind you need is any brand featuring rangetop burners that can be pulled out (unplugged). You can replace the element at your electric company repair headquarters or a well stocked commercial repair shop for about $12 to $25. (Take the old element along to match for size.)

Before doing anything, unplug the whole range if possible. If not, shut off the range's electricity in the basement or utility room fuse box.

You don't know how to tackle the fuse box?

Find out before you need to from someone who knows. Fuses for the range are usually separate from regular fuses for the rest of the house. They are sometimes in a yank-out section above the other fuses; sometimes in a box of their own with a shut-off handle, sometimes something else.

At the very least, make sure all control knobs on the range are turned to "off."

Flip up the ailing burner just as you would to clean it. Remove the bright metal ring around the burner and the drip shell beneath it. You should now be able to see the place where the burner connects to the stove.

If wires seem to run into a block of porcelain or glass at the connecting point, you probably can't remove the burner yourself. But removable burners plug into the range just like a large lamp or radio plug.

Give the burner a slight tug if you can't tell exactly which it is. But not too hard.

Many plug-in burners have a little sign saying so. It's printed on the disc in the middle of the burner. Another indicator is the angle at which the burner flips up. A plug-in doesn't move as freely as the other kind.

Assuming you can unplug the burner, you still have to figure out where the trouble lies—whether in the burner itself or the wires running to it.

A simple test will give you the answer. Unplug a burner that you know to be good. Insert it where the defective one was. Turn the range back on and see if the good burner will heat in that location.

If the test burner heats, the one you removed is defective. If neither burner will heat, you have trouble somewhere else and should call a serviceman.

A tip: Large burners won't plug into outlets for small burners. But vice-versa will work for a test (not for actual cooking).

44 / How to fix a faulty refrigerator thermostat

You say your Jello won't jell; your fruit mold molds; you've got more sour cream than you ever bought? And all because the refrigerator lost its cool.

Or maybe your refrigerator is working overtime and freezing everything.

In either case, the problem could be in the thermostat—the device that tells your ice box when to run or not run.

You may be able to change your own thermostat and save a service call. It depends on how accessible the device is on your refrigerator—different brands have different arrangements.

If the refrigerator is running all the time, yet never seems to get cold enough, the thermostat is not to blame. It's something else.

If the refrigerator is running all the time and everything is freezing, the thermostat probably is to blame.

If the refrigerator is not running at all, unplug the fridge, remove the thermostat and tape the ends of the two electrical wires together (explanation to come). Plug the fridge back in. If it runs, the thermostat is bad. If it doesn't run, there's something else wrong.

Unplug the refrigerator before fooling with anything. The thermostat is located directly behind the temperature control knob on the side or back wall inside the refrigerator. The temperature control knob usually pulls off, like the knobs on a stove.

The thermostat may be further concealed by a plastic shield that snaps out or is held with a couple of screws. Remove the shield.

The thermostat, when you finally see it, will look like a small metal box (about 2 inches by 3 inches) with two wires and a skinny tube running from it. It may be held to the refrigerator wall with a couple of screws or it may just snap into place with prongs.

Disconnect the two electrical wires. Some are held to the thermostat with terminal screws (just loosen the screws); some are attached with pull-off clips or little plugs. (Freezer compartment controls sometimes have three electric wires. Make sure you hook up any new thermostat the same way the old one was attached.)

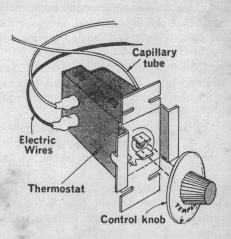

Capillary tube

Electric Wires

Thermostat

Control knob

The skinny tube you see is called a capillary tube and is made of metal. It cannot be detached from the thermostat.

The end of the capillary tube is sensitized to test

the temperature inside the refrigerator. Thermostats on new refrigerators usually have capillary tubes that just stick out into the air and sample air temperature. The capillary tubes on older refrigerators often run from the thermostat, through the refrigerator wall, and attach to the cold plate or cooling coils inside the refrigerator compartment.

It may take you a while to locate the cold plate. It can be almost anywhere inside the refrigerator compartment and may be covered by a plastic shield. It can also be located in the freezer section.

If you have the older kind of capillary tube, detach it from the cold plate and fasten a heavy string or lightweight wire securely to the end of it.

Pull the thermostat and capillary tube out of the refrigerator, allowing the string to follow the "cap" tube up through the wall. This is easier said than done.

Jot down the make and model number of your refrigerator. Take this information, along with the old thermostat, to a well-stocked repair shop for a replacement.

Reverse the whole procedure to install the new thermostat and cap tube. (If there are just two electrical wires for the thermostat, it doesn't matter which one fastens to which terminal screw.)

If the new cap tube is too long, do not—repeat, do not—cut it. It won't work any more if you do. Curl up the excess near the thermostat or the cold plate.

If you lose the string for this Hansel and Gretel act, you can simply run the cap tube to the cold plate without threading through the refrigerator wall. It will work; it just won't look so great.

A No. 5 setting on one thermostat is not always the same as a No. 5 setting on another. Set the temperature dial where you think it should be; wait 24 hours, then make any necessary temperature changes.

45 / First aid for a plugged washer

Have you ever had a washing machine cough up its socks? It's not a very pleasant happening and usually means a service call unless you know what to do yourself.

The inner tub of a washer (the place where you put the clothes) rotates within an outer tub or shell. Both tubs hold water. The washer drains itself through a hole and hose at the bottom of the outer tub.

Occasionally, especially on older models, something light like a baby sock will float up and out of the inner tub. It travels over into the outer tub and down into the tub drain, blocking the flow of water.

If the garment is very small and light, it will actually get sucked through the tub hose into the pump itself.

If your machine is not pumping water out, you can test for blockage.

Take the drain hose from your laundry basin and lay it down flat on the floor to drain by gravity. If water gushes out, your pump is probably bad and you need a repairman. If water only trickles out and you know the washer tub is full, there is some kind of blockage in the hoses.

Turn off and unplug the machine before doing any work on it. Also allow as much water as possible to drain from the machine by gravity.

You want to unhook at least one end of the drain hose from either the bottom of the tub or the beginning of the pump. To do this, you must remove the washer's access panel.

The access panel may be the whole front of the washer, the whole back, or parts thereof. You'll just have to explore and get to know your own machine.

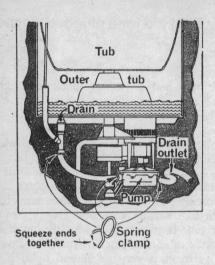

Look for a combination of screws and clips holding the access panel in place.

The insides of the machine, once exposed, will look quite confusing. But you can trace the path you need to follow.

Look for a fat black hose coming from the bottom of the outer washer tub. It runs to the pump—a gismo about the size of a cottage cheese carton. If you can't find what you want, start from the other end. Trace the last stage of the drain hose backward. It also connects to the pump.

A simple washer will have two hose connections at the pump. A washer with a lint recirculator will have four. But the two main drain hoses (see sketch) should be slightly fatter than the other two. It doesn't really matter if you unfasten the wrong hoses anyway. It will just take you more time and sweat to find the sock.

Disconnect the hose from the tub where it joins the pump. Do this by loosening the clip that holds the hose. Some clips have a screw you can undo. Other clips look like the one in the sketch. (Pinch that style with pliers and twist the hose loose at the same time. You don't need to take the clip clear off.)

Explore with flashlight and a mirror if needed. Remove any obstruction with needle-nose pliers.

Part III:

Common Problems in Plumbling, Heating and Cooling

46 / Some handy plumbers' tips

Plumbers know all kinds of handy little hints you never see in repair books—things they have just picked up through the years.

None of the hints involve a lot of "doing." They're just little stop-gap measures until major repairs can be done—or tips on how to keep things running right.

Here are a few for you:

Repair of a leaky faucet sometimes has to wait till the weekend. Or a faucet may start leaking heavily all at once. If the faucet is on a basement tub, where the end of the spout is usually "threaded," borrow the nozzle from your garden hose. Screw the nozzle onto the end of the faucet spout and turn the nozzle to the off position. This will contain the drips until you can tackle them on a permanent basis (see sketch).

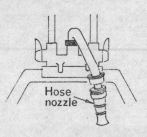

If the faucet spout is not threaded (a bathroom sink, for instance), look underneath the sink for small faucet handles on the pipes leading up to the sink. (There should be one handle on the hot line and one on the cold, if provided at all.) Turn the appropriate one to the off position. This shuts off the hot and/ or cold water supply to the sink faucet until you can make needed repairs.

Automatic clothes washers that discharge into laundry tubs often cause drain problems because of all the lint in the used water. Find an old nylon stocking and put it over the end of the washer's discharging hose. Fasten it with a heavy rubber band. Leave the stocking long, so the foot of it dangles onto the bottom of the laundry tub. This keeps the weight of accumulated lint from pulling the stocking off the hose (see sketch).

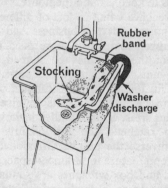

Kitchen sink drains may never give you trouble if you simply take the time to rinse soap scum and food particles out of them after washing dishes. You don't need to use hot water; cold or temperate will do.

Let the soapy water run out of the sink. Fill the sink again with clear water, then pull the plug. This works better than just running the faucet. What you want is a strong rush of water all at once. Rinse the drain every time you do dishes or maybe a couple of times a week, depending on how much junk you put down your drains.

47 / Some handy dandy wrenches and how to use them

Wrenches are nearly indispensable for any kind of plumbing job. And they come in handy for other home repair work too—any time you need to hold a nut or bolt steady or turn it.

Here's a run-down of the most common and handiest wrenches to keep around the house.

Socket wrenches come in lots of different sizes with different handles. But the business end of the thing is a sturdy tube, an inch or more deep (see sketch). The inside of the tube may be shaped to fit square nuts or any nuts having up to 12 sides. The tube is designed to fit down into hard-to-reach places. Socket wrenches can be bought in sets to give you several different head sizes. Some handles have what is called a reversible ratchet. You flip a little button (see sketch) to reverse the pulling direction of the handle —another good feature for cramped spaces.

Open end and box wrenches are similar and can be bought separately or in combination. Both types come in various sizes and are not adjustable. That is, the size of the business end cannot be changed. Both are fairly light weight and have reasonably small heads that fit into close quarters. (Good for removing the nuts around sink faucets, for example, where a bulky wrench won't fit between faucet handle and spout.)

The open end type has a sort of C-shaped head. The box type head is closed all the way around (see sketch). The box type head, giving you a slightly better grip than the open end, should be used for final tightening or freeing of "frozen" nuts.

Adjustable wrenches are very versatile in that a dial device allows you to change the head size. The wrench itself is available in lengths anywhere from about 4 inches up to 24 inches and has a C-shaped head see sketch). The bigger and longer the wrench

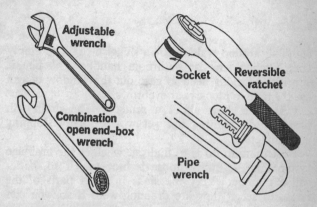

is, the harder the job it will handle. A medium sized one is good to have around the house, especially for jobs like removing rings or nuts from drain pipes.

Adjust the wrench jaws to fit snugly against the sides of any nut or bolt you are turning. Allowing the wrench to slip can round off the edges of the nut, making it almost impossible to turn.

Pipe or Stillson wrenches are a bit like adjustable wrenches in that you can change the head size or jaw span. But the jaws are shaped more like an open-sided box instead of a "C," and the edges of the jaws usually have teeth (see sketch). Pipe wrenches are designed for grabbing and turning round smooth objects like pipes (surprise!)—thus the teeth. When gripping a pipe, don't force the pipe all the way into the wrench head. Confine the gripping work to the two toothed surfaces.

One general rule: Pull a wrench rather than push it, whenever possible. This will save you from skinned knuckles should the wrench slip.

48 / Unplug that slow drain

Standing around waiting for a sluggish drain to empty your kitchen sink or bathroom handbowl is fine if you feel a driving need to gaze out the window or can use the time to pluck your eyebrows.

Otherwise, how about a remedy? The drain will probably do nothing but get worse, finally stopping up completely.

First thing to do is to find out whether the drainage system for the entire house is blocked (if so, better call a plumber). Try the sinks in other parts of the house to see if they are draining well. If so, you can go to work:

Trying simplest things first, use a plunger (plumber's helper). If the sink is full to the brim, dip the water out of it into a bucket until three or four inches of it remain in the sink. Smear the bottom edge of the plunger's rubber cup with petroleum jelly to make a better seal. Stuff a damp rag into the little overflow drain on the side of the handbowl. This concentrates all the pressure of the plunger on the drain hole.

Work the plunger up and down vigorously over the drain hole several times in a row. Don't give up too soon.

If you have a pop-up drain stopper that rides high in the open position and interferes with the action of the plunger, better take it out. That's the next step anyway, if the plunger has no effect.

At this point, some people recommend using a chemical drain cleaner. Do so if you wish; but there are risks involved. If the household pipes are very old, some plumbers say a chemical solvent can eat right through them. Solvent should also be avoided if the drain is totally blocked, with no movement of water at all.

To remove the drain stopper, take hold of it in the "open" position, turn it, then lift up. If jiggling around does not free it, then it's the kind that must be released from underneath the handbowl.

Place a bucket under the sink to catch any water while you are working.

Underneath the handbowl toward the back, there should be a rod coming down from the stopper handle. This first rod joins a second one (at a 90-degree angle) which runs to the bottom part of the stopper. The second rod is secured to the drainpipe with a nut, which can be turned counterclockwise with a wrench and removed. (See sketch.) Once the nut is loosened, slide the rod out a couple of inches, freeing the stopper.

(When you pull the rod back, you will probably bring with it some water, a small spring and a rubber or plastic washer—a little ring. Don't worry about these. Just put them back the way you found them at the end of the job).

Now remove the stopper and clean it of all hair, suds and other extraneous items. If, after this, you go back to using the plunger, be sure to screw the stopper nut back in place or you will squirt water all over the flow.

If this still doesn't help the drainage, next step is to take the trap apart—the trap being that gooseneck-curved portion of the drainpipe.

Look at the very bottom of the gooseneck curve. If you see a smallish nut screwed into the pipe like a plug, you're in luck. Unfasten it with a wrench. This will let out all the water in the trap, so make sure that bucket is still in place.

Poke around inside the drainpipe, in all directions, with a straightened coat hanger or—better yet—a plumber's auger or "snake." These are sturdy but flexible metal rods with a handle attached and range in price from $2 to $21. The cheapest models are generally good enough for amateur plumbing jobs.

If there is no nut at the bottom of the gooseneck, you will need to take the trap apart. This is done by unscrewing the two slip nuts (again, counterclockwise) which encircle the drainpipe at each end of the curve. (See sketch).

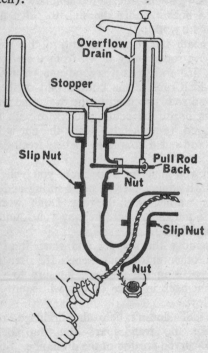

Under each slip nut, you will probably find a rubber ring or washer or some string-like wrapping. Be sure to put these back or replace them when putting the trap together again.

With the trap removed, go through the bit with the "snake" or straight coat hanger, cleaning out both the trap and the rest of the pipe.

If none of these measures has any effect, you may need a professional plumber (plus the shoulder of someone to cry on).

Handy hint: When screwing the slip nuts back in place, smear the threaded grooves with petroleum jelly. They will be easier to remove in the future.

49 / How to speed up sluggish drain

An individual drain in your house may run slowly, telling you it needs to be cleared. But in some houses, all the drains are slow. What's more, they cough, gurgle and act in general as if they're going to "spit up." The performance is sometimes accompanied by fluctuation of the water level in the toilet bowl.

This problem may indicate, among other things, a partially blocked vent stack.

The drain system in your house has to breathe. When water flows down the main pipe, the moving mass creates a suction behind itself. Unless air flows after the water, or chases it, the water slows down and gurgles and creates suction in all the drain pipes, including the toilet bowl.

A vent stack provides the needed air. The stack is simply an extension of the main drainpipe that runs up through the house and out the roof, like a small chimney (see sketch).

Most vent stacks are installed without any kind of cover. Thus leaves, branches, dead squirrels and any number of things can collect in them, partially cutting off the air flow.

If you don't mind climbing around on the roof, you can check the vent stack yourself for any obstructions.

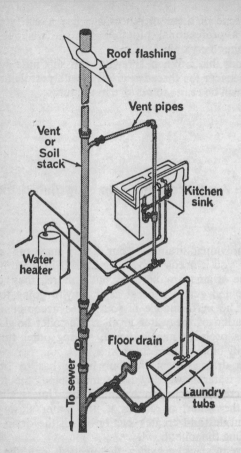

But if you can't see anything in the stack within reach, you'll probably need to call a professional. The job can cost anywhere from about $50 to $100.

Some people put wire mesh over a vent stack. But this has drawbacks too, since the mesh itself can collect leaves and debris.

While on the subject of drains, here's a handy thing to know:

If your basement or guest bathroom "smells funny"

or has an odor of sewer gas, you can often cure the problem with a few cups of water.

Basement floor drains have a trap curve like the kind you see under a sink—except in this case the trap is under the floor (see sketch). There should be water in the trap to keep sewer odors from drifting up the main drainpipe back into the house. If a basement floor drain has not been used for several months, it is possible for the water in the trap to evaporate.

Pour a gallon or so of water down the drain. Then pour a cup or two into it every month. Do the same with the bathtub and handbowl in a seldom-used bathroom.

50 / Liquid drain cleaners—handy, dangerous

With its typical penchant for new household aids, the American public has latched onto chemical drain cleaners as quick cure-alls for clogged plumbing.

Chemical cleaners do have a place. Used sparingly and sensibly as preventive medicine, they can keep a drain from stopping up. And if there is absolutely no way of getting into a drainpipe or of taking it apart, a chemical cleaner can be handy if used properly. But the list of drawbacks is significant. And anyone who tries home drain repairs should know about them.

For starters, liquid and granulated drain cleaners are among the most dangerous chemicals to be found in a home. Most are marked "poison" and/or "extremely harmful if swallowed." They must always be kept out of reach of children and pets.

These chemicals are designed to eat through things— grease, fat, hair, soap scum. But they don't stop there.

If accidentally splashed on you, they will eat through clothing, burn skin and cause blindness. Consumer experts suggest that the user wear rubber gloves, old clothing and protective eye goggles when using a drain cleaner.

Some brands, particularly those marked "enzyme," are milder and safer to use. But there is a tradeoff in efficiency, according to some experts. The stronger drain cleaners are based on either sodium hydroxide, caustic potash or sulfuric acid.

In dealing with these, instructions must be followed to the letter. Many chemical cleaners—particularly the granules—create heat when mixed with water. When instructions say to add cold or lukewarm water, there is a good reason. Hot or boiling water, added to some brands, can turn a drainpipe into something like a rocket. According to one professional plumber, it can create enough heat to split the pipes.

The problem is that most labels do not give sufficient warning of what can happen if directions are not followed exactly. Home repair manuals say, "Don't use a plunger (rubber suction cup) while chemical is in the drain." The sloshing, spurting action of a plunger could easily send caustic chemicals onto the user.

But enough about safety.

Based on articles in consumer magazines and on interviews with professional plumbers, garbage disposal dealers and a chemistry professor, the following practical drawbacks are noted:

Some cleaners that work fine on grease make nothing but trouble in bathroom tubs and sinks, where blockage is usually caused by accumulated hair and soap scum. Various plumbers say they have seen hair turned into a glue-like substance which stays in the drain and continues to collect debris.

If a liquid cleaner fails to clear a totally blocked drain, you are faced with a pipe full of caustic chemical. About the only remedy is to remove the drain trap, making sure there is a bucket to catch the chemical.

If a granulated cleaner is used on a completely

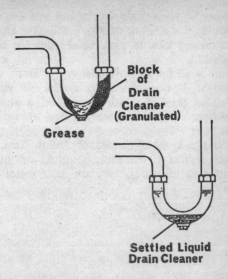

Block of Drain Cleaner (Granulated)

Grease

Settled Liquid Drain Cleaner

blocked drain and does not work, the problem is different. Some types, after the original chemical reaction calms down, will "form up," just like concrete.

Some will do this anyway, even on a partially clogged drain, if enough water is not added.

Other granulated cleaners have aluminum added, which causes temporary violent agitation and prevents solidification for a time. But one byproduct of the chemical-aluminum reaction is hydrogen gas—highly flammable. Drop a cigarette ash down the drain and you're likely to get an explosion.

Some makes of drain cleaner on the market will ruin a garbage disposal unit. Exceptions are the mild enzyme cleaners. But as one disposal dealer says, "If it's mild enough to be safe for a disposal unit, it probably won't do much to help the drain."

Liquid cleaners are mostly formulated to be heavier than water. So they sink to the bottom of the U-shaped pipe trap and stay there unless flushed out thoroughly. Some brands are so strong they warn on the label, "May reveal weakness in pipes." If you have old pipes, the cleaner may eat right through if not flushed out. Even brands that are not so strong will have an eventual effect on any kind of pipe metal when the chemical base is caustic.

To sum it all up, one plumber says, "Drain cleaners are all right, I guess, if used correctly. But you know people. They think if a little bit is good, a whole lot is even better. And that's where they always get in trouble."

If you use a chemical cleaner, follow directions to the letter. If it says "one tablespoonful," or "flush with tap turned to full blast," or "use cool water"—do it that way.

51 / Stop that big drip

A dripping faucet is more than an annoyance. It's also a drain on the budget.

The most common causes of faucet leaks are worn washers, deteriorated packing or corroded valve seats. If water comes out around the handle, it's generally the packing; if water drips from the spout, it's probably the washer or seat.

The following directions apply to the normal, turn-type faucet. Lever-style faucets are something else again—the subject of another essay, or a call to a plumber.

1. Most important, shut off the water supply before you take the faucet apart. Unless, of course, you plan on a new decor for your apartment—Early Everglades. Shut off the supply at the water meter. This you will probably find in the basement or utility room close to the wall. The meter itself looks like a bulbous metal

growth on the water pipes and may have a flip-top lid protecting the numbered register. There should be a shut-off valve right next to the meter (it may turn just like an outside hydrant or it may require a wrench).

2. Turn on the ailing sink faucet to let the remaining water drain out. If you have a lower story to the house, turn on a faucet there too. That will take care of any seepage through the water meter valve. Then close the drain or put a towel in the basin so you won't lose dropped screws.

3. The first thing you need to remove is the top screw that holds the faucet handle in place. If you don't see it, don't despair; it's there someplace: Unless you have very fancy faucets, there is probably a little disk on the top that has an "H" or a "C" on it. This disk snaps up (or sometimes screws off) to reveal the screw. It usually fits pretty close to the handle, however, so you may need something like a metal nail file or the point of an ice pick to get under the edge of it.

A tip: As you take the faucet apart, set each piece in a row as removed to avoid confusion when putting it back together.

4. Next, unscrew the bonnet or packing nut with a wrench. (To protect the finish, wrap nut with tape beforehand.) In some faucets, there may be a decorative shell over the whole affair, which will have to be removed first.

Rubber washers and packing material cost only a few cents, so you may want to replace both at the same time. But different faucet styles use different sizes; so take the disassembled faucet stem to the nearest hardware store and ask them to match the pieces you want replaced.

The packing inside the packing nut may look like string, reinforced cardboard or graphite (the color of pencil lead) and can be pried out.

5. After the bonnet has been removed, take the faucet stem out by turning it in the same direction you would to turn the water on. On the bottom of the stem,

you will see a small washer held in place with a screw. Undo the screw and replace the washer with a new one of the same size and shape (some are flat and some are rounded on one side). If the washer is rounded on one side, make sure the new one is installed facing the same direction as the old one.

6. If replacing the washer or packing does not help, the trouble may be a corroded or damaged valve seat. (See sketch.) It is possible to buy a little tool to grind

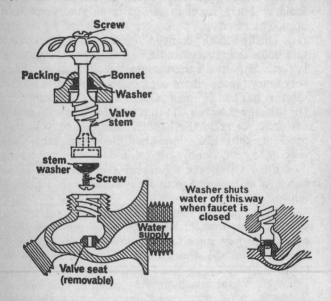

the surface of the seat (they come as cheap as $1). But if you don't know what you're doing, it it easy to grind too long or at an angle—which ruins the valve seat.

So it is often smarter to just buy a new seat (less than $1). If the seat has a square or hexagonal hole in it, it is usually removable. But for this, you will need an Allen wrench (not really a wrench at all, but a solid metal rod, bent at a 90-degree angle and tapering to a hexagonal end). Insert this into the valve seat to unscrew it. Again, have the hardware store match the new seat to the old one.

7. Reassemble the faucet, screwing everything back together securely—but without forcing. As you begin screwing the bonnet nut back in place, you should be able to jiggle the stem freely up and down within it. If the stem is already screwed down against the seat as far as it will go, screwing the bonnet nut back on may force the stem right through the seat. Just make sure the faucet is in the open position as you reassemble it.

Note: If the faucet assembly is so old and badly corroded that it breaks apart in your hands (or looks like it might), take it to a hardware store and have it matched with new equipment.

52 / Noisy pipes? There's a reason

Do your water pipes thump and clank like Marley's ghost when you turn the faucets off? Plumbers call this condition "water hammer."

Here is what happens: Water flows from an open faucet with considerable pressure and momentum. When you shut the faucet off quickly, the water is stopped short with no place to go. Unless there is a "cushion" somewhere in the piping system to absorb the shock, it causes the pipes to thump and vibrate.

Most plumbing systems built in the last thirty years have shock-absorbing cushions in the form of air chambers. These are pipes that usually rise perpendicularly from the main water pipe, going nowhere, just sticking up in the air about 18 inches.

These pipes are filled with air. Air will compress; water will not. So when the fast-moving mass of water is stopped short, the excess sort of whooshes up a little way into the air chamber, with the air acting as a compressible cushion.

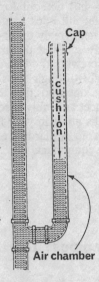

The problem is that after several years of this pressure, the air can gradually be forced out of these chambers through minute leaks in the caps. They then fill completely with water and become useless as cushions.

The remedy, in most cases, is simple. You drain the house water pipes of all water. This lets air into everything (except the hot water tank). Then, when you turn the water back on, the air in the chambers is trapped right where it is supposed to be.

To drain the system, first find the water meter in your house. If you have a basement it is surely there. Otherwise look in the utility room. It is always located within a few feet of the point where the water pipes enter your house from outdoors.

The water meter itself is a fairly large, bulbous, metal affair with a gauge on top that is sometimes covered with a flip lid. Somewhere near the water meter, on the pipe running to it or from it, you will find a faucet handle. It usually resembles an outdoor hydrant handle.

Turn it to the off position.

Now go to every faucet in the house—whether tub or sink—and open each one on both the hot and cold side. (Don't forget the basement faucets, if there are any.)

Leave all the faucets open for at least fifteen minutes. Then shut them. Go back to the water meter and turn the pressure back on. Then go to each faucet in the house and turn it on until water starts coming out and it stops sputtering.

53 / "Backwashing" hot water faucets

Older homes with galvanized or ferrous plumbing pipes sometimes display a curious phenomenon: At a given sink or tub, the cold water will run just fine. But you can barely get any hot water at all from the very same faucet.

A common reason for this is corrosion and sediment in the hot water pipe running to that sink. For some reason, hot water corrodes pipes faster and leaves much more sediment than does cold water.

Sediment and corrosion build up to a stubborn layer in the pipes, with bits and pieces occasionally breaking loose and floating around to collect at "elbows" or narrow points in the pipes.

The only long-term remedy for this problem is having the old, ferrous pipes replaced by a professional with something like copper that is less subject to corrosion.

But there is a simple trick you can try that works to clear blocked hot water faucets about 50 percent of the time. It's called backwashing. It doesn't take any special equipment; but it is simpler on faucets where both hot and cold come out of a single spout.

The first step is to shut *off* the water pressure at the hot water tank. To do this, look at the two pipes extending from the top of the hot water tank. One of them should have a faucet handle resembling the kind you see on outdoor water spigots. The handle is usually located on the pipe that feeds water into the tank (see sketch). Turn the handle to the closed position.

Next, turn *on* the hot water faucet at a sink or tub that lies between the blocked sink and the hot water tank. Leave that faucet on through the whole procedure.

For example, let's say it's an upstairs kitchen sink faucet that is giving you trouble. If you have a basement laundry tub, it is probably directly below and on the same hot water pipe as the kitchen sink.

Turn on the hot water faucet of the laundry tub. If the faucet spout of the laundry tub happens to have an aerator (bubble maker) on the end of it, unscrew and remove the aerator.

Now go upstairs and turn *on* the hot water faucet of the kitchen sink. Also remove any aerator on the end of that water spout.

Place your hand or a rag firmly over the end of the kitchen water spout and turn on the cold water at the same sink. Turn it on with as much force as you can control without spraying the whole room.

Leave your hand over the end of the spout and leave the hot water handle of the sink *open*.

What happens is this: The cold water, unable to escape through the faucet spout, travels over to the opened hot water valve and flows backward down the hot water pipe to the opened spigot of the laundry tub

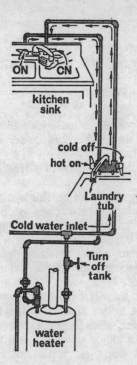

downstairs. As it goes, it takes loose sediment and corrosion with it (see sketch).

After you have backwashed for three or four minutes, shut both faucet handles at the kitchen sink. Then go and turn the hot water pressure back on at the water tank. Let hot water run out of the laundry tub tap for a minute to clear that pipe of air. Then turn on other hot water faucets in the house, one at a time, to clear them.

One caution: In backwashing hot water pipes, you may simply chase the obstruction from one faucet to another. So keep that in mind and choose the lesser of two evils.

54 / How to thaw out frozen pipes

Frozen water pipes are often tricky to thaw out. But there are a few things the homeowner can try before calling a plumber.

Professional plumbers say two freezing points are most common.

1. The pipe running to an outside hydrant.
2. Pipes running to a kitchen or bathroom sink. These traditionally pass from the basement wash tub right up past the basement window.

Outside hydrant pipes typically freeze when the homeowner forgets to shut off the water supply to the hydrant in the fall.

Hydrant pipes usually branch off from a major line, so you may not notice that the pipe is frozen until it ruptures. (Water, when frozen, expands.)

Blockages on a major water line will be immediately noticeable. You won't get water out of a particular sink—or maybe two. And for some complicated reason, hot water pipes freeze faster than cold water pipes.

Check the basement walls along the entire pipe system for any small cracks or holes. Cracks around basement windows or holes in the glass are notorious culprits.

A small, concentrated stream of cold air will freeze nearby pipes more readily than will a big general blast of cold air (as through an open garage door). But the pipe left open to winter weather is vulnerable.

If the line for your kitchen sink runs up from a basement tub, try the tub faucet. If the tub faucet works and the kitchen faucet doesn't, the freeze point is somewhere between the two locations.

Now comes the job of thawing.

Leave the main water line open, maintaining normal pressure with the sink faucets open. This will let you know immediately when the thawing process begins to work because the water will start moving.

The idea behind thawing is to heat the pipe—but not so hot that the water turns to steam. Steam, if trapped on either side by ice, will rupture the pipe.

Towels dipped in boiling water and wrapped around the pipe are safe. If there's no water to boil, get some from the neighbors or melt some snow.

A hair dryer, the air stream directed up and down the side of the pipe, is also good. But when using any electrical appliance, keep your hands off the pipe. You will be a path for electricity from the appliance to the pipe if the appliance develops a short circuit.

Other sources of heat are electric light bulbs, sunlamps, space heaters, and heating pads. Keep sunlamps and space heaters a few inches back from the pipe.

Do not try using a blow torch unless you are an expert.

A handy and inexpensive gadget is a pipe heating cable—an insulated flat cord that puts out low, constant heat and runs less than $1 a foot. One end plugs into an ordinary electrical outlet and the rest wraps around the pipe.

Directions for use are on the package. The main thing to beware of is a crack in the wire insulation.

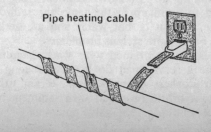

Pipe heating cable

This could electrify the water pipe. Install the cable when it is warm and pliable to avoid cracking.

Heating cable not only thaws pipes; it keeps them from freezing again. Other preventive steps include patching all wall and window cracks and wrapping exposed pipes with insulating material available at any building supply store.

Letting faucets drip during a particularly cold night will keep the water moving, sometimes avoiding a freeze-up.

If your frozen pipes are located in the crawl space under the house or are hidden inside the walls, your best bet is to call a plumber.

55 / Drain your water heater

There's probably no such thing as Be Kind to Your Water Heater week. But your water heater does need some loving attention to keep on working the way it should.

The only things you need to worry much about are keeping the area around the water heater clean and well-ventilated and draining the water out of the heater every six months or so.

This draining helps remove sediment from the tank. If allowed to build up in the tank, the sediment will reduce the amount of hot water you are getting and will cause other more serious problems.

If you have not drained your water heater in two years, have a serviceman do it. In that long a time, the rubber washers or rings in the drain valve may have become brittle or caked with sediment and you may not be able to get the valve completely shut again if you try it yourself. After having the serviceman out, you can do it yourself once every six months.

This is the procedure:

Up at the top of the water heater are two pipes. One feeds cold water into the tank. The other sends hot water out of it. You can tell one pipe from the other by touch after you let about a gallon of hot water run out of a faucet somewhere in the house. Each pipe has a handle on it to shut off the flow of water. Turn off the flow of cold water into the tank. Leave the hot water pipe alone.

If you have a gas heater, look on the side of the water heater for a squarish box with a temperature dial on the side of it and one or two buttons on top of it. The box may be located near the floor or at eye level. It may also have a removable protective shell over it.

The typical control box has, as mentioned, a temperature dial (see sketch B), a red button used for reigniting the pilot light when it is out and another dial with the words on, off and pilot printed on it. It's the "on-off-pilot" switch that you're interested in at this point.

Turn the dial to "pilot" (do not pass "off" in the process or you will extinguish the pilot light). This keeps the gas burner from coming on while you are draining the tank.

Electric water heaters usually have switches located on the house wall near the water heater or near the household fuse box. They look like ordinary light switches. There may be one or two. Turn them both off.

Draining the water heater will be much easier if you open a hot water faucet somewhere in the house—preferably upstairs. This allows air to replace the water that is leaving the tank.

Get a length of garden hose to attach to the drain valve. You will be dealing with quite a bit of water and an ordinary bucket just won't be satisfactory. Drain valves vary somewhat in style, but most are made to take a garden hose connection. Run the hose to the basement floor drain, or out the door. Try to keep the end of the hose low. Water in the tank will drain to a level no lower than the end of the hose.

The drain valve itself should be on the side of the water heater, near the floor. It usually looks just like an outdoor water hydrant (see sketch A). Turn it to

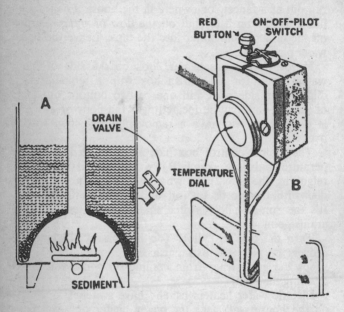

the open position and let all of the water leave the tank.

The bottom of the water tank inside the water heater is dome shaped as in sketch A), allowing sediment to collect in the low places beneath the level of the drain valve. It's no great tragedy if that sediment never gets entirely cleared out.

But you can get rid of some of it by the following steps: After all the water is drained from the tank, turn on the cold water inlet valve on the pipe at the top of the water heater. Turn it on full blast to stir up any loose sediment in the bottom of the tank. Let it run just until water is coming out strongly from the drain valve, then shut it off and let the tank drain down again. Do this two or three times until the draining water runs fairly clear.

When the job is finished, shut the drain valve. Turn on the cold water inlet valve and leave it on. Go upstairs to the hot water faucet that you left open; wait until water starts coming out of it and then close it. Go to each additional hot water faucet in the house, turn it on until water comes out and then shut it. This removes air from the system.

Finally, return to the water heater and turn the on-off-pilot dial back to "on" (or flip the electric switches).

56 / How to fix a rackety radiator, cold boiler

If you have a steam system, the thing in the basement or utility room that you call a furnace is actually a boiler—a big tank of water with a heating element attached. As the water boils, steam rises up a main pipe, called a header, to warm the radiators, condense back into water and run back down to the boiler. (See sketch A.)

Boilers come in many different shapes and sizes and use different fuels. But they have several things in common.

One is the gauge glass, a clear tube hanging on the side of the boiler (see sketch B). The water level in the gauge glass corresponds to the water level in the boiler. If the boiler has an automatic feed device,

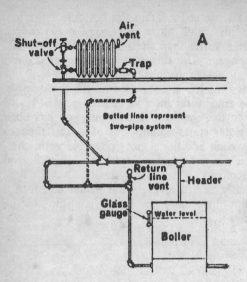

the water will stay at about the one-third level on its own.

But if the boiler has a manual feed—and most small to medium homes do—you should keep the water level about half way up the glass. Some boilers may need filling once a day; Others maybe once a week. Check yours once a day until you learn its cycle.

To fill the boiler, find the refill valve (looks just like the handle on an outdoor water hydrant) on the water line leading into the boiler (sketch B). Wait till the heat has been off about 10 minutes. Turn the valve just a bit, until you can hear water running SLOWLY into the tank. DO NOT turn the faucet on full blast. This floods the warm or hot tank with a sudden volume of icy water, creating stress that could crack the boiler.

Even worse is adding water to a hot boiler that has run dry. If, when you check, you can see no water

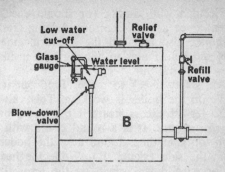

at all in the glass, turn the household thermostat way down and wait for the boiler to cool.

If the boiler is standing free, wait till you can put your hands on it without being burned; if it's enclosed in a metal cabinet, wait until the cabinet is no longer warm. Again, add water slowly.

Boilers should not actually run dry. There is a safety device on many of them that is supposed to shut off the heat when the water level gets low (see low water cut-off, sketch B). But sometimes this device becomes fouled and quits working.

To keep this from happening, you should clear the dirty water and sediment from the cut-off mechanism once every two to four weeks by opening the blow-down valve.

This is a faucet-looking handle (sketch B), spring loaded (which means it will close by itself if you let go of it), and may or may not have a long pipe "spout" attached to it. Turn the household thermostat up to test the cut-off while draining it. Make sure the glass gauge is at the halfway mark. Place a bucket under the blow-down valve and let the water out of it until the water runs clear. The heat should shut off as the water level gets low. Afterward, bring the water level in the glass gauge back up to half.

There is also a way to drain the actual boiler. But unless the water in the glass is the color of chocolate milk, it is best to leave this to the judgment of the serviceman who checks (or should check) your equpiment once a year. Reason: Adding fresh water to the boiler also adds all the chemicals that water contains and contributes to "liming" the inside of the boiler.

A good safety check to make: Find out if the relief valve on the boiler is working. This valve is designed to let off excess steam if the boiler builds up too much pressure. It is a round gismo with a small lever on top sometimes found atop the boiler, sometimes on the side (sketch B). While the heat is on, lift up or push down briefly on the lever. It should hiss. If it doesn't, have the valve replaced or repaired.

Now to the radiators. There are two different kinds —one-pipe and two-pipe. Sketch A shows, basically, a one-pipe system; the dotted lines show where outlets are in a two-pipe system.

With one-pipers, you should keep the shut-off valve (sketch A) either all the way open or all the way closed. Incoming steam and outgoing condensate use the same opening; if it isn't open wide, the steam and water will "fight" each other, causing all kinds of racket.

The radiator air vent (sketch A) lets air flow out as steam flows in. When hot steam hits the air vent, it's supposed to close; so if you see steam coming from the vent, the temperature control inside it is broken and the vent should be replaced (about $3 to $6; take it along for the hardware store to match).

If the air vent is clogged, the radiator will be cold because the steam can't get in. To check the air vent, turn the radiator OFF, let it cool, unscrew the vent and try to blow through it. If you can't, get a new vent.

To help remedy loud pounding in a one-pipe system, check the return line vents (see sketch A) near the boiler. They are somewhat like the radiator vents. Also, prop the legs of the radiator so that it's either exactly level or tips ever so slightly toward the single pipe.

A two-pipe radiator usually has no air vent. Rather, there is a fist-sized trap on the outflow line at the bottom of the radiator (sketch A). This, like a vent, helps control how much steam enters the radiator and has a temperature sensitive device inside.

If it breaks down or fails "open," the affected radiator will heat like crazy while others are relatively cool—because steam is going through and through the radiator with nothing to stop it. One of the return line vents near the boiler will probably also be spouting steam.

If the trap fails "closed," the radiator will fail to heat. A serviceman can replace a trap or you can unscrew the top of it with a wrench and take the top to a dealer for replacement. But turn the radiator off first and let it cool.

Two-pipe radiators should be either level or tipped just slightly toward the lower outflow pipe. The shut-off valve on a two-piper CAN be set halfway open or closed, since condensate leaves by the lower pipe.

57 / How to clear blocked garbage disposal

You're in the midst of preparing company dinner.

You flip the garbage disposal switch to clear the sink of egg shells and pomegranate seeds and . . . the silly thing just hums at you for 20 seconds and then dies.

There's an 80 percent chance that a simple obstruction is keeping the unit from whirring happily. Before frantically calling a repairman, consider this: Most garbage disposal warranties do not cover service calls on obstructions.

So you might as well try a few simple things first on your own.

First, turn off the wall switch. If your unit plugs in to an electrical outlet under the sink, pull out the plug too for good measure.

Now remove everything from the disposal until you can see the flat plate at the bottom (you'll need a flashlight). On most models, you will see two metal protrusions or "lugs" toward the outside edge of the bottom plate or turntable. These, in combination with the whirling plate, reduce the garbage to bits.

Try to spot what has obstructed the progress of the lugs. To free the mechanism, you will have to reverse the action of the turntable.

Some garbage disposals have a reverse-action switch, labeled as such, on the bottom part of the unit under the sink.

If yours doesn't, you will have to manually prod the turntable backwards. This is traditionally accomplished with a broom stick, but a sturdy wooden spoon does just as well.

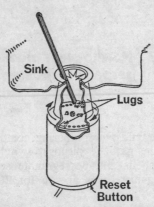

Just one catch. Not all disposals turn in the same direction. Most of them run counter-clockwise; so you will try to turn the lugs clockwise.

But to double-check, see on which side of the lug

the obstruction or remaining garbage has accumulated. The build-up will be on the forward side of the lug—the direction in which the grinder was turning when it quit.

Place your chosen prod at an angle against the obstructed lug and push or rap "smartly." Garbage disposals will take considerable abuse; but don't hammer with all your strength (unless you're a real weakling) and don't push straight down (it accomplishes nothing).

All is not over. There is a button on the very bottom of many disposals (under the sink) called a reset switch. It is a safety device that automatically turns the unit off when a jam or overload occurs.

The unit will not start again until you push the reset button. These buttons are normally recessed for protection; so use a pencil eraser or something similar to poke the little dear back into action.

If your garbage disposal has no reset button, it probably resets itself automatically.

If whirrs are still not forthcoming, make a final check in the household fuse box. The fuse or circuit breaker controlling the garbage unit may have blown. Replace the fuse or flip the circuit breaker.

Some disposals require that the lid be properly in place before they will start, so check the lid too.

58 / Mixed-up showerhead and how to fix it

If your showerhead sprays water every way but straight, the little holes through which the water comes may be clogged with chemical deposits.

You can try poking into the holes with a straight

pin or needle. This may work for a while, but the sediment is actually still knocking around in there. So the best thing is to take the showerhead apart if possible.

Showerheads come in perhaps hundreds of styles. But all are held onto the shower pipe with a main collar nut. (See sketch). In between the collar nut

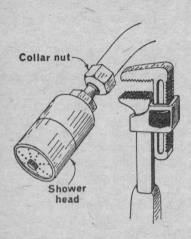

Collar nut

Shower head

and the end of the assembly, most showerheads come apart at various places—so you don't have to take the entire head off to clean it out.

It's hard to say where to start but anything that looks like a seam probably unscrews and comes apart. Sometimes the little spray disc is held in place with a twist-off ring; sometimes a screw runs up through the middle of the disc; sometimes it can be approached only through the back by taking the showerhead apart somewhere in the middle.

If water is leaking up around the collar nut, or if the showerhead flops around uncontrollably, chances are you need to replace the little rubber 0-rings or washers in it.

The main collar nut will probably require a wrench for removal. If it is stuck, don't twist so hard that you bend the water pipe. Put a little oil or rust dissolver along the edges of the nut and wait an hour or so before trying again. Put tape over the nut if you don't want to scratch the finish.

Some collar nuts on cheaper models are not hexagonal but are perfectly round, with little ridges on the outside. These are, frankly, very difficult to remove. If the wrench keeps slipping, try the handy dandy jar top and bottle cap remover you have in the kitchen. Replace the washer under the nut.

There should also be a washer under the second nut or casing in line from the collar nut. This second connection covers the ball joint—the round knob that lets you swivel the showerhead.

Take the removed washers to a hardware store and have them matched for size.

If you need to replace the whole showerhead, most of them come in just one pipe size. Screw-on adapters can be bought for odd-size pipes.

59 / How to fix shower doors that leak

People with leaking shower stall doors generally have very clean bathroom floors. But that's not much compensation for all the bother.

Remedies for leaking shower doors are either very simple or very complicated. We'll stick to the simple ones here. If they don't work, you had better call in an expert.

Hinged shower doors (the full-length ones that go on shower stalls rather than bathtubs) vary in style. But most have a rubber strip or gasket along the bottom edge to keep water from running out over the threshold of the stall.

If that rubber strip deteriorates or no longer makes a snug contact with the threshold, it can be replaced at shops specializing in bathroom equipment.

Also located at the bottom of the shower door (on the inside) is a short metal ledge or tray called a drip cap to guide water back into the shower stall after it runs down the door.

Some rubber gaskets are held in place behind the drip cap, which may be fastened with screws to the door. If this is the case, it should be fairly simple for you to unfasten the drip cap and remove the old gasket. (See sketch A.)

With other shower doors, the gasket slides into a groove in the bottom of the door. In this case, you may need to remove the entire door to get at the gasket.

Most shower stall doors hang from a metal frame which is fastened to the wall with screws. If you look

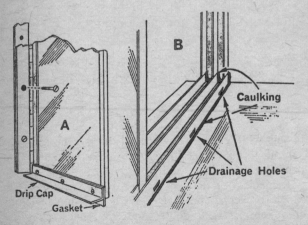

at the frame strip, you will probably see countless little brads the whole length of it. Interspersed will be three or four slotted screw heads. These are the things you're interested in. Remove these screws and take the door and attached frame strip away. (See sketch A.)

When you finally remove the old gasket, take it with you to the store so they can match the type.

If the door still leaks with a new gasket, check the line where the door frame meets the shower wall. You can often see daylight between frame and wall. Depending on the direction of your shower spray, you may need to lay a thin line of tub and tile caulking along that seam. Put it on the inside of the stall, not the outside. Silicone caulking that comes in a squeeze tube is probably the easiest to apply.

Sliding doors along the top of a bathtub don't have drip caps and bottom gaskets. Instead, they slide in double-channel tracks installed along the top of the tub. Small holes along the inside edge of the track allow water to drain out of the channels.

This track should have been applied to the tub edge with caulking. If not—or if the caulking has deteriorated—apply a thin line of tub and tile caulking to the inside edge of the track where it meets the tub surface. Be careful not to clog the drainage holes in the track. (See sketch B.)

Water sometimes collects in the end corners of the door track. This happens if the track is not perfectly level. What you want to do is to somehow make this little pool of water run back down the track toward the drainage holes.

Try pushing a blob of tub and tile caulking into the end corner of each channel (See sketch B.) Smooth the caulking with your finger and slant it toward the middle of the track. Don't use so much caulking that the sliding door will run into it.

60 / How to fix a "singing" toilet

There are few things more annoying than a "singing" toilet. The sound of water constantly running through a toilet tank is music to no one's ears—especially since it increases the water bill.

Two basic assemblies control the water in a toilet tank—the flushing mechanism and the refill mechanism. We'll talk about half the equipment in this chapter and the other half in the next chapter.

The flushing mechanism may be your culprit. This is certainly the case if you have to jiggle the toilet handle each time to stop the toilet from running.

First, take the top off the tank and flush the toilet once to watch what happens. If your toilet is of the most common style, you will see a rubber stopper, called a flush ball, rise from the bottom of the tank to let the water out.

Next, look for a small, faucet-type handle on the water pipe leading to the toilet and shut off the water supply coming into the tank. Flush the tank once more to clear it of all water.

Now begin checking.

Lift the flush ball and examine it to see if it was deteriorated. If the surface has become rough and crumbly, buy a new one; the old one unscrews from the wire stem. It's a good idea to also give the rim of the flush ball seat (the drain hole at the bottom of the tank) a quick scrubbing with steel wool to keep it smooth.

Working back along the system, check the lift and linkage wires to make sure they are not bent. If they

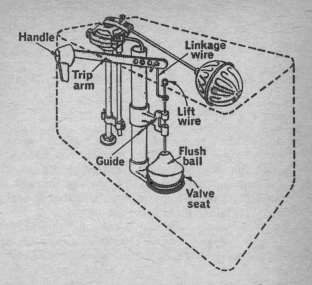

are, you can buy new ones at any hardware store for a dollar or less. (Sometimes, if they don't seem to be sliding well, a thin coat of petroleum jelly helps, too.) If you install new wires, make sure the linkage wire gives the flush ball leeway enough to drop back down completely onto the valve seat.

If the flush ball is not dropping back squarely onto the valve seat, check the wire guide—the little metal clip with an eye in it that holds the lift wire straight. Loosen the screw holding the guide in place and move the guide back and forth until the flush ball is dropping the way it should. (Be sure to tighten the guide screw again when you are through.)

Finally, determine whether you need a new handle. (The handle on the outside and the long metal trip arm on the inside are all one unit.) The handle assembly shouldn't rattle back and forth very much. A nut screws onto the back side of the handle, just inside the tank wall. If tightening this nut doesn't help the situation, the handle assembly is inexpensive to replace and one size fits most toilets.

61 / Another cause of a "singing John"

The only "John" that continuously sings and whistles around your house should be a person by that name not your toilet. But unfortunately, the number of malfunctioning toilets seems to be so high that when you mention repairing your own, you're bound to hear one or two friends chime in with their stories.

The most common problem is the toilet that keeps filling and filling, making singing, hissing noises all the while. There can be two causes for this performance.

The flush ball may not be reseating properly (that's the stopper that rises when you push the flush handle and lets the water out of the tank). Flush mechanisms vary according to manufacturer and have been dealt with in another chapter.

The other cause can be a refill mechanism that needs a few new parts. They do wear out eventually.

There are many different styles in refill units. One found quite commonly these days is a diaphragm device. There are different styles even among these. But the principle of operation is similar in all:

The float arm (that longish rod inside the toilet tank arm with a floating bulb at the end) rises as the water level in the tank rises. As the arm changes attitude, the end of it pokes down on a plastic or nylon "plunger" (nothing but a solid little rod about an inch long). The plunger, in turn, presses down on a flexible rubber disc (the diaphragm) that covers the opening where the water comes into the system.

This rubber diaphragm sometimes gets cut or otherwise deteriorates and needs to be replaced. It can't cover the water opening (called the seat) satisfactorily unless it is smooth and flexible.

Different makers use different size diaphragms. So look at the top of your refill device (known in the trade as a ballcock) and take down the brand name and any numbers you see. Don't go by the brand name of the actual toilet body; it may be something else. A good plumbing contractor or supply house should have replacement diaphragms for several brands.

The one shown in the sketch is a Mansfield 07A.

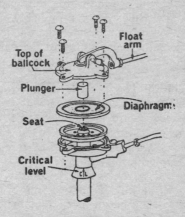

It does not have a seat that you can replace easily yourself. Some brands do. (They need to be replaced if cracked or chipped.) The diaphragm on this model, however, is very easy to replace.

First step is to shut off the water supply to the toilet. Look underneath the toilet for a metal tube with a handle on it. Turn the handle to the off position; then flush the toilet to clear the tank of water.

You do not need to remove the float arm from this model in order to replace the ballcock diaphragm. Some models do require this; but it is usually easily done by loosening a couple of screws.

The only things you need to unfasten in this model are the four screws holding the body of the ballcock together (see sketch).

Lift off the top of the ballcock (with float arm attached) and the little plastic plunger should drop right out of the middle of it into your hand. Set these things aside; then lift off the rubber diaphragm, exposing the water spout or seat beneath.

Run your finger around the rim of the seat. If the rim seems caked with water chemicals, give it a swipe with some fine steel wool.

Look closely at the new diaphragm you plan to install and you should see the word "top" printed on it somewhere. That side, as you probably can guess, faces upward toward you. Center the diaphragm over the seat; replace the plunger, top of the ballcock and screws and you should be ready to turn the water back on.

It is possible, if you know what you're doing, to replace an entire old refill unit with a newer model like this. Just one word of advice to such advanced home handymen: Look for a marker immediately below the ballcock with the letters "CL" inscribed. The letters stand for "critical level."

Many city codes require that the tank water be no higher than this mark AND that the top of the neighboring overflow tube be an inch or more lower than the "CL" mark. Check your own city code.

62 / How to fix a toilet fill unit

If you are treated to the high-pitched serenade of water running through the toilet tank day and night, and you've determined that the problem is not in the flushing mechanism, water may be escaping through the overflow pipe.

The last chapter dealt with the flushing mechanism. This one looks at the refill unit.

Take the top of the tank off and check the water level inside. It should stop about a half inch short of the top of the overflow pipe. If it doesn't, there is probably trouble in the inlet valve which, as its name implies, lets water back into the tank after flushing.

The inlet valve is controlled by that long metal arm with the float at the end of it. As the water level rises, so does the float arm, eventually shutting off the water before it runs over the top of the overflow pipe.

So as a first step, while water is still in the tank, lift up slightly on the float arm. If this stops the "singing," adjustment will be fairly simple.

Locate the faucet-type handle on the pipes leading into the toilet tank and shut off the water supply. Now flush the toilet to clear the tank of water. Unscrew the float from the end of its arm and shake it. If it has water inside, it is leaking and should be replaced.

If the float is in good shape, try bending the float arm downward from about the middle until the bulb rides a half inch to an inch lower. Then turn the water back on to see if the problem has been remedied.

If not, you may need to replace the washers on the plunger.

The sketch shows a common mechanism style. There are others. But to change the plunger on this

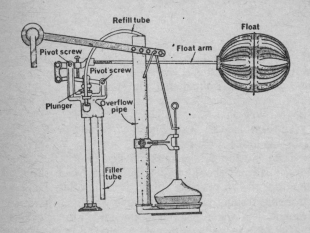

system, remove the two pivot screws that hold the linkage end of the float arm onto the valve brace which looks sort of like an uneven tuning fork. The linkage itself runs through the slotted top of the plunger. Remove the float arm and its linkage, sliding it out of the plunger top.

Pull the plunger up to remove it. On the bottom of the plunger (or sometimes down in the recess) is a rubber or leather washer (small disk), with another washer at about the halfway point on the plunger. Replace these with the same type washers. To be sure, you might take the old washers to the nearest hardware store and ask the clerk to match them.

When you put the equipment back together, make sure the refill tube (see diagram) is feeding into the overflow pipe. This arrangement keeps a correct water level in the waste pipe trap, preventing sewer gas from escaping into the house.

63 / How to repair that ailing bathtub

The only thing most people know about bathtubs is how to climb into them and get clean.

But there are a few simple things that go haywire with bathtubs and can be fixed by an amateur. One of them is the lever (part way up the side of the tub) that opens and closes the drain.

There are generally two major styles in drain levers for modern tubs. One kind of lever moves up and down. The other is more like a handle and flips in a half circle from one side to another.

The flip-type handle doesn't go on the fritz too often. So we'll talk for a minute here about the up-and-down type of lever.

A lever will occasionally become looser and looser until it won't hold its position at all.

Behind the lever, there is usually a spring and washer device that travels over a triangular bump or pivot point welded to the back of the overflow plate. (The overflow plate is simply the decorative shield that covers the hole in the tub.)

The point of this triangular bump gets worn down after a time and allows the lever to slip.

All you need to do is replace the overflow plate (at a well-stocked plumbing supply house).

First, copy down any brand name you can find on the lever, overflow plate or drain. Then remove the two screws holding the overflow plate.

Pull the whole lever mechanism out toward you. It is hinged in various places so it can bend and come out. About 3 inches past the overflow plate, you should encounter a hinge or joint held together with a cotter pin (looks like a sturdy bobby pin). Pull out the cotter pin with pliers, freeing the overflow plate from the lever.

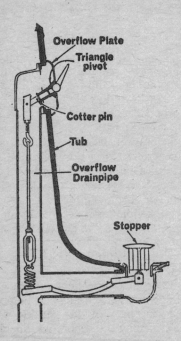

Overflow Plate

Triangle pivot

Cotter pin

Tub

Overflow Drainpipe

Stopper

Take the overflow plate with you (along with the note on brand name) to the plumbing supply house. Reverse the whole procedure to put the thing back together.

Note: Most overflow plates have a slot or notch along part of the edge. This slot is the overflow drain entrance. Make sure the slot is facing down toward the bottom of the tub when you fasten the new plate in place.

Occasionally, a lever will work progressively harder instead of getting loose. (This also happens to the flip-type handles.)

This usually means there is sediment, corrosion or some kind of obstruction down around the drain area of the mechanism.

Again, unfasten the two screws holding the overflow plate and start pulling the lever mechanism up and out. Don't worry about any cotter pins this time. Just pull the whole strung-out lever assembly from its hole. (If you have a different style from the one pictured here and can tell that the far end is attached to something, don't force it.)

At the end of the lever assembly, you will probably find a large spring or a weight or a plug-like cylinder. Clean it off with steel wool. Apply a coat of petroleum jelly.

You can also probe down the drainpipe for obstructions before reassembling the lever mechanism. But that's involved with cleaning the whole drain and will be discussed in the next chapter.

64 / How to unclog a slow bathtub drain

No Rosie likes to play ring around the bathtub. But that's the game plan—even after a shower—when the bathtub drain is slow. Sluggish water leaves enough grime behind to run you out of both cleanser and patience.

Unclogging a tub drain is tougher than tackling a sink drain. With sinks, you can usually reach the trap pipe underneath (that curved portion) and take it apart. With tubs, there is sometimes a removable access panel to the pipes through the back of the linen closet. But even so, you probably won't be able to see the trap—much less reach it.

The best an amateur can do is probe for obstructions in the drainpipe itself, use a plunger or use chemical drain cleaners. You don't need to approach the pipes from the access panel in any case.

The key to the whole operation is the cover on the overflow drain—that chrome disc behind the drain lever on the side of the tub. You need to remove it to use either a plunger or a probe (sometimes called a "snake"—one of those long springwire devices with a handle).

Unfasten the two screws that hold the overflow cover in place (see sketches). Then pull the cover, lever and the whole long linkage behind it up and out of the tub.

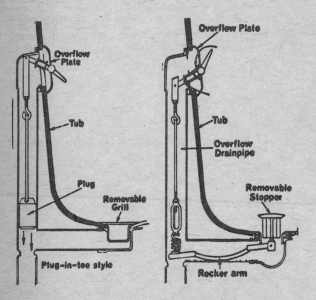

Modern tubs generally have one of two drain plug styles. One is a plug-in-tee arrangement (see sketch). The other is a pop-up device (other sketch).

If you have a plug-in-tee drain, you will automatically remove the plug when you pull the lever and its attached pieces out of the tub. A cylinder at the end of the lever linkage normally drops down across the "tee" of the drain and seats against a rubber-rimmed ledge see sketch). The drain grill you see in the bottom of the tub doesn't actually do anything except filter hair and soap chips.

If you have a pop-up drain plug, you will usually find either a weight or a heavy spring at the end of the lever linkage. The weight of spring normally presses down on the end of a rocker arm when you flip the drain lever (see sketch). This rocks or pops the drain plug up.

The end of the rocker arm is not usually attached to the weight or spring. So after you remove the lever assembly, pull the pop-up stopper out from the bottom of the tub.

Insert any probe or snake from the overflow drainpipe entrance (where the lever used to be). This gives you a straight shot down the drainpipe—at least as far as the trap.

If you decide to use a plunger instead, you need to plug the overflow drain hole with wet rags. This gives the plunger more force by blocking the escape of air or water. (Also remove the grill over the the drain hole in the bottom of the tub if you have a plug-in-tee arrangement. The grill slows down plunger action. Some are held with screws; some can just be pried out.)

Partially fill the tub with water before using the plunger.

Is a chemical drain cleaner your choice? Don't use it if the drain is completely blocked. You won't have any way of getting it out of the drain. Flush the pipes well with water after using a chemical.

65 / How to get rid of the drip in that bath faucet

A dripping bath faucet can send hard earned pennies down the tube—er, tub. But bathtub faucets are more difficult to fix than sink faucets.

In either case, the problem is usually a worn rubber washer on the end of the faucet stem. (When the faucet handle is turned down to the "off" position, the washer covers the hole through which the water flows.)

Sink faucets stick up above the level of the sink and are easy to reach. But you'll find, upon taking it apart, that a large portion of a tub faucet is located back behind the wall's tile facing.

There's another slight problem, too. Many tub faucets don't have any shut-off valves on the pipes leading to them. (Sinks generally do. Look for small handles on the pipes directly under the sink.)

If your tub has an access panel to the pipes through the back of the linen closet, take a look. If there are no shut-off handles, you'll have to turn the water off further down the line.

(Shut off the hot water at the hot water tank. Shut off the cold water anyplace where you can find a handle on the cold water pipe running to the bathroom. That failing, you can always turn off the entire water supply at the water meter. You needn't cut off both hot and cold if you are just working on one system.)

Now you can disassemble the tub faucet. Look for a screw holding the faucet handle in place (see sketch). The top screw may be covered by a decorative disc; it usually pries off. Some older faucets may have a small "set screw" or nut on the back side of the handle. It needs to be loosened before the handle will pull off.

Behind the handle there is a decorative shield called an escutcheon plate. Unscrew this from the faucet stem. The escutcheon plate may be held in place on the stem with a screw-on retaining ring or chrome nut. It is also held to the tile wall with putty, but should break away with minimal pressure.

You will now see a hole in the tile and main portion of the faucet stem. You may have to chip away the edge of the tile hole to get at the faucet. It depends on how well the faucet was originally installed. If you choose to chip, make sure you don't enlarge the hole so much that the escutcheon plate will no longer cover it.

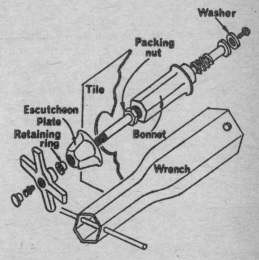

On the faucet stem itself, you should see a wedding-cake tiered set of two hexagonal nuts (see sketch). Ignore the smaller first one (the packing nut). Go for the second or larger one (the bonnet) and unscrew it, freeing the whole faucet stem.

This is easier said than done because of the tile facing. You may need a special kind of wrench called a plumber's deep socket (see sketch). A plumber's deep socket is just a hexagonal tube that will reach behind the tile and has room in its hollow center for the faucet stem. A rod shoved through the end of the socket wrench acts as a handle or lever.

Plumbers' deep sockets are hard to find in regular hardware stores. And you probably wouldn't want to buy a whole set anyway. Go to a well-stocked plumbing supply house or a friendly plumbing contractor and see if he'll rent you a deep socket for the day. Some places do that. Measure the exact width of the nut you want to loosen (from flat side to flat side) so you will know what size deep socket to get.

Note any brand names on your faucet handle. Take the removed faucet stem (and other removed parts) to a good plumbing supply house. You may need to replace part of the faucet assembly as well as the washer, and there are about two hundred different sizes in tub faucets. You will have a better chance of getting the right replacement equipment if you have the old stuff with you at time of purchase.

Before replacing the stem in the wall, make sure the stem, in its surrounding nut, is turned as much as possible to the open or "on" position. If the stem is screwed down or "off" as far as it will go, you can run the risk of jamming it as you tighten or turn down the main nut.

One more thing. Smear some plumber's putty (available from most plumbing houses in cheap amounts) on the back edge of the escutcheon plate before putting it back against the wall. Failing to seal the plate against the tile will allow water from the shower to run behind the plate and into the wall.

66 / How to care for a septic tank

If you are buying a house that has a septic tank, there are things you should know about the sewage system.

Septic tanks work well if they are taken care of. If they are neglected, they can smell up the neighborhood and even back sewage up into your home.

In general, septic tanks are buried concrete tanks that vary in capacity from one thousand to two thousand for residential use. The tank collects liquid and solid waste from the home and breaks down the solid material through bacterial action over a period of months. Solids settle to the bottom of the tank. Water drains off the top portion and seeps into the ground through either a "drain field" or an adjoining dry well.

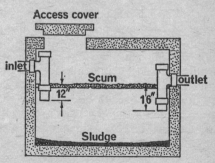

As the solids decompose or break down, they form a scum material over the top. If the scum gets deeper than about a foot, it clogs the drain field, causing all kinds of problems.

This is why a septic tank should be cleaned out professionally about once every two years.

To make sure your septic tank operates the way it should, avoid putting strong chemicals through it or things that will not break down readily.

For instance, no disposable products heavier than toilet paper should go into the system. This means no flush-away diapers, tampons, cloth, plastic or cigarette butts.

Garbage grinders can be used with a septic tank. But you should put only vegetables and meat scraps down the garbage grinder—no bones, egg shells or coffee grounds. They won't break down satisfactorily. Also try to keep grease and fat to a minimum.

A garbage grinder may also mean that your septic tank will have to be cleaned more often, depending on the tank's capacity. A garbage grinder adds significantly to the input of solids.

If you have a mechanical water softener, the salty back-wash of the machine's regenerating process should not go into the septic tank.

Laundry detergent should be bio-degradable. It is all right to use chlorine bleach, toilet bowl cleaner, tub cleanser and drain cleaner in moderation. It is not particularly good for the septic tank, but the volume of such chemicals is generally low unless you are some kind of cleaning neurotic.

Most people who move into a place with a septic tank do not know the capacity of the tank. The best procedure is to have the tank cleaned by a reputable licensed firm to determine the tank's capacity. The company should then be able to recommend a cleaning schedule to fit your tank's capacity and use.

67 / Keep portable humidifier clean

Portable humidifiers do not require much attention. But an occasional cleaning will keep the device adding moisture to the house efficiently.

The most common design for portable humidifiers is a rotating drum covered with a removable strip of foam. The drum turns—much like a mill wheel— through a pan of water at the bottom of the humidifier.

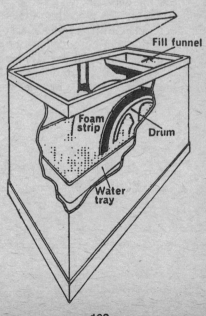

A small fan then sends the moisture collected in the foam out into the air.

When the foam strip around the drum gets caked with mineral deposits, it does not function properly. The strip should therefore be kept reasonably clean and pliable.

Manufacturers recommend replacing the foam (available at heating-cooling supply stores) once a year. You can also remove the strips periodically and wash them in mild detergent or a baking soda solution.

To do this, it is often easiest to remove the entire drum. Different manufacturers give different instructions. But in many cases the drum simply lifts off the wheel-like braces on which it rests. Unplug the unit before removing the drum.

You should also clean the water tray occasionally to get rid of mineral deposits and stale water. Unplug the unit and check the back side of it for a removable panel that will give easy access to the water tray.

There are liquid chemicals on the market (from humidifier dealers) that can be added to the humidifier's water to inhibit mineral and bacteria formations. But even with these chemicals, the unit should be cleaned and freshened at least once or twice each year.

68 / How to beat the dampness in your home

Wringing your hands over wet weather and what it does to your belongings?

There are some tricks to help beat the dampness. The most efficient of these is to buy a portable dehumidifier. But if you are planning to buy or already have one, there are a few things to keep in mind.

The water collection tray on a dehumidifier should be emptied once a day (more often if needed) or else the device will be working to extract the same water it took out of the air that morning. Once a year, you should also remove the cover on the machine, unplug it and wipe clean all reachable surfaces to maintain efficiency.

One portable dehumidifier will not have much effect on an entire house. It works best when confined to a one or two-room area that can be shut off from the rest of the home. Close the windows in that area, too.

Warm air holds more moisture than cold air does; so open all windows to air out the house on cool, dry evenings. Also ventilate (with exhaust fans if possible) all areas where cooking, laundering and bathing is carried on. These activities can add as much as two gallons of water to indoor air in a day.

Sometimes a basement is the only available storage area. Wrap any sweating pipes in some sort of insulating material; a variety can be had at lumber stores. If basement walls become damp, patch any cracks with mortar and paint the walls with a waterproof covering (available with directions at paint and lumber stores).

Mothballs inhibit mildew in stored clothing.

But sometimes things are used occasionally through the summer and the mothball treatment is unsatisfactory. For items kept in plastic bags, try adding a handful of either regular or instant rice to the bag.

Try putting cones of carpenters' chalk on the shelves of the linen closet. When the chalk gets damp, dry it out in the oven at low heat, 300 degrees or under. Carpenters' chalk can be found in lumber stores.

Large department stores and a few hardware stores sell boxes of moisture-absorbing flakes. Like carpenters' chalk, they are baked when saturated. Read directions; some of the substances can be corrosive.

Burning a constant, low-watt bulb in a closet will

help keep down moisture. Spray the closet occasionally with a mildew-retarding air freshener.

If clothing does mildew, wash it in detergent and bleach with water as hot as is safe for the fabric. If the fabric won't take bleach, an option is applying lemon juice and salt to mildew spots and drying the clothing in the sun.

69 / Properly maintain your oil furnace

Basic maintenance steps for an oil furnace and checkpoints in case of unexpected trouble are much the same as for a gas furnace, described in another chapter. But there are a few differences.

As with a gas furnace, changing dirty air filters (if you have a forced air system) is perhaps the simplest and most important maintenance step. This should be done two or three times each heating season.

The blower motor should be oiled sparingly once a year. Look for one or two little quarter-inch holes (sometimes capped) near each end of the motor.

Your equipment should be checked by a serviceman at least once a year.

If an oil furnace stops unexpectedly, take the following steps:

1. Check the oil supply to make sure you're not out of fuel. The oil tank may be located in the basement, garage or sometimes outside the house. A gauge on the tank will show whether it is empty. But to make sure the needle isn't stuck, give the gauge a slight tap or give the side of the tank a whack near the gauge.

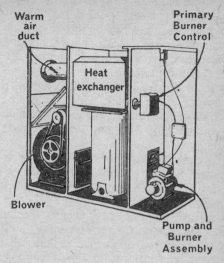

Warm air duct

Primary Burner Control

Heat exchanger

Blower

Pump and Burner Assembly

2. Check the household fuse or circuit breaker box to see whether the fuse controlling electrical portions of the furnace has blown. If so, replace it (or flip the circuit breaker back to "on"). Before replacing the fuse, turn the home thermostat down low; after the new fuse is in place you can turn it back up. If the fuse blows again right away, there may be a wiring problem requiring a serviceman.

3. Look for a switch (looks just like a light switch) on the side of the furnace or on the wall or rafters nearby. This also controls electricity to the furnace and may have been turned off by someone.

4. A box about eight inches square, called the primary burner control or relay, is often located just outside the furnace, sticking out of the smoke stack. On some newer furnaces, it is inside near the pump-burner assembly. There is a button on the primary control box to restart the furnace.

Wait 20 minutes after the furnace stops; then push this button (or move it sideways). The waiting period is important, as this gives oil fumes in the furnace a chance to clear—a safety factor.

Some repairmen say the button should be pushed only once; others say twice is all right. But no more than twice; and you should wait another 20 minutes before the second attempt.

5. Sometimes there is an overload button or switch on the burner pump motor, which is located on the outside wall of the furnace or, in newer models, just inside (see sketch). This button (often red) should be pressed once.

If, after pushing these various buttons, you are not sure whether the oil is burning, you can look into the firebox through a little spring-trap door—the observation port (see sketch).

But wait five minutes after pushing the button before you open the port. Oil sometimes "puffs" when it catches fire. If you don't give it that five minutes, you may get a face full.

6. Finally, check the household thermostat by running it up five degrees over the present room temperature. If the furnace does not react, clean the contact points in the thermostat as described in the chapter on gas furnaces.

70 / Maintain gas furnace at peak efficiency

Among the most common heating setups is a gas furnace hooked to a forced air system.

A gas furnace should be checked by either the gas company or a heating contractor at least every other year. Once a year is even better.

Any adjustment of valves controlling the gas and air mixtures in the furnace should be left to an expert. He should also check the safety device that shuts off the gas flow in case the pilot light goes out. (You should, by the way, leave the pilot light on all year to avoid condensation in the furnace.)

But there are a few simple things the home owner can do to keep the system efficient. Chief among these is changing the air filter, a large square of woven fiberglass strands framed in cardboard and usually covered with a metallic mesh. It should be changed two or three times during the heating season. See sketch A.)

The filter is generally located just inside the cold air return duct, where air enters the furnace to be warmed and, later, sent back into the house. A dirty filter will slow circulation and sometimes make a furnace run twice as long as it should.

To find the filter, look in the blower compartment of the furnace. This is sometimes at the bottom. Just open all the little doors and snap-out grille · sections on the furnace until you find it.

The blower area is the one that contains a large, round metal device that looks like an enclosed squirrel or gerbil cage. In different models the filter sits at different angles. But it should be in plain view.

The size of the filter should be printed on the cardboard frame. If not, measure the filter by length, width and thickness (the replacement must be the same size).

When installing the new one, check the cardboard frame for a little arrow marked "air flow." Turn the filter so that air flowing into the furnace from the duct will follow the direction of the arrow.

The blower motor should also be oiled once a year, unless it is the sealed type, which has no oil holes.

If it can be oiled, you will see a little hole (about ¼-inch in diameter) on the motor body near each end. These holes are usually covered with a flip-top or snap-off cap and are sometimes marked "oil." Two to three drops of light motor oil a YEAR will suffice.

Now to emergencies. What do you do when the furnace suddenly won't operate?

With gas fuel, which is highly explosive, most remedies should be left to the gas company, which will send a man out to reignite pilot lights (sometimes for free, sometimes for a fee, depending on the company).

But first check to see whether the pilot light is still burning. To find the pilot, follow the gas line to where it enters the furnace, remove the nearest panel and look in the burner section (sketch A) for a

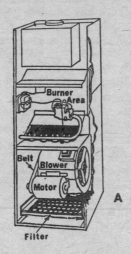

skinny, ¼-inch aluminum tube with a flame at the end of it. The flame should be fairly visible, so if you see no fire in the burner section at all, the pilot is probably out.

If so, and if you can smell gas, it is a good idea to shut off the gas to the furnace.

This can be done with an L-shaped handle located near the furnace on the gas line. (This handle will also help you identify the gas pipe, which is about the same size as a water pipe.) If the handle is turned parallel to the pipe, the gas is on; turning it at a right angle to the pipe shuts the gas off. (See sketch B.)

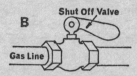

If the pilot light is burning, look for a switch (just like a light switch) on the side of the furnace or located on the wall nearby. It controls electricity to the motor and may have been turned off by a child. (Not all furnaces have such a switch.)

Next check the circuit breaker or fuse for the furnace. This is usually located with or near the other household fuses, and should be labeled. Flip the circuit breaker "on" or replace the blown fuse. If it blows again right away, there may be a serious problem in your wiring.

Finally, check the thermostat. Remove its cover. If

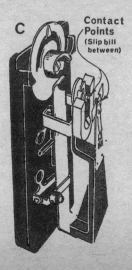

you see a little capsule of liquid, you have a mercury vial control and there is likely no problem with it (nothing you can do about it anyway).

But if the device is a sort of U-shaped prong, turn the dial higher until you see two contact points (about the size of a pin head) come together. If these points are dirty, they may not be functioning. So slip a crisp dollar bill or a business card between the points; hold the points together and slide the bill back and forth to clean the surfaces. (See sketch C.)

If none of these measures works, call a serviceman.

71 / Sizzling over high utility bills?

Steamed up over utility bills? You can save a few cents—maybe even dollars—by cutting the heat loss from your water heater and/or radiator heating system.

The trick is to insulate the hot water (or steam) pipes in your basement or utility room.

The decision whether to insulate has to depend on your own common sense. If you are selling your house next year or if the heated pipes in your house are exposed for only a very short distance, you could spend more on insulation than you would ever recover in lowered fuel bills.

The whole idea of insulating hot pipes is to help preserve the warmth that you have spent fuel in creating. If the pipe from your hot water tank traverses the open air of the whole basement before entering the walls, the hot water in the pipe is cooling off by a few degrees for the whole distance. The same holds true of pipe leading from furnace boilers.

There are many different kinds of pipe insulation for

many different prices. The sources are hardware, lumber and department stores. Of the three, lumber and department stores are likely to have the largest selections.

The easiest type of insulation to use is a pre-formed, tubular piece of foam with a slit down the side for slipping it over the pipe. (Know the diameter of the pipe you're covering before you go to the store.)

The foam sleeve is sometimes covered with paper (as in sketch). You just glue the overlapping flap of paper and seal the sleeve in place over the pipe like an envelope. Some sleeves are not covered in paper. You have to buy tape to seal the slit edge.

The disadvantage is expense. The foam sleeves, even without paper covering, run about $1.25 for 4 feet on ¾ inch pipe.

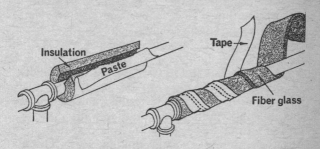

Probably the cheapest (yet effective) commercial pipe insulation is fiber glass wool. You can buy it in rolled up strips about 4 to 6 inches wide. A roll of wide tape for covering the fiber glass is usually included in the package.

One package costing about $1.30 to $1.60 will cover about 20 feet of ¾ inch pipe (depending on how wide the fiberglass strip is).

There are disadvantages. It takes time to wrap the fiber glass in a spiral around the pipes and then tape it (see sketch). And fiber glass gets into your skin and clothes. Wear gloves and long sleeves for the job.

You will see various kinds of insulating tapes on the

market, too, in addition to the above products. Most of them are more expensive than the fiber glass, but handier to install.

The best advice is simply to shop around. Try several different stores; one place rarely carries more than two kinds of pipe insulation.

72 / How to insulate your attic

Fuel costs being what they are, it might pay you to look into your home's insulation. You may be able to lower your heating or air conditioning bills.

One insulation man says he would put at least 3½ inches of blanket insulation in the side walls and 6 inches in the ceiling (attic floor), if he were building his own house.

But if your house is already built, your options are limited. Adding insulation to the side walls would involve one of two things: either tearing the walls apart from the inside to install blanket insulation, or having a contractor drill holes through the outside of the walls to blow in loose insulation. (Deal with a good company. Blown insulation can settle inside the walls if improperly installed.)

About the only practical thing for a homeowner to tackle, in a house that's already complete, is the insulation in the floor of an unfinished, unheated attic.

You will probably encounter a variety of insulation styles at department, discount or builders supply houses. There are stacks of loose fill that you can sprinkle around. There are batts—square pieces of (usually) fiber glass wool backed on at least one side with heavy paper or foil. There are also blankets—

rolls, really—of fiber glass wool. Blankets can be entirely covered in paper or just have paper on one side. Blankets and batts also come in various thickness.

You need to know the distance between joists (beams) in your attic floor before buying blanket insulation. Most joists are either 16 or 24 inches apart. Insulation is manufactured in the same widths. If, for some reason, your joists are a weird measure, you'll have a messy cutting job with blanket insulation. Consider using the loose fill type.

Another thing to check is the building code for your city. Some specify thickness, use of vapor barriers, and materials.

A vapor barrier is designed to keep condensed moisture in the insulating material to a minumum.

On blanket or batt insulation, the vapor barrier is part of the paper backing. The borders of the backing stick out a little bit, giving you an edge you can staple to joists, etc. So even if the entire blanket of insulation is covered in paper, you can distinguish which side is the vapor barrier by looking for the extended border.

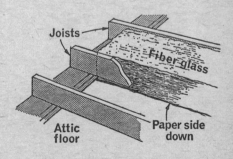

Joists — Fiber glass

Attic floor — Paper side down

Loose or blown insulation doesn't have any backing—thus no vapor barrier. Some companies put down a layer of plastic sheeting as a vapor barrier; some don't. It depends on the climate and the building code.

In any case, the vapor barrier is supposed to face the warmth.

That means, in the case of your attic floor, you should lay the paper backing toward the living room downstairs. You won't be able to staple the insulation operating this way, but it will stay in place. (If you are doing walls, the backing or barrier faces inward toward the room you are heating.)

You can lay one blanket of insulation on top of another older one. Just pretend the old layer isn't there and proceed as normal. You can also add loose fill on top of a blanket.

Batts can come in handy for partially covering trap doors into the attic. (The more complete the layer of insulation across the floor, the better.)

Fiber glass particles are quite irritating. So avoid dragging the insulation through the house any more than you have to on the way to the attic. Wear work gloves. A surgical mask isn't a bad idea either. It will protect you against both glass fibers and the dust that accumulates in an attic.

73 / How to keep your fan in running order

Attic fans and large window fans are fairly reliable creatures than don't require much upkeep. But there are a few things you should do at the beginning and end of each summer to keep them running right.

If there are any louvers or shutters that open when the fan is running, oil the pivot points or the pins on which each little panel swings (light motor oil or machine oil should do the job). Wiggle the louvers open and closed a couple of times to spread the oil around and make sure the louvers operate freely.

Next, look for an instruction plate attached to the

fan telling how and where the fan should be lubricated. If there is no plate, look for a couple of small holes (about ⅛ inch diameter) on the motor. These are usually for oil and may have the word printed near them. Sometimes the openings have little flip-top caps over them.

A motor on a large fan may be off to the side, connected to the fan shaft by a belt. Or it may be a "direct drive" motor with no belt, built in as part of the hub of the fan. If you see no oil points on the motor, with either style, it is probably the sealed variety and requires no lubrication.

Oil any points where the fan shaft runs through the support structure or the turning mechanism. Do all this oiling twice a year to keep moisture from corroding working parts in the fan.

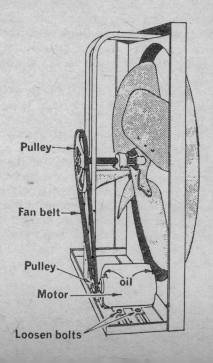

Check the fan belt, if there is one, for cracks, crumbles or a shiny glaze on the underside. Any of these symptoms should send you to the store for a new belt. (Take the old one along to match for size.)

The belt needs to have the right tension, too. Press down in the middle of one span of the belt. It should "give" 1/2 to 1 inch under moderate pressure.

To tighten a fan belt, remove an old one, or install a new one, you will probably need to move the fan motor. This is not a big job in most cases. Look for a couple of bolts holding the motor to the fan frame or to a couple of little slotted tracks (see sketch). Loosen the bolts and slide the motor to the point where you want it; then tighten the bolts again.

(Any new belt you buy will probably be slightly V-shaped. That is, the inside edge of the belt will be a bit narrower than the outside edge. The narrow edge is supposed to nestle into the grooves of the belt pulleys.)

If the fan does not operate when you turn it on, check the fuse or circuit breaker for that part of the house. If the fan runs but seems to be laboring, even after oiling, call a serviceman.

A noisy or vibrating fan may have become loose in its mounting. Check any nuts and bolts holding it in place. The fan blades may have become loose on the shaft, too, although this happens infrequently. Loose fan blades will rattle noisily as they turn.

To tighten them, look for a bolt right in the nose of the fan or a small hole in the side of the fan nose. This little hole usually contains a recessed set screw. You will need an Allen wrench to tighten the set screw. (An Allen wrench is just a hexagonal rod with a handle. You can buy a whole set of them cheaply at any hardware store.)

74 / More efficiency from your air conditioner

You can make portable or window air conditioning units much more efficient in cooling your whole home by turning on the furnace fan (without heat, naturally). This keeps air circulating throughout the house and distributes temperatures more evenly.

All you need is a forced air heating system—the type of fuel used makes no difference. And this whole discussion concerns heating systems that don't have air conditioning built in.

Turning on the furnace fan or blower is easy. Just push, pull or flip a switch.

Finding the switch is the hard part. It can be on, in or around the furnace. Or sometimes in an entirely different part of the house. (One acquaintance recently located his furnace switch in the linen closet.)

First step is to make sure the household thermostat is turned down to about 50 or 60 degrees. This prevents fuel ignition and heat production in the furnace. (You should leave any pilot light on all season to prevent moisture condensation.)

If you have a furnace ten years old or more, it will probably be pretty easy to find what's commonly called the summer switch. It often looks like a light switch and is located on the outside of the furnace (or on the wall near it). If you have an electric furnace or some arrangement where there is more than one switch, simply listen as you turn each one. You'll hear the fan after you flip the right one.

If you have a newer furnace and don't see a switch on the outside of it, you'll have to start removing the snap-in metal panels that cover the furnace.

Every company makes a different style furnace. The styles also vary according to the fuel used. But the accompanying sketch shows some of the major things you would encounter in one type of oil furnace.

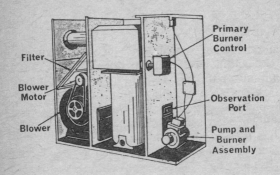

Primary Burner Control

Filter

Blower Motor

Blower

Observation Port

Pump and Burner Assembly

The blower or fan in almost any furnace looks like an enclosed squirrel cage. This is the thing you want to activate. It is usually located near the filter—a square of mesh-enclosed fiberglass strands.

The burner area is usually in a separate compartment. If you can locate a tiny flame (the pilot light) you have found the burner.

The heat exchanger is generally just above the burner. And now we're getting close to home. The air that heats your home flows around and through the heat exchanger and then into the main duct that feeds the different rooms.

The little control box for the fan is usually located somewhere between the heat exchanger and the point where the body of the furnace joins with the main, warm air duct. Under automatic conditions, the control "samples" the air flowing from the furnace into the house. When the air gets hot enough, the fan turns on. When the air cools down, the fan turns off.

You want to switch the fan operation from automatic to full time or manual.

When you find the control box, it should have a

button or switch on it marked "auto" for one position and "on" or "man" for the other position.

If you have trouble during this search distinguishing the cold air return duct from the warm air duct, the cold air duct is usually the one that feeds right into the fiberglass filter. As a last resort, turn the thermostat up to about 80 and let the furnace run for a minute. The warm air duct will be warm.

One caution on oil furnaces: There is often a small metal box on or near the burner pump. This is called the primary burner control and usually has a button on it.

If you mistake this for the fan control and push the button, nothing disastrous will happen (although the oil inside the burner may flare for a minute). But don't keep pushing it if the fan doesn't come on immediately —you're filling the burner with oil instead of operating the fan.

Part IV:

Working with Wood

75 / How to use the right hammer
for right job

To do almost any repair job around the house you need a hammer. But what hammer?

Most people have the Old Reliable, a claw hammer, that they use for hitting anything and everything. But using the right hammer for the right job will give the best results.

Following is a list of four common hammers that householders find most useful. The list is meant not only as a guide for buying. It is also a brief catalog for the amateur who wanders into or inherits a workshop and wonders, "What in the world is that thing for?"

Claw or nail hammer: This is what most people picture when they think of a hammer. It is versatile and can do a lot of different jobs but is designed expressly for driving regular nails into wood or for striking a nail set (a metal prod that drives the nail down below the surface of the wood). It's not actually supposed to be used on masonry nails, chisels or any extra-hard surface of this nature. The claw at one end is for grabbing and removing old or bent nails from wood.

Ball peen hammer: This hammer is often (but not always) smaller than the average claw hammer and has a round knob where the claw would be. Ball peen hammers are exceptionally hard. Thus, they are the choice for striking things like masonry nails or chisels and for shaping metal.

(Those "distressed" pieces of hardware like door latches, etc.—the ones with lots of dents—have often been finished with a ball peen hammer.) Most ama-

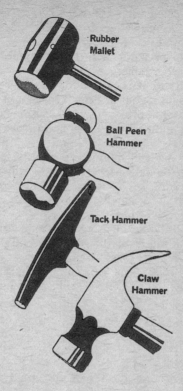

Rubber
Mallet

Ball Peen
Hammer

Tack Hammer

Claw
Hammer

teurs won't have any call to use the knob portion; just the hammer face. The hammer's smaller face and lighter weight make it less than ideal for ordinary, nail-and-wood carpentry.

Magnetic tack hammer: If you see a smallish hammer made with a split end that doesn't look quite like a claw, it is probably a magnetic tack hammer. The split end is the magnet—sort of like a skinny horseshoe magnet. You pick up the tacks by their heads (carpet tacks, for instance) with the magnet end of the hammer. You "set" or lightly tap the tack into place. Then you turn the hammer over and finish driving the tack with the regular face of the hammer.

A tack hammer's light weight and small striking face make it unsuitable for driving heavy nails or working against very hard surfaces.

Rubber or plastic mallet: This hammer looks like a small sledge hammer, except with a hard rubber or plastic head. It is meant for use on surfaces that you don't want to mar or dent. Typical uses are pounding hub caps into place on wheels, pushing out dents in a car body, setting brick or stone in place or working on furniture.

A rubber mallet should never be used to drive nails or strike spikes or chisels. Doing so will tear up the hammer head. The hammer won't do that job anyway. But it is a handy thing to have around the house.

One general rule in using any hammer: It's smart to invest in a pair of plastic goggles (good protection in lots of home repair jobs). Hammer faces can chip. But even more likely, an amateur hitting a nail at a strange angle can make the nail do all kinds of flips and unexpected tricks.

76 / Keep wood from turning to dust while sawing

It's fine to read about easy build-it-yourself projects like bookcases and tables. But all involve sawing wood.

If you're an amateur at this sort of thing, the simple job of sawing often turns out to be so discouraging that the whole project is scrapped—just like the lumber you've chewed up.

The most common types of hand saws are crosscut and rip saws. A crosscut is designed for cutting across the grain of a board; a rip saw is designed for cutting with the grain. If you don't know what your saw is, it is probably crosscut. It is the most common and useful. If you are getting ready to buy a saw, an eight point crosscut will be a good all-purpose one. (Eight point means there are eight teeth to the inch.)

A crosscut saw can be used to rip. But not vice versa.

First of all a saw should be sharp. If you suspect it isn't, have a professional sharpen it.

Mark your prospective path with a pencil. To begin your cut, brace the saw blade with the thumb of your free hand (carefully) and draw the saw up toward you a couple of times to just make a nick in the wood. Now you are ready to work in earnest.

Hold the saw at about a 45-degree angle to the wood. Grip the handle firmly, extending your forefinger along the handle as a sort of guide or brace.

Most beginners make the mistake of trying to cut with both strokes of the saw. Cutting should be done only on the down or push stroke. The up or pull stroke is just to get the saw back in position. Do not bear down on the saw when cutting. Just push it and let the weight of the saw itself do most of the work. On the up stroke, you can even lift slightly.

Make long strokes, using as much of the blade as possible.

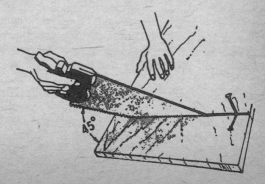

After you get a good distance into the wood, the saw may begin "binding" and you will have trouble moving the blade. This is because the wood is closing in on itself after the cut and holding the saw blade like a vise. The remedy is simple. Insert a nail or a small wedge of wood into the cut (as shown in sketch). Move the nail toward you gradually as you get deeper into the wood.

If you wander off of the pencil mark you have drawn, take the saw blade back to the point where you deviated. Take short strokes along the line until you are back on the track. This is easier than trying to "bend" back into the proper cutting line from somewhere outside it.

77 / Shimming made easy

Skriiiiitch! There it goes again—that door that hangs crooked, scraping on the door jamb or the floor.

Before you take the door down to plane or sand the offending edges, try "shimming out" the hinges. It is easier to do and, in many cases, takes care of the problem. Translated into regular English, shimming a hinge means simply sticking something like thin cardboard behind the hinge leaf if it is set too deeply into the door jamb. This makes the door hang "square" again.

If it's hard to tell where the door is sticking, run a piece of paper between the edge of the door and the jamb while the door is closed. The paper should move freely all the way around the door except at the sticking points.

Next, open the door wide enough to get at the

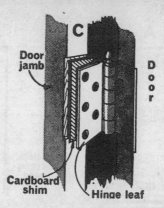

Cardboard shim · Hinge leaf

screws in the hinge leaves. (See sketch C.) Make sure all the screws are turned down as tight as they will go. If they simply won't stay tight, chances are the screw holes are "chewed up" or enlarged and need to be repacked.

First, place a book or a couple of magazines under the end of the open door. Then, when you unfasten one hinge, the door won't suddenly sag to the floor, putting a strain on the remaining hinge. Unscrew the hinge leaf from the door jamb. To repack the screw holes drilled into the jamb, try tapping a couple of wooden match sticks or toothpicks into the holes. A little glue stuck in there with them doesn't hurt. The hinge leaf can then be fastened back in place.

If tightening all the hinge screws still doesn't help the door, you can try shimming one of the hinges. The hinge you pick depends entirely on where the door is sticking. See sketches A and B, picking the one that applies in your case.

Let's assume you're shimming out the bottom hinge. Again, prop the end of the open door with a magazine or two. Unscrew the hinge leaf from the door jamb. Next, cut a piece of thin cardboard to about the size of the hinge leaf—but just a hair smaller all the way around. An old show box is almost the perfect weight for the cardboard you want.

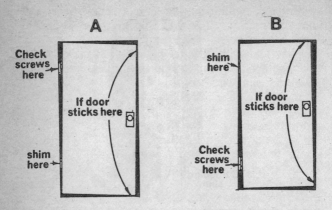

Slip the piece of cardboard behind the hinge leaf before screwing it back in place. If one thickness of cardboard is not enough, one or two more can be added.

78 / How to take the "squeak" out of stairway

Unless you need a sneaky way to monitor late hours kept by family members, you probably find squeaky stairs a slight annoyance.

This mouseland serenade is often caused by movement or friction between the tread and the riser. The tread is the flat board you step on. The riser is the up-and-down board that supports the tread.

The tread sticks out an inch or two past the riser and underneath this "lip," covering the seam between riser and tread, is generally a rounded strip of moulding for looks.

Pry the moulding away with a screwdriver, trying not to break it, since you'll want to nail or glue it back in place when you're through.

Look under the edge of the tread and see if you can tell whether the tread is held to the riser with nails or if it is a tongue-and-groove affair.

If you are not sure, poke upward with a knife blade along the face of the riser. The blade will slip part way up into the body of the tread in a tongue-and-groove, or "dadoed" construction.

To reinforce a nailed tread, measure the distance from the edge of the stair lip to where the riser meets the underside of the tread. Measure this same distance from the lip edge on the tread's top side, adding between a quarter and a half inch so the nail will come through into the riser instead of in front of it.

Have a neighbor or someone stand on the stair to hold it together firmly. Drive finishing nails (those skinny ones without heads) through the tread into the riser at angles to each other, forming wide V's.

Countersink the heads. That means drive the nails down deeper than the wood surface so you can cover the nail top with wood filler for a smoother appearance.

Countersinking is usually done with a nail set, which looks like an all-metal pencil with a dull point. But you can do nearly as well with another nail turned head down against the one you're driving.

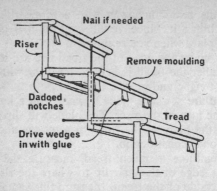

If the stair is grooved, drive thin wood wedges into the seam. Dip the skinny end of the wedge in glue first for a better hold. After the glue has dried for a couple of hours, trim off the excess portion of the wedge with a sharp utility or pocket knife.

If you're lucky enough to be working on a free-standing basement stairway, you can do much of this work from the back side.

79 / How to rebuild broken stairway banister

A staircase banister that's losing its vertical spindles looks about as appealing as a person who's losing his teeth.

There are different ways to build a banister. But two methods are probably most common.

The first is with channels and spacer blocks. The vertical spindles in a banister are called balusters. In this construction, the ends of each baluster fit into channels or grooves that run the length of the stair line and the underside length of the handrail.

Between the ends of balusters is a small piece of wood called a spacer block. It is sunk into the channel and held in place with glue or nails. The same arrangement is used in both stair line and handrail channels. The ends of each spacer block are slanted or beveled to accommodate the slant of the stairway (see sketch A).

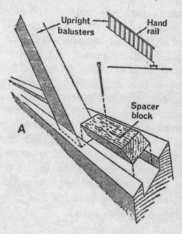

When a baluster falls out, it is usually because a spacer block is loose or has come out entirely. The remedy in this case is simple. Either tack the old spacer block back in place or cut a new one. Pry another block out of the channel to use as a pattern for the replacement. (A thin putty knife or screwdriver will usually work the block loose.)

If all the spacer blocks are in good shape, chances are your whole staircase is starting to sag, widening the gap between stair and handrail. The only permanent solution is to have a professional carpenter or contractor shore up the weak portions of the structure. But, in the meantime, you can try making a temporary repair by removing a spacer block and slipping a thin square of cardboard (a "shim") under the bottom end of the affected baluster.

This may raise the baluster enough in its bottom channels that the top end of the spindle will once more come within the channel of the handrail.

Some banisters do not use slanted channels and spacer blocks. Instead they have balusters that appear to sit flush against the stepping surface of each stair. (The handrail may or may not have spacer blocks in it.)

In this construction, the bottom end of the baluster usually has a small knob or dowel on it that fits into a hole drilled in the stair surface see sketch B).

It is more difficult to repair one of these balusters. Check for any loose or missing spacer blocks in the handrail. But if the diagnosis is a sinking staircase, you may want to slip a circle of cardboard into the hole in the step.

The problem is that you will create a gap between the "finished" portion of the baluster and the stair step (as shown in sketch B). You may be able to hide this to an extent by cutting thin wooden pieces to fill in the gap. But it will require some very exact measuring, some sanding and painting; and the repair may always look a bit rough.

There is one more thing to check before giving up and calling a carpenter.

Curving handrails are often put together in sections, each section held to the next with some kind of complicated internal gismo. If the connecting rod becomes loose, the balusters can start falling out.

Find the seam in the handrail (it should be readily visible from the top side). Then look on the bottom side of the handrail near the seam for a hole. Inside the hole, you should find a nut (as in nut and bolt).

Turn the nut to tighten the connection. This is easier said than done, since the nut is generally recessed and hard to reach. Try using needle-nosed pliers or a small screwdriver and hammer.

80 / How to tighten sagging cane chairs

Cane bottom chairs are both a joy and a grief to those who buy or inherit them. The intricately woven strands of cane look great but are expensive to replace.

When a cane seat starts to sag with use, extra strain is put on the strands around the chair edge. It doesn't take a crystal ball to see a broken seat in the near future.

Bringing the cane up tight and level again will help preserve the chair. It's a simple process of soaking and drying.

Mix as much warm water and plain glycerin as you will need, using a ratio of one ounce glycerin (available at drug stores) to two quarts water.

Soak two towels in the solution for each chair being treated. Place one wet towel on the corner or edge of a table; turn the chair over, resting the seat on the towel; put the remaining wet towel on the upturned underside of the chair seat. (See sketch.)

Towel

Towel

Let the cane absorb the water and glycerin for about half an hour or until the fibers are flexible. Then simply set the chair aside to dry for about 24 hours; the cane shrinks as it dries. An electric fan will speed the process.

Cane that has been varnished will not absorb the water and glycerine. But check the underside of a varnished seat; it may not have been painted. If it appears untreated, try a wet towel against just the one side. It will often still do the job.

81 / How to mend joints in creaky chair

Do your joints creak when you sit down?

You may not be able to reverse the aging process within your own body, but you can reinforce the joints in squeaking wooden chairs.

A loose rung on a chair is best repaired when it can be removed entirely. After removal, scrape the old glue from the rung end and from the hole in the chair leg. Try not to enlarge the hole in the process.

New glue can then be applied liberally to both surfaces. (White vinyl, epoxy or formaldehyde glues would be good choices.) But if the hole is too large for the rung, you can "fatten" the end of the rung in a couple of ways.

One method is to apply glue to the rung end, then wrap the end with a length of sewing thread (you can also use a strip of nylon stocking or a couple threads of steel wool.) Allow the glue to dry; then put fresh glue over the threads and inside the hole.

Another way is to install a wedge in the end of the rung, forcing it to expand as it's inserted in the hole (see sketch A). Saw a slot in the end of the rung and

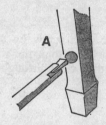

insert the cut-off end of a wooden clothespin (skinny end first). Coat the rung and hole with glue as before. When the rung is positioned in the hole, give the outside of the chair leg a good rap to secure the rung and drive the wedge back into the sawed slot.

A rope tourniquet will help hold the joint firm until the glue dries. Tie a rope loosely around the outside of the chair legs, protecting the finish with scraps of cloth or paper. Use a stick or pencil to twist the rope tight across the center, bracing the stick against the rung to keep it from unwinding. (See sketch B.)

If the offending rung cannot be removed for repair try drilling a hole into the joint through the side of the leg. Drill only as far as the rung end; then inject glue as forcefully as possible into the joint. Special "squirters" are available at some hardware stores; or you might want to try an old ketchup or mustard dispenser. Fill in the hole with wood putty that matches the chair finish as closely as possible.

These procedures also apply to legs that fit a socket in the bottom of the chair seat.

Wobbly joints where legs are attached to the corner of the seat frame can best be fixed with corner braces as shown in sketch C. Secure the braces with both glue

and screws. Prepare a path for each screw by drilling a hole slightly smaller in diameter than the width of the screw. Be careful not to drill clear through the side of the chair into the finish.

82 / Building bookshelves? It's easy to do it right

There comes a time in everyone's house when a bookshelf is needed. The fastest and easiest remedy is to buy a finished, ready-made shelf and have it delivered.

The other option is to put your own shelves together. This presents a wide range of possibilities. There are some styles you may not have thought of—and some things to keep in mind when putting bookshelves together.

You can go the traditional route of buying lumber and building and designing your own bookshelf. The ways of putting a wooden bookshelf together and supporting the shelves are so varied, it is best to check some books out of the library and review several building styles to pick the way that looks easiest for you.

If you want a wide shelf (to hold a record player in addition to books), you will probably have to go to 3/4-inch plywood. The edges of plywood are rough. You may want to apply a layer of wood filler to them before painting to give an even surface and better appearance.

Prefinished shelves made of pressed wood and covered with a hardwood veneer are available in lots of hardware, lumber and do-it-yourself stores these days. Some of the newer products combine the shelves with carved wooden spindle supports that come in various lengths and styles.

The shelves come with holes already drilled at the four corners. Spiral wooden or metal pegs fit through the holes. The spindles screw onto the pegs.

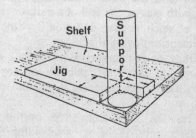

You might consider acrylic plastic sheeting and tubing. It can be used for a modern, airy appearance, combining clear plastic shelves cut to order with hollow plastic cylinders turned on end to act as supports. Sheeting 3/8 inch thick may suit your needs. But a heavy load may require sheeting 1/2 inch thick. The tubing can be had in several diameters.

The cut edges of the plastic can be left rough or sanded with even finer grades of wet-or-dry sandpaper used wet to keep down dust and heat. A special plastic glue that sort of melts and then bonds the surfaces can be used to secure the supporting cylinders to the shelves.

Whether sticking, drilling or nailing any support into place between shelves, there is a fast and sure method for always locating the supports in the same spot under every shelf.

The method is to use what's called a "jig." Experienced carpenters say you are sure to make a mistake if you rely on measuring say, 2 inches in and 4 inches back, with a ruler at the corners of every shelf.

Figure out how far in from a given shelf corner you want your support to be. Then cut a chunk of those dimensions from the corner of a piece of board or even heavy cardboard, as shown in sketch. This is your jig.

Line the jig up square with the corner of the shelf. Snuggle the support piece into the corner of the jig and mark around the base of the support piece with a pencil or, with plastic, the end of a nail.

Do this at each corner and you'll come up with the same dimensions every time.

More things to remember: Bookshelves carry tremendous weight. Test the flexibility of any material you plan to use before ordering it cut and paying for it.

Bookshelves that hang from strips on the wall must be fastened securely. If the screws holding the slotted strips to the wall go into plaster, hollow wall or brick, you'll need anchors for sure.

These are "sleeves" made out of plastic or any number of materials on the market. They fit into drilled holes; the screws then go into the sleeves. With hollow wall construction, it is best to use some type of "molly" bolt—a metal winged gismo that flares out on the back side of the wall as you tighten the screw it is attached to.

83 / How to make furniture blemishes disappear

Children can't seem to avoid skinned knees. Tables can't seem to avoid collecting a water mark or cigaret scorch here and there in a lifetime of use.

If there were an easy or foolproof way of fixing such blemishes, professional furniture doctors would be out of business. They aren't. And there isn't.

But it's worth trying a couple of things yourself, if the mar is not too serious.

Col. Edward R Gilbert, chief conservator of Greenfield Village and Henry Ford Museum, says his favorite all-purpose cleaner and polish for varnish and spirit-finished wood is as follows: A half pint each of boiled linseed oil, cider vinegar and pure turpentine, with one teaspoon methyl alcohol added.

This last ingredient is sometimes available from solvent companies but is pretty scarce these days. You can substitute denatured alcohol (sold as shellac thinner) for it.

To remove a water mark or a scorch, rub the blemish with 4-0 steel wool (the finest grade) dipped in this polish. Use only moderate pressure and work with the grain of the wood. Confine your treatment to the affected area. (On pale blond furniture, use white paste wax instead of linseed oil polish.)

As an alternative, try blending the finest grade of

pumice (from hardware stores) with vegetable or mineral oil to form a paste. The paste is rubbed over the blemish with a soft cloth pad in the same manner.

With either treatment, wipe the area frequently with a dry cloth to check what's happening.

Steel wool and pumice accomplish about the same thing; the wool is just easier to find and easier to work with.

If you get carried away with either of these procedures, you may lighten the finish in the area right around the blemish. This is certainly true of old furniture—the finish has usually darkened with age anyway.

If this happens you can sometimes redarken the spot (on brown or dark furniture) by applying a half-and half mixture of boiled linseed oil and turpentine to the lightened area once a week for some time. Linseed oil tends to darken a bit after it "cures."

Apply the darkener; let it stand for five minutes; then wipe it away with a dry cloth. (This, incidentally, is the same way the linseed formula polish is used—five minutes; then wipe dry.)

Because of the problem with rubbing away the finish it is extremely difficult to treat any burn that is deeper than a brownish scorch. The area of a real burn is depressed. By the time you get down to it, you may have a rather large discolored area instead of a small one. Better send the table to a professional or put a lamp over the mark.

84 / Get the best use out of your drill

It's hard to do much of anything constructive around the house without a drill.

Most people who confine themselves to odd jobs around the house have either a small electric drill or a hand crank drill (it has a little wheel you turn, sort of like a hand egg beater).

Any decent hardware store has a whole rack full of drill bits (the removable rod that actually does the drilling). Different sizes, different purposes and shapes. What do you need? What does it look like?

There are three things you need to know upon entering the store: The size of the chuck on your drill (explanation to follow), the size of the hole you want to drill and the type of material you will be working on.

Most hand drills are ¼-inch drills. This means the chuck (the nose opening where you insert the bit) will accept nothing larger than ¼ inch in diameter. It will, however, close down to accept anything smaller.

Inexpensive electric drills are mostly either ¼ or ⅜-inch drills (again, referring to the chuck size). They have an advantage over hand drills in that they provide more muscle and can be adapted as sanders and buffers with special attachments.

If you have a hand crank drill, you need an assortment of ordinary high-speed steel bits (see sketch). They can be bought singly or in sets that drill holes anywhere from $\frac{1}{16}$ of an inch to ¼ inch. If you are drilling a hole larger than ¼ inch, you can get a larger bit that has a shank or stem that is cut down to fit into a ¼-inch chuck.

The very cheapest bit sets are made of carbon steel and will drill wood easily. But it is smarter to invest a couple of dollars more and get high-speed bits. They will handle wood, thin sheet metal (like kitchen cabinets), plaster and plastic. This is all you really need with a hand crank drill, since you can't get enough leverage to drill concrete or masonry with it anyway.

The same basic kind of high-speed steel bit set should be bought for a light-duty electric drill. But in addition, there are a couple of extra options because of the higher turning power of the electric.

One of these is a flat-blade bit (see sketch). It is

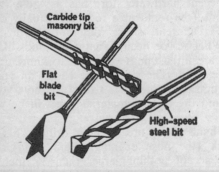

meant for drilling wood only and should be your choice if you are drilling any hole larger than ¼ inch in wood. The reason is that a flat-blade bit is cheaper (past ¼ inch) than a spiral bit of the same diameter.

The other bit that you will probably buy eventually is a carbide-tipped bit for masonry, brick and concrete. This kind of bit looks much like the plain spiral bit for wood and metal. But the tip of it has a wedge inserted into it that looks almost like an afterthought (see sketch).

Some masonry bits are slightly more expensive than plain bits and should be bought singly after you determine how large a hole you want to drill. Like the larger diameter wood and steel bits, they are available with cut-down shanks so they will fit into the drill.

85 / Make drilling easier

There's something very frustrating about watching a person drill into a wall or door frame, get the drill bit stuck in there and then try to get it out. The person in question usually pulls and tugs at the drill until it suddenly comes loose and he flies across the room—or until the drill bit breaks.

It's frustrating to watch because the remedy is so simple. If you are using a small hand crank drill (the kind that looks sort of like a heavy-duty egg beater), you simply turn the crank wheel in the opposite direction, reversing the action of the drill bit. It is then easy to back the bit out of the hole.

If you are using a hand electric drill, it may or may not have a reverse button on it. Many simple models don't. But just give the drill a little spurt of power in the regular forward direction while pulling the drill back at the same time.

You ought to pull a drill out of its hole every now and then anyway if you are drilling anything an inch or deeper. (Keep the drill turning as you pull it out.) The reason is to clear the hole of chips and debris. These chips not only make drilling harder, they can even enlarge the hole in some cases.

There are other handy things to know about drilling. For instance, you really should have a gismo called a center punch. This is sort of like a fat nail or spike that you smack with a hammer to make an initial hole or dent in either metal or wood. Center punches are available at hardware stores, often for less than a dollar. The purpose of the hole or dent is to give the drill bit something to home in on until it bites into the material.

Unless you need to drill a hole at an odd angle, a drill should be held at a 90-degree angle to your work. And don't press too hard. Just keep moderate pressure on the drill and let the bit set its own pace through the material. This is especially true with a small electric drill, which can overheat if you strain it.

(The exception is in drilling masonry with a carbide tip, where you press hard and turn the drill slowly. An electric drill with variable speeds is best for this. If your electric has just one speed, be careful of burning it out on masonry.)

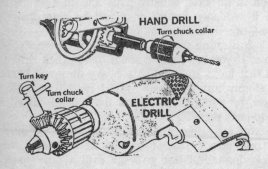

Are you an amateur who has inherited a used drill without directions? Then you'll need to know how to change the drill bits.

The business end of a drill—the part that holds the drill bits secure—is called a chuck. It expands and contracts to hold bits of various diameters (although small hand drills don't usually expand to more than ¼ or ⅜ inch).

The chuck on a hand crank drill is very simple to operate. Hold the crank wheel and body of the drill firmly with one hand to keep the wheel from turning.

With the other hand, rotate the metal collar of the chuck counterclockwise to loosen, clockwise to tighten (see sketch).

The metal collar of the chuck on an electric drill also turns. But there is an additional securing mechanism because of the higher speed of the electric drill.

Just in front of the collar on the electric chuck you will see three holes. There should also be, with the drill, a metal "key"—sort of an exaggerated version of a skate key (see sketch).

Insert the key into one of the holes and turn it counterclockwise to loosen the jaws of the chuck. Then turn the chuck collar to the diameter you want. Insert the new drill bit. Close down the chuck collar and tighten the loosened jaws with the key. (Not too tight. You won't get it undone again.)

Don't change bits while an electric drill is plugged in. You could chew up a finger.

Part V:

Working on the Outside

86 / Exterior painting to do? Here's what you'll need

You've probably put that exterior house painting job off just about as long as you can now. If you don't start fairly soon, your house will face one more season of winter peeling and your spirits one more season of doldrums.

There's a good deal to be said about exterior painting. So we'll split the discussion into three chapters —equipment, surface preparation and actual painting.

The first important supply you'll need is ambition. House painting is a time consuming, tiring task. It helps to remind yourself that you're saving money, if you do the job right. But if time is more important than money to you, hire a professional.

Assuming your resolve is high, you will need the following equipment:

• An extension ladder long enough to allow you an easy reach to the roof-edge gutters. One sliding section of an extension ladder overlaps the other section. When the ladder is extended as far as you need, the two sections should still overlap each other by two or three feet.

• A step ladder for lower middle areas of an outside wall. Professionals don't use a step ladder over eight feet tall outdoors. A six-footer is best. The standing surface outdoors is usually not reliable enough for a very tall step ladder.

• A good pot hook from which to hang the paint bucket on the ladder. Paint stores sell pot hooks for less than a dollar. Don't try to use an ordinary bent coat hanger. It won't hold more than a few minutes before dumping your expensive paint to the ground.

• Drop cloths for shrubs and sidewalks. The old canvas-type covers are always good. Or get some of the cheaper disposable drop cloths made of plastic or paper.

• Paint scrapers. There are many different kinds, but two are basic. One is a straight paint scraper and is actually just a very stiff putty knife (see sketch)—a wedge-shaped metal blade in a wooden handle. Don't buy a blade wider than 2½ or 3 inches. Exterior boards usually have a slight curve. A

wider blade won't fit the contours of the board as well.

The other kind is called a wood scraper or hooked scraper. It looks a lot like a straight paint scraper except for the end of the blade. It is bent down at about a 90-degree angle. The best hooked scrapers have a long handle. Many have a double-faced blade (see sketch). You can get very good leverage with these things by holding the end of the handle in one hand and pressing down just behind the head of the scraper with the other hand.

There are also special little paint scrapers shaped to fit corners and even the fluted edges of columns. None of them costs a fortune.

• A stiff wire brush. Get the kind with a long handle rather than a rectangular "scrub brush" model. The long handle will help save your knuckles. Don't buy a brush wider than about 1½ inches. It should be skinny enough to fit between iron railings and behind the edges of gutters.

- Sandpaper in at least two grades—coarse and medium. Add fine grade as a third if you're a perfectionist.
- Wipe cloths for misplaced paint drips on house and hands.
- Sturdy shoes with good arch construction. The rungs of a ladder come right across the middle of your foot. You'll be screaming after an hour if you try to wear tennies.
- Finally—a couple of good paint brushes. One should be narrow, about 1 inch or 1½ inches for window sashes. The other should be 3 or 4 inches wide for the sides of the house. Get synthetic brushes if you plan to use latex paint. Get natural bristle for oil base paint. Rollers aren't generally used on houses, except on brick or stucco faces.

87 / Preparing your house for paint job

You've collected ladders, brushes and other paraphernalia and you're ready to prepare your house for painting. This is the time when your home, no matter how modest, is going to loom larger and larger.

It takes a lot of work to prepare the exterior surface. But keep reminding yourself that a careful, thorough job now will save you work in the long haul. The new paint will last a lot longer.

The first step is to scrape away all the old blistered and peeling paint from the house. Use a paint or wood scraper (listed as needed equipment in the previous chapter) on wooden surfaces. A stiff wire brush will help you in tight corners. But it's not too good on open, flat wooden surfaces, since it can put grooves in soft wood. A wire brush does work well on metal surfaces.

Some houses carry so many layers of old paint that any new coat is going to look bad over the old cracked layers. If yours fits that picture, you may need to invest in paint and varnish remover—a goop that you paint on, then scrape off with a stiff putty knife or paint scraper. (Follow product directions for removal of final traces.)

Peeling gutters and drain pipes are a particular nuisance. If the old paint can be peeled from them easily, chances are the gutters were painted without proper preparation when they were new. New galvanized gutters have a light film of oil on them. They should be washed well and painted with a special primer for galvanized metal before they are painted to match the house.

If that procedure was neglected, you will probably have to take all the old peeling paint off with paint and varnish remover and start from scratch.

After scraping the old peeling spots from the house, you will need to sand the edges of the scraped places to blend them with the rest of the surface. Start with coarse paper and follow with medium.

Then—hateful though it may be—lightly sand all the old paint surfaces: the whole blessed house. You don't need to go right down to the wood. Just give a once-over with coarse sandpaper and follow with medium. The purpose is to create a good bonding surface for the new paint.

You may need to wash the area under the house eaves before sanding. Dirt tends to collect there. Sanding and then washing with chlorine bleach and water will usually get rid of any mildew spots.

Wipe or brush the sanding dust away with a cloth or old paint brush. Just hosing down the side of the house won't remove the dust satisfactorily.

Spot prime any areas that have been scraped down to the bare wood. Use an oil-based product labeled as an exterior primer or base coat for wood. (A finish coat of either latex or oil base will work fine over it.)

Metal and masonry require special primers of their own. Check with your paint man, especially if the masonry has a chalky or dusty surface.

Wood surfaces covered with old paint don't require a primer after sanding, if your planned new color is about the same as the old color. But if you are putting a light color over a dark color, you will be smart to put a primer coat over the whole house—preferably a shade lighter than the finish coat will be.

Primer is slightly thinner than finish paint, goes on easier and dries faster. And it is physically much easier to apply your final coat over primer than it is to put the finish coat over a layer of itself.

If you are painting aluminum siding on which the finish has deteriorated, wash the siding well with a mixture of trisodium phosphate (available at paint stores). Then give the entire surface a coat of the same oil-base primer you would use on wood.

88 / Now it's time to paint the house

The scraping, sanding and priming are finished. You're almost finished, too. And the time is finally here to put that gleaming coat of new paint on your house.

Any primer coat should be dry before you apply a finish coat of the exterior paint you want. But try to do the finish coat within a week of priming. If the primer gets too hard or dirty, you run the risk of painting over a bad bonding surface and your nice new paint job may peel.

The amount of paint needed varies considerably according to the surface being covered. Brick takes more than flat wood, for instance. Consult your paint dealer.

Either exterior latex or exterior oil-base paint will work well. One professional interviewed recently prefers oil-base. He says you can tell right away how well it is covering the old color. With latex, he says, you sometimes don't know until the paint dries. But latex does have the advantage of easy cleanup (just soap and water).

There used to be many exterior paints on the market labeled "self cleaning." Some are still available. These paints are designed to "chalk" or powder slowly over the years, the surface powder (and dirt) washing away in the rain. Do not use such a paint where the painted surface is situated over a portion of something like natural brick. Rain will wash the paint powder down onto the brick, making white or colored streaks.

A cheap paint will sometimes chalk whether designed to or not. So will a paint that has been thinned too much. Over-thinning or buying poor quality paint is a dubious savings, considering your investment in time and effort.

Start painting at the top of the house and work down. When working from a ladder, hang only a quart of paint in a gallon container from the hook on the ladder. If you should happen to spill or drop the bucket, the mess and money loss won't be disastrous.

Do use a brush (although rollers are all right for masonry surfaces). You want to "work the paint in" slightly by stroking a few times over the same area. This blends the paint with any light dust on the wall. Just laying the paint on top of the dust (as a roller would) risks later peeling.

Don't paint in excessive heat (100 degrees or over). Although if it's that hot, you probably won't feel like painting anyway. High temperatures make the liquid evaporate quickly from the applied paint before it has a chance to really bond to the surface. Remember that dark colors absorb heat much more than light colors.

(In winter, freezing temperatures will ruin latex paint. It separates like bad Hollandaise sauce and never is the same again. Oil paint won't exactly freeze. But it will become unworkably stiff.)

Rain will wash either wet latex or oil base paint off of a house. But most people don't start painting with a thunderhead on the horizon. A much more common mistake is painting too soon after a rain. A house must be completely dry before painting or the residual moisture will cause the paint to peel.

Don't paint much past late afternoon with gloss paint. If dew settles on the wet paint, the gloss will be gone in the morning.

89 / Some easy rules on ladder safety

Whether you're climbing Jacob's ladder or your own, there are a few rules to follow:

Test the soundness of a straight wooden ladder by placing it on the ground and stepping in turn on each of the rungs. Also examine the side pieces for any rotten or cracked areas. (Never paint your wooden ladder. The paint hides weak spots.)

The side pieces of aluminum stepladders sometimes buckle. They can be bent straight again, but are never really reliable afterward. It's better to buy a new one.

Learn to carry a ladder correctly. Carry the ladder by one side piece, right in the middle at the center of gravity. Some people attach an old screen door handle or window handle to the side of the ladder at that point. It makes toting much easier.

The angle of a straight ladder against the house is important. If the foot of the ladder is out too far, your weight may break the ladder or it may slide down the face of the house. If the foot is too close to the house, you and the ladder may topple over backward like a felled tree.

The distance between the house and the base of the ladder should be one-fourth the length of the ladder. In other words, the base of a 12-foot ladder should

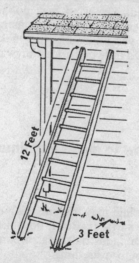

be 3 feet from the house; the base of a 20-foot ladder should be 5 feet from the house (see sketch).

The base of the ladder should rest evenly and on a firm surface. Some surfaces, like concrete, are too firm and tend to be slick. Fill a couple of small burlap sacks with sand and stick the feet of the ladder into them. Secure the sacks with wire or string around the legs. This is a good way to avoid slippage. Another is to nail hunks of old tire to the bottoms of the ladder legs.

Glueing strips of old carpeting to the top pieces of a ladder will protect the paint finish of your house while the ladder is against it.

A wide rubber band or strip of inner tube wrapped around the top leg or top shelf of a ladder makes a handy holder for small tools.

Never climb higher than the third rung from the top of a straight ladder (or the second step from the top on a step ladder).

Don't reach far to the side when working from a ladder. Move the ladder instead.

And—as silly as it may sound—don't use a ladder in a high wind. The wind may not affect the ladder much. But it can supply enough lateral push on your body to throw you off balance and make you fall, when your footing is a little precarious anyway.

90 / How to clean aluminum siding

Aluminum siding may require less care than many exterior home surfaces. But it does need some upkeep —especially in industrial areas where corrosive pollution globs onto everything.

Siding should be washed with mild detergent, water and a soft brush about twice a year in normal areas. In industrial areas, change that schedule to four or five times a year.

But suppose you move into a house where the aluminum siding has been neglected for several years and is really caked with dirt and oil. Advice gleaned from four companies dealing in siding is as follows:

All aluminum siding has a paint covering that is baked on at the factory. But different brands use different kinds of paint. And the paint thickness is not always the same either. So whereas one brand may stand up under pretty harsh cleaning, another may not. The answer is to spot test and experiment a bit before tackling the whole house exterior.

Start with mild detergent and warm water used with a soft brush. (Those long-handled brushes that attach to hoses for washing the car are good for doing siding.)

If the mild detergent doesn't work, go to a stronger detergent. A liquid cleaner normally used on floors, in a strong concentration with warm water, will usually do the trick.

If that doesn't work, about the only alternative is powdered bathroom cleanser used with a soft rag. But this, if used time after time, will take the finish off even the best siding. Using an abrasive compound like cleanser should be a last resort. Don't scrub too long in one spot. And keep in mind that you may have to paint the siding if the cleanser ruins the finish.

Whatever you use to clean, wash from the bottom of the house up. And try to pick a cloudy day for the work.

Working from the bottom up helps prevent streaks. Sure, you will get dirty water dripping down over the areas you have just cleaned. But that is better than soapy water making tracks down through the dirt on lower panels if you start at the top. Clean streaks are harder to get rid of than dirty streaks. A cloudy day simply keeps the streaks from drying so fast.

It is essential to rinse the finished cleaning job well with a hose. Swipe along with the brush, too, to remove all traces of soap. Otherwise, you will have a mess the next time it rains.

If aluminum siding has corroded so badly that dirt has embedded itself in the surface, you probably won't ever be able to get it clean. The only option then will be to paint the siding, if you want a shining clean surface again.

Most companies recommend exterior latex paint for painting over aluminum siding. There shouldn't be any special preparation needed except thorough cleaning, rinsing and drying before the paint goes on.

If siding is extremely corroded, the worst spots are generally up under the eaves of the roof, where rain has not washed the surface. A light sanding with fine-grained sandpaper in those areas may be needed.

Once you do paint aluminum, the surface will eventually require repainting, just as any painted surface does. It should, however, last a bit longer than a paint job on wood, since the expansion and contraction of wood is not a factor.

91 / How to caulk your home

Caulking and weatherstripping will help seal your home against drafts. Since caulking cannot be applied when the outdoor temperature is below about 40 degrees, it's best to do it on a mild day.

Caulking is the putty-like substance used to cover the little cracks between the body of the house and the window sash (or the door frame). It is usually applied when a house is built, but it should be scraped away and reapplied after a few years have dried and cracked it.

Caulking can be bought in bulk. But do-it-yourselfers usually prefer either cartridges or giant tooth-paste tube containers. The squeeze tubes are for small jobs and generally roll up at the end with a key.

Cartridges require a caulking gun, sold separately at hardware stores. (Don't try to use a cartridge without a gun. The plunger inside the cartridge is too hard to push by hand.)

The plunger on the caulking gun is a central rod with teeth or ratchets on one side of it. Turn the rod ratchet-side-up and pull it back as far as it will go (see sketch). Insert the cartridge; then turn the rod

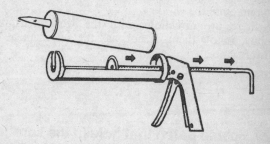

so the ratchets face downward (otherwise the trigger won't engage them to push the plunger forward).

Snip the nozzle of the cartridge at a 45-degree angle; there are little marks on the end to show you where. Also stick an ice pick down the nozzle to break the inner seal where the nozzle joins the cartridge. Then pump the trigger to force out the caulking.

Apply the compound in a continuous "worm" over the crack to be covered. After allowing the caulking to dry a couple of days, a coat of paint over the compound will help keep it flexible. Caulking compound will stick to metal, wood and masonry, but only if the surfaces are dry and fairly clean.

Plain old architectural grade caulking costs 50 or 60 cents a cartridge. Latex and butyl rubber compounds are both more expensive—about $1.40—but are reputed to stay flexible longer.

Weatherstripping comes in many different designs. Some must be nailed into place. But the easiest to handle are flexible, adhesive-backed strips of felt, vinyl or foam rubber.

There are no strict rules about where weatherstripping is to be applied. The idea is simply to stop the drafts.

Stick-on foam strips, for example, can be applied to the window-sill, snug up against the face of the closed window sash. If you don't like the way the stripping looks inside the house, put it on the outside of the window or even inside the groove where the window sash fits—if that won't make it too hard to open and close the window.

If there are directions with the weatherstripping you buy, follow them. If not, ask the salesman at the hardware store.

92 / How to patch that hole in the screen

Grisly thought putting up and taking down screens and storm windows.

While you're taking down and putting up, you might as well do needed minor repairs like patching holes in the screens and painting or caulking the storm sashes.

There are little screen patching kits you can buy at hardware stores. They come with directions. Just try to match the metal of the patch to the metal of your screen. Some metals fight each other, causing unsightly staining—copper and aluminum, for instance.

But you may have a chunk of old screen lying around the basement or workshop—which means you won't have to buy anything at all. Cut a square patch at least twice as large as the hole you want to cover. Then remove some of the wire strands along each side of the patch, much as you would pull threads to fringe a piece of cloth.

Check the edges of the hole. Either even the edges with wire cutters or straighten the loose strands, with the idea of weaving them into the patch later.

Bend the fringe edges of the patch to a 90-degree angle and apply the patch to the screen, poking the fringe ends through the mesh of the existing screen (see sketch).

Screen Patch

Mash down the fringe pieces of the patch to secure it. Weave any loose strands around the hole itself into the mesh of the patch. A pair of old tweezers or needle-nose pliers will be helpful.

All this mashing and weaving will put a strain on your screen unless it is lying flat with a board or some kind of raised support placed under the patching area.

Aluminum sashes or frames should be cleaned occasionally with mild detergent and fine steel wool. Put a coat of car wax on the frames it you wish, to help protect them.

Wooden sashes or frames should be painted now and then for looks and to keep moisture from entering the wood and swelling it.

Sand the old paint surface a bit with medium grade sandpaper. This accomplishes two things. First, it roughens the old paint enough to make a good bonding surface for the new paint.

Second, it makes room for the new coat of paint. If you keep adding layers of paint to the sashes, they will eventually get too "fat" for the windows or doors they are supposed to fit. Keep any new coat of paint moderate in thickness for the same reason. Don't apply so much paint to the sides that it runs down and makes little globs.

Those of you who have hanging brackets on the sashes are in luck. Suspend the sash by its brackets (by wire to something sturdy, or drive nails into a wooden basement beam). That way, you can reach all the wooden surfaces without turning and propping the sash.

Suspend a brick from the bottom hook of the sash to steady it and give it more "heft" while you're painting.

Sashes don't have any brackets? You'll have to dream up your own tricks. Maybe thin wire strung at two points through the screening close to the wooden edge?

93 / How to clean greasy garage floors

Grease and oils stains on an unpainted garage floor are among the most stubborn things to get rid of. They rank right along with athlete's foot and chronic borrowers.

There are commercial preparations available—usually at auto supply stores or the auto sections of department stores.

However, if they are hard to find or prove to be unsatisfactory, there are a few other things you can try. The idea is to use something that is either dry or like a paste to stay put for some time and "draw" the oil or grease out of the concrete. Concrete is porous; so grease and oil sink down into it if left.

Trisodium phosphate is a supercleaner sometimes available at industrial paint stores or building supply

Trisodium phosphate

Sawdust

houses. A strong mixture of it with water and sawdust (to hold it in place) is supposedly quite effective if left on the spot for a couple of hours.

Wear rubber gloves. When the job is done, scrape up what you can of the mixture and dispose of it in the garbage can or incinerator. Then flush the cleaned area with water.

Another method is to put down a half-inch layer of cement powder and let it sit for a day or two. Then sweep it up. Cement powder is very fine and absorbs well. It should draw some of the oil out just by itself. But if it doesn't, put down another layer of cement powder and saturate it with mineral spirits (available at paint stores).

The mineral spirits not only dissolve grease and oil; the evaporation helps the powder "draw." Mineral spirits will not cause the cement powder to harden.

Antifreeze or rust stains from overflowing car radiators are even harder to remove than grease marks. They reportedly can be removed by scrubbing the spot with oxalic acid and water (wear rubber gloves). Oxalic acid is not all that commonly available; but a good pharmacy should be able to order it for you.

Both oxalic acid and trisodium phosphate will open the pores of concrete somewhat or etch the surface, leaving it more susceptible to stains. So you should really apply a coat of clear concrete sealer after you get the floor clean. If you are moving into a new house, apply a sealer coat before you ever start using the garage or driveway. It is available in well-stocked paint stores and building supply houses.

With any of the above cleaning methods, make sure pets and babies are kept out of the garage while cleaning substances are on the floor.

94 / How to treat a power mower

Every summer adults and children are injured by rotary power mowers—usually through carelessness.

Cutting blades are not the only danger—stones, glass and other debris can be hurled many feet by a rotary mower—with deadly effect.

Make sure you aren't involved in a mower accident this year—follow these safety rules:

Know your controls; read the owner's manual carefully and learn how to stop the mower engine quickly in an emergency.

Keep children and pets as far away from the mower as possible.

Disengage all blade and drive gears before starting (on units so equipped). Start the engine carefully with feet well away from the blades.

Check all nuts, bolts and screws often to be sure the mower is in safe operating condition.

Do not operate the engine where carbon monoxide fumes can collect.

Never cut grass by pulling the mower toward you.

Be extremely careful when using a riding mower on slopes. It can turn over.

Make sure the lawn is clear of sticks, stones, wire and other debris.

Do not overspeed the engine or alter governor settings. High speed is dangerous and shortens mower life.

Never leave inertia-type starters in a wound-up position.

Stop engine and disconnect spark plug wire before checking or working on the mower.

Add fuel before starting the engine—never while the engine is running.

Do not allow anyone to operate mower without instructions.

Stop the engine before pushing mower across gravel drives or walks. Also stop it whenever you leave the mower, even for a moment.

Don't drive too close to creek or ditch edges and watch out for traffic when near roads.

Stay alert for holes and other hidden hazards.

Keep all shields and safety devices in place.

Do not carry passengers on a riding mower.

95 / How to keep a power mower working properly

Power lawn mowers are only used six months out of the year, and often they don't get proper maintenance during the lawn-mower season. Why not check your power mower now, before the day of reckoning comes along and you find the blankety-blank thing won't start?

Before doing any cleaning or checking, make sure all mower switches are turned off and the spark wire is disconnected. Otherwise the blades might give a turn or two unexpectedly.

The spark wire? This is a little electric cord that hooks to the top of the spark plug which, in turn, fires the engine. Motor styles vary from size to size and maker to maker. But the spark wire (and top end of the spark plug) are generally somewhere on the outside of the motor, accessible without taking the housing apart. The Briggs & Stratton motor shown in the sketch is an example.

Spark wires sometimes just clip or slide into place over the plug end; others are held in place with a screw.

While in the neighborhood, you might as well check the spark plug. It unscrews. There is usually a copper gasket or washer around the screw-threads of the spark plug; be sure not to lose it, as it is necessary for a proper fit.

Spark points
(scrape clean)

At the threaded end of the spark plug are two little metal points across which the spark is supposed to jump (see sketch). These should be free of all carbon and corrosion. Scrape gently to clean. Look carefully at the two points; they should have nice straight edges and squared-off ends. If they are jagged, the plug probably needs to be replaced (not expensive) with the same style plug.

Try not to widen the gap between the points while cleaning; it's hard to set right again without a specially-made measuring tool. If for some reason you have further separated the points, however, the thickness of a dime will approximate what the measure should be.

Clean dust, dirt and grass clippings from cutting blades and from the rotating screen and cooling system (this should be done after each use).

The air filter should be cleaned or replaced. A common type of filter used today is a piece of foam rubber-like material contained in a small metal box closed with a nut and bolt. Remove the foam; squeeze it out in a container of kerosene. Dry the foam by squeezing it in a cloth; then soak it with engine oil, squeezing it once more to remove excess oil and replace in its box.

Air filters are found in various places, but should be marked on the mower itself. Clean or replace for every 25 hours of operation or according to owner's manual directions.

Lubricate the wheels by putting a few drops of oil where the axle sticks through the hub of the wheel

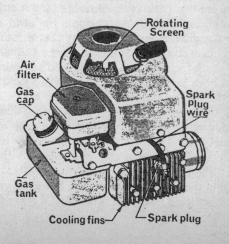

(some wheels have a little hole in the hub for adding a few drops).

Cutting blades should be well sharpened. They can be unbolted with an adjustable wrench and either sharpened at home (with a 10-inch heavy file or a grinding wheel) or taken to a shop, where the job is quickly done for a small fee.

The height of the blade can be adjusted on many mowers by moving little levers located at each wheel to raise or lower the whole mower.

Check the air vent of the gasoline tank (air has to get into the tank as gas flows out). Some mowers have a little hole in the gas cap, some have a tiny cap on top of the main cap. If your style is the latter, the small cap has to be loose while the mower is running. In either case, swizzle the gas cap around in a container of kerosene to loosen dust and dirt in the vent.

Some mowers have what's called a settling bowl—a little glass or clear plastic cup set into the fuel line between the gas tank and the motor to catch gunk in the gasoline. The settling bowl should be removed and cleaned with kerosene. But FIRST close the gas line shut-off valve (usually a little butterfly or wing nut) on the fuel line at the bottom of the gas tank.

There are two basic types of power mower engines— four-stroke and two-stroke engines. No need here to explain the difference except to say that a four-stroke generally uses straight gasoline and has a special crankcase or sump for motor oil. (Oil should be drained and changed once every 25 hours of operation or sooner if owner's booklet so states.)

With two-stroke engines, on the other hand, the lubricating oil is usually mixed with the gasoline right in the fuel tank. The point is—if your mower is a two-stroke, you should not add raw gasoline to the tank. The gas should be mixed with motor oil in a ratio specified in the owner's booklet. (If, however, you have lost the booklet, a backyard rule is half a pint of oil for every gallon of gas.)

Here's a handy little idea for keeping leaves and twigs out of basement window wells.

A mesh cover spanning the recessed area of the window well can save you an unpleasant cleaning chore later.

A variety of materials can be used—screen wire, a wider meshed wire or plastic coated mesh available at hardware and building supply stores.

With a frame house, you can tack or staple the mesh to the bottom edge of the wooden siding; then secure the far edge of the mesh at the outside rim of the window well using bricks, little stakes or whatever is handy and seems safe. See sketch.

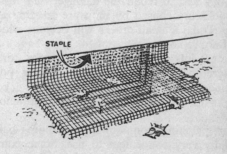

STAPLE

With a brick house, you may be able to tack the top edge of the mesh to the top of a wooden window sash.

A brick wall and metal window sash may necessitate building a lightweight wooden frame to fit over the space and hold the mesh in place.

Prefabricated plastic or fiber-glass "dome" covers are supposedly available for basement window wells. But they are a bit difficult to find.

Other possibilities include building a rigid wooden cover which could be removed in summer, or constructing a miniature greenhouse by covering the window well with wood-framed panels of clear plastic or glass. But avoid using glass if the neighborhood is full of children. Rigid covers are always a temptation for children to stand on.

97 / How to patch minor cracks in concrete

Did the winter leave your sidewalk, patio or concrete stairs cracked and crumbly?

If so, it's best to repair the damage while it's minor. Such cracks are caused by moisture freezing and expanding. Today's small cracks will become wider next winter if not repaired.

There are lots of products on the market for patching concrete. The old standby is regular portland-type cement mixed with sand and water (you can buy sacks that already contain the right amount of sand).

Newer patching compounds are more expensive, but usually very convenient to use. Some come in a puttylike consistency in little buckets. Some are latex based and use a special liquid instead of water. Some are epoxy types that have yet another special liquid plus a hardening agent, and so on.

Whatever you choose, preparation of the old concrete for patching is pretty much the same. The trick is to create as clean a surface as possible.

First brush and scrape away all the loose and crumbled concrete that you can. Then, with a hammer and chisel, form the sides of the crack into a rough "V" (see sketch A). Brush away the new debris you have created. A wire brush is good for this. Get all the dust out too.

Most repair manuals say to chisel the crack in a reverse "V" form—wider at the bottom than at the top. But this is almost impossible to do. And worse yet, you run the risk of trapping air bubbles in the crack when you patch it because you can't see exactly what you are doing.

If you are working on a vertical surface like the face of a step, just scrape away all the crumbly material you can. If the seam looks unsound where the vertical portion meets the horizontal surface of the next step, chisel that seam into a small "V" It also helps to drive a couple of masonry nails into the seam as flat up against the vertical surface as possible (see sketch B).

This helps give the patch something to cling to.

If you are using some of the newer concrete patching compounds, follow the directions for use on the package and stick to the mixing proportions they recommend.

If you are using a regular portland cement and sand mixture, follow these recommendations:

Blend the concrete and water to a fairly stiff mixture. It should hold together in your hand in a sort of loose ball if you squeeze it. The more water you mix with concrete, the more it shrinks as it dries; and that's something you don't want.

Next, dampen the surface you'll be patching. Don't make a big puddle; but get the area thoroughly damp. This keeps the old concrete from stealing moisture from the new patching material and gives a better bond.

Plop the patching material into the "V" with a trowel or something similar. Use a generous amount. Poke it and wiggle it around a lot to work it down well into the crack and remove all air bubbles.

Level off the surface of the patch with the edge of the trowel or a board. If working on a vertical surface, create the shape you want with the edge of the trowel. A fairly stiff patching mixture should hold its shape without any wooden forms or bracing material.

Check the patch periodically until it has begun to harden. Then place a piece of cloth or burlap over it and dampen the cloth with a fine spray from the garden hose.

Keep the cloth damp for several days until the concrete patch is completely set or "cured." This is important to keep a portland patch from drying too quickly and developing cracks of its own.

98 / Quick ways to mend a leaky hose

Most people have at least one length of old garden hose which has enough bulging tape wrapped around leaking sections to make the thing look like a skinny snake that has swallowed the family pet.

To make your hose a little less bulky and a little

more watertight, try these inexpensive tricks. If they don't work, you haven't lost much time or money.

Small cracks in rubber hose can sometimes be helped by a generous coating of rubber glue—available in small bottles from any dime store.

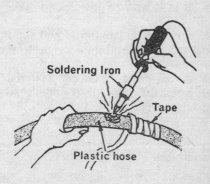

Soldering Iron

Tape

Plastic hose

First clean and dry the cracked area thoroughly.

Spread a blob of rubber glue over the crack and bend the hose back and forth a little to let the glue work down into the damaged area. Apply one or two more coats, waiting 15 minutes between applications.

Then wind an overlapping strip of rubber or plastic tape around the repaired area and set the hose aside 24 hours before using.

Small cracks or holes in plastic garden hose can sometimes be helped with a soldering iron. Hold the heated iron to the damaged area briefly until the plastic begins to melt. Spread the soft plastic back and forth until the crack or hole is plugged.

Reinforce the repair job with a length of overlapping plastic tape.

Neither of these methods will work for long on a major break. For that, you may have to cut out the damaged section and insert a metal splicer or clamp Consult the nearest hardware dealer before launching on this project.

If the hose leaks at its connections, new washers are probably needed (little rubber rings seated just inside the metal cap at the end of the hose). Prying the old washer out and turning it over will sometimes help until you get to a hardware store.

When a garden hose gets so old that repairing it is senseless, there are still uses for it:

Poke holes in it with an ice pick to make a soaker hose.

Slit a section of hose lengthwise and slip it over the cutting edge of your handsaws for protection during storage.

A hose makes great "bumper" material too, for everything from the rims of children's swing seats to boating dock edges.

99 / How to care for metal lawn chairs

Pity the poor aluminum lawn chair that sits out in the rain and pollution all summer. You can help preserve the originally shining aluminum with a mixture of elbow grease and paste wax.

Some advertisements say aluminum furniture requires no care. But it doesn't take long—especially in an industrial city—for air pollution and weather to roughen and pockmark the armrests and other metal surfaces.

The unsightliness may not bother you but rough metal against bare arms is unpleasant. Against sheer summer sleeves it can be downright destructive.

If lawn furniture is still bright and new, wash it with a soft cloth, detergent and water. Then rinse and dry it. Apply two coats of a good paste wax (either for furniture or cars).

If the metal surface already looks and feels corroded, use a steel wool soap pad and water to smooth the surface as well as possible. Then go through the wax bit.

A really industrious polisher can unfasten the screws that hold the strips of plastic webbing in place (see sketch), thus getting a clear shot at all alumi-

num portions.

Wax is also good protection for painted wrought iron. But spray wax is sometimes best here for reaching all the twists and curlicues.

When it comes to replacing the plastic webbing on aluminum lawn chairs, there are at least two common attachment methods.

One is with screws, as mentioned before. Packages of webbing are available at large hardware, department and outdoor furnishings stores but the packages usually contain no eyelets. Directions simply say to poke a hole through the folded end of the web. But this leaves the edges of the hole ragged and prone to unravel.

The remedy is to go to the nearest fabric or sewing shop and get a packet of quarter-inch metal eyelets to rim the hole (available for about 60 cents with a little tool for mashing the eyelets flat).

Another way to fasten webbing is with a simple tube-like clamp available in large hardware stores (see sketch). Directions are printed on the package. The clamps require no screws and can be pried off with a screwdriver when need arises.

Some playground equipment was never made with child safety in mind.

Open-ended metal tubes often have rough edges and make good places for fingers to get caught. The tubes come in various diameters, but some of them can be fitted with the plastic caps (available in hardware stores) you often see on the bottom of kitchen chair legs.

The chains on swing sets often break near the top or the bottom at stress points. You can install safety chains on the top bar and on the seat as shown in sketch A. Drill through the top bar two or three

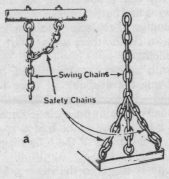

Swing Chains →

Safety Chains

a

inches to the outside of the regular eye bolt and install a second eye bolt. Leave a bit of slack in the safety chain so there will be no wearing strain on it.

Installation of the extra chains on swing seats will depend on how the original chain is situated. Sketch

A shows safeties for a chain that joins the middle of the seat. If the original chain splits into a Y at the seat, you would run a single safety chain down the center of the Y. Again, leave a little slack to avoid strain.

Plastic swing seats are generally light enough that they don't present a great hazard to tots standing nearby.

But the combination of absent-minded kids and flying metal or wooden swing seats can result in a real goose egg on the noggin.

As a precaution, measure the perimeter of the swing seat and cut a like length of old garden hose as a bumper. Drill holes for nuts and bolts around the overhanging edge of the seat—two or three to the long side, one or two on the short side.

Slit the hose lengthwise and drill matching holes in the side of the hose that will be against the seat. Keep in mind the slit should face down toward the ground to avoid pinching children's legs. (See sketch B.) Prying the hose open at the slit, install bolts and metal washers (0-rings) securing them with nuts.

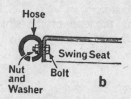

Some parents also install rubber hose "sleeves" on swing chains for a distance of two or three feet near the seat. This keeps little fingers out of the chain links.

Some playground equipment is designed to simply set on the ground without any anchoring device. If the equipment tends to tip over, you can improve matters by buying a few lengths of chain and some of those corkscrew-like stakes sold in pet stores.

Dampen the ground around the equipment braces, twist the stakes as far as possible into the earth and run a chain (either wrapped or bolted) from selected braces to the stakes. This, unfortunately, still allows some movement of the equipment but it at least forestalls a total topple.

Children can aid stability of a swing set by not swinging in the same direction in unison.

Check equipment for any S-hooks and pinch them closed with pliers. Tape any sharp edges on slide boards and look for possible splinters if the side supports are wooden. (The remedy is sanding and repainting—with lead-free paint.)

Gliders—those double bench seats that swing—often display a scissors or knife action between the supports and undercarriage. Designs vary from maker to maker, but check out the possibility of installing a plywood floor on your child's glider to cancel all chance of foot or leg injury.

A strip of wood nailed across the middle of the new floor will give the children a brace against which to push to get the gilder going. You may need to leave slots in the floor for movement of metal support pieces. Make the slot long enough so that the support piece, at the outside limit of its movement, will not hit the end of the slot.

A bar striking the end of the slot will eventually loosen the floorboard and could also pinch a child's fingers or toes.

101 / How to clean a dirty barbecue grill

You're hauling out the portable barbecue equipment in the spring. And what do you know! "Somebody" put the thing away dirty last fall.

The meat rack or grill is caked with congealed

grease, burned-on food and dust. The standard way of removing all this is to launch an attack with soap, water and a scouring pad. But this is really messy. And invariably, a removable grill won't fit all the way into your sink.

There are a couple of other options you might consider. One of the best is the children's sandbox. Sand is a super cleaner and you don't need water.

Just flip the grill over in the sand a couple of times to get it well coated. The more sand that sticks to the grease the better. Scrub sand up and down each rod with your fingers and you'll be surprised how fast the grill comes clean. If you have delicate hands, use an old cloth.

If you have an old fork that you don't care about, it makes a good scraper. The tines fit around the rods of the grill.

Spray-on oven cleaner is another option. (A similar spray made just for barbecue grills is also on the market.) Most meat racks for portable sets are made of chrome, stainless steel or cast aluminum and have a hard enough suface that oven cleaner shouldn't harm them. Heat the rack a bit first before spraying it, if possible. But this isn't always essential; check directions on the spray can.

Spray the grill; let it stand for about 15 minutes; then spray it with the garden hose. Stubborn spots may still have to be scraped.

After you clean the grill, you can make future cleaning easier by spraying it with that vegetable-based no-stick spray used for pots and pans.

Permanent brick barbecues often have a heavier type of grill made from cast iron. These grills can and do rust if they don't have a coat of oil on them.

You can scrape the worst of the rust off the surface with an ordinary house brick. But you'll have to follow up with something like steel wool or a wire brush. Use the garden hose as you work with the steel wool to rinse away the rust as you go.

As the water dries, it will create little rust spots

of its own, of course. But you'll need to finish by coating the iron grill with a layer of cooking oil anyway. Use a cloth to do this and you will wipe away remaining light rust spots as you go.

Don't wash an iron grill after every use. Just wipe it clean to keep the oil film intact.

Further repairs may be in order for your barbecue equipment. If a brick or masonry barbecue pit has developed cracks during the winter, patch the cracks during the spring with cement to prevent further damage next winter.

Check the owner's booklet on your portable grill to see if any hinges, cranks or controls are supposed to be oiled periodically.

If the paint on the shell of your portable barbecue has been chipped or is flaking away, sand the flaking spots. Then wipe the whole shell clean with paint thinner and spray it with high-temperature paint designed for barbecues.

102 / How to rid your house of wasps

The planning sessions for D-Day were probably nothing compared to the cumulative hours invested in strategy each summer by Americans Against Those Darned Wasp Nests.

Everyone has his pet method for attacking a wasp nest (which always seems to appear in the least desirable place—in the attic, on the back porch, under the second-story eaves). The most common method, however, is to let somebody else do it.

Here are some hints for the brave.

One "handyman" book suggests hanging strips of

flypaper around an indoor nest, changing the flypaper frequently until all resident wasps have been trapped. Then the nest can be knocked down, doused with kerosene or lighter fluid and burned.

For an outside nest, the book says to put a ladder up (if needed) during the day. Then at night, while the wasps are snoozing in the nest and dreaming of the people they'll sting, you put on a hat, veil, gloves and long-sleeved shirt. Under cover of darkness, you climb the ladder, clip the nest free and let it fall into a plastic or heavy paper bag.

The book then says to "immediately douse the nest with kerosene and set it on fire." One assumes, however, that this is best done after descending from the ladder.

E. C. Martin, professor of entomology (bugs) at Michigan State University, says these procedures sound overly complicated to him. His first bit of advice is to pick up a can of wasp spray at the grocery or drug store. NOT an all-purpose bug spray, but one specifically marked for wasps, hornets and bees.

He says there are three common wasps: Hornets, which build big round flakey-looking nests up in trees; yellow jackets, with the yellow and black striped bodies, and Polistes wasps, which are a sort of russet color and are sometimes called red wasps.

A hornet nest has a hole in the bottom of it about an inch in diameter. Wait until night, when the hornets

are alseep and spray up into the hole for as long as your nerve lasts. Give the outside of the nest a parting shot with the spray before you run like the devil. The idea is that the hornets will not fly out the hole against the spray.

The same theory applies to yellow jackets, which nest in the ground (often near tree roots) and have about a one-inch opening to the nest. Again, wait until evening and then spray into the hole.

Red wasps are different. Martin says it is best to attack their nests during the day while the adults are out gathering food. If you get to the nest in early summer while it is small, the population of the nest may be only two or three adults. The longer you wait, the more wasps develop.

Once you have knocked down the nest, spray the area if possible to prevent a return engagement. Then keep an eye peeled for the returning adults and knock them off one by one with the spray. Also install screen wire over all attic vents.

As for burning the nests, this is fine. But Martin says he just stomps on them.

103 / How to get rid of pesky ants

Despite their reputation for thrift and industry, ants are unwelcome guests in most homes. Aside from being disconcerting to a good housekeeper, ants can actually cause damage.

Carpenter ants, for instance, have a nasty habit of munching on wood. These large black ants normally live outdoors in an old tree trunk. But for some unknown reason, they can suddenly decide to move convention headquarters to your house (usually the structural wooden supports).

Pavement ants (little brown ones), for another instance, sometimes nest in cracks of the house foundation and make forays into the kitchen.

John Newman, a research technician for the department of entomology ("bugology") at Michigan State University, says there are at least eight varieties of ants that can be a nuisance to homeowners. Some make sandy mounds in the middle of your lovely lawn. Some make themselves at home.

There are, of course, chemicals or pesticides on the market (read any directions very carefully).

But Newman is an organic gardener himself and a sort of modified "ecology nut" and says there is a much simpler, safer way to get rid of ants.

All you need, he says, is a jar or old pop bottle with a bit of sticky, half dry pop or sugar water in the bottom (or put the sugar water in a small cap in the bottom of the jar). This is a trap the ants should go for in a big way. Turn the bottle on its side or leave it straight up.

Ants, according to Newman, usually invade a house in search of goodies. And they have a definite sweet tooth (or what ever it is ants have instead of teeth).

They are highly intellectual insects and have little scouts runing around all the time looking for food. If one ant finds something promising, he will gallop back and tell his friends and lead the whole troop to the spot, regardless of whether you've cleaned it up in the meantime.

The aforementioned trap, left out overnight, should have a good many ants in the bottom of it. All you do is slap a cover over the jar or bottle and then drown the ants by filling the jar partially with water. Kerosene works even better and faster.

Then sweeten the trap again and put it out once more (after washing away any kerosene traces).

It seems you would keep attracting even more ants this way. But Newman says no. He says a colony contains just so many individuals. You may need three or four days in succession to trap them all. But eventually, he says, enough workers will be killed off so that the colony can no longer sustain itself.

The sweet trap method, he says, works either indoors or outdoors.

He also knows a similar trick for getting rid of slugs in a vegetable garden—a half buried sauce dish filled about half way with beer. He says he once found about 40 slugs that had drowned themselves in the beer in one night. Funny—his description sounds like a story heard before, but without the vegetable garden as part of the plot.

104 / How to start and keep a compost heap

Many cities now have laws against leaf burning. Even if yours isn't one of them, there is no point in sending something as valuable as dry leaves up in smoke.

Try making a compost heap for your garden instead.

Compost is nutrient-rich matter that is formed by piling organic waste like leaves, grass cuttings and even garbage together, then adding water and a high-nitrogen fertilizer. After a time, the whole mixture decomposes to a fine-textured substance that garden plants just love.

For most home gardens, a compost heap about 5 feet in diameter and 5 feet high is plenty big. Plan to put it in a far corner of the yard. A well-kept compost heap doesn't knock you out with its odor, but there may be a slight "fragrance."

It is best to build some kind of low frame for a compost heap to keep it from spreading out and blowing around. Use chicken wire, wooden snow fence or whatever comes to hand.

Start the pile on loose soil or gravel which allows water to drain and earthworms to enter the compost heap.

The first level should be about a 6-inch layer of shredded leaves and weeds. Use the power mower as a shredder; but remember it will blow the leaves around quite a bit. You don't absolutely have to shred the material anyway.

Cover the bottom layer with a 2-inch layer of manure, if available. Or use a commercially prepared high-nitrogen fertilizer like urea (about two pounds).

Dampen (not until soggy) the two layers with water. Compost heaps start "working" or decaying best when the outdoor temperature is 50 degrees or above. But you can start yours in nippier weather if you use warm water to sprinkle the layers instead of cold water out of the garden hose.

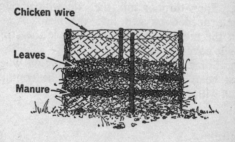

Repeat the layers and the water until the pile is about 5 feet high, mixing in as many different kinds of organic matter as feasible. The last layer should be leaves rather than fertilizer. The top of the compost heap should be fairly flat with a slight "dish" in the middle. Cover the finished pile with about a 4-inch layer of straw as insulatation. Then cover the straw with a loosely fitted sheet of plastic to protect the heap against winter winds, evaporation and the cold water of melting snow.

Moisture, oxygen and nitrogen are essential for the compost heap to do its thing—that is, to compost. The process of decay should begin with just the elements listed above. Initial composting will be speeded up with the addition of commercial "starter" material. But good luck finding it. Some stores listed in the Yellow Pages under "fertilizer" carry it, but not all of them. Call first. The best starter is a bucketfull of leftover compost from last year.

You'll know your compost heap is working when it begins generating heat, a by-product of decay. The temperature inside the heap should be about 140 degrees when it is decaying properly. It should reach this temperature three days to a week after being constructed. To test it, scoop out a small section at the side of the heap and insert a meat thermometer.

If the temperature has dropped below 100 degrees, it is probably time to turn the pile over—a chore you should perform once every six weeks anyway.

Remove the straw from the top of the pile and set it aside. Then turn or mix the pile with a pitchfork. This gets needed oxygen into the heap. Add some water if the mixture looks dry. Replace the straw and the plastic cover when finished.

Note: Some cities have laws designating whether a compost heap is legal and what can be contained in it. Check with city hall.

105 / Prudent pruning calls for planning

There's a classic sequence in animated cartoons that has one of the characters sawing a limb off a tree. The cartoon character, naturally, is sitting on the limb he is sawing.

Most (although not all) people are smart enough to avoid this situation when pruning shade trees or removing limbs that have become bothersome or damaged. But there are some hints for doing the job properly.

To begin with, remember there are professionals who do this sort of thing. Risking your neck is neither smart nor economical. If you can't remove a tree limb by standing on the ground or a low stepladder, consider having someone else do it. And do not stand directly under any limb you are removing.

There is quite a bit of equipment available to the gung-ho groundskeeper. You can buy as much or as little of it as you need; but one thing you should have is a hand "speed" saw. This is not a power saw. It is a handsaw with its teeth spaced in such a way that it cuts a fairly wide path through wood and does not bind and get pinched halfway through the limb you're working on.

The idea in removing a tree limb is to damage the tree as little as possible and protect it from invasion by insects and disease.

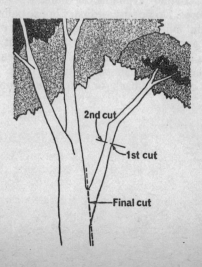

The bark on a tree has a degree of self-healing capacity. So what you want to do is trim a branch off flush with its main limb (or a main limb off flush with the trunk of the tree), leaving an area over which bark can construct itself.

But if you start cutting a large heavy limb from the top side, it will often begin tearing away from the tree, taking a big strip of bark with it. To avoid this, cut the limb off to a manageable stub first. Cut from the bottom side of the limb initially, as shown in the sketch. After cutting about halfway through the limb, start cutting from the top side. As your second cut nears the first cut (the one you started from the bottom), the branch will break off cleanly, leaving a short stub.

Some people leave the job at this. But the cut end of a stub cannot mend itself and is a good avenue for insects and decay. Air and water start deteriorating the stub and then continue on into the heart of the tree.

So trim the stub off flush with the tree trunk (or main limb) with the saw (as shown in sketch). Then seal the cut against water and air with a paint-on or spray-on coating available at nurseries and garden supply stores. Do not use ordinary house paint.

Keep in mind that it is dangerous to expose too large an area of the tree trunk to constant sun when that area has become accustomed to heavy shade. Trees, like people, can suffer sunburn or "scalding" that can cause die-back or extensive wounds to the bark.

Part VI:

Taking Care
of Your Car

106 / How to replace car blinkers

Most gas stations will change burned-out turn signal blinkers on your car. But some don't want to bother.

It seems too small a problem to warrant taking the car into a dealership. Yet the police will stop you if turn signals or brake lights aren't working.

You can change a bulb yourself without much trouble, which means you can buy a couple of spare bulbs. Keep them in the glove compartment and make the change when it's convenient.

Bulbs used in the front parking and blinker lights are the same size as those used in the rear brake and blinker lights. One size also fits most cars.

They are called double-filament bulbs and come in two intensities, commonly indicated by numbers. In the rear, 1157 bulbs are used. Weaker 1034 bulbs are usually used in the front. But the two intensities are interchangeable in an emergency.

The red plastic covering over a rear light is called a lens. Front blinker lights have to be amber, according to police regulations. So if the front lens is clear, buy an amber bulb. If the front lens is amber, buy a clear bulb.

Lenses that fasten in place with screws make it easy to change the bulb.

Remove the lens and expose the bulb. To remove the bulb, press in on it, turn it and pull out. Reverse the procedure to install a new one. (See Sketch A.)

The stem of the bulb itself is not threaded. Instead, it is smooth, with a couple of little bumps on the side that fit grooves in the socket.

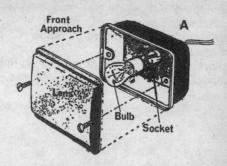

These bumps are not even with each other. So if the new bulb will not snap into the socket one way, turn the bulb 180 degrees and try again.

If the lens over your blinker or tail light does not fasten with screws, you will have to approach the bulb from the back side. This means from the trunk, from under the front hood or, in some cases, from underneath the bumper area.

Look directly behind the light for the back end of the light socket. It is encased in plastic or metal and has wires running out the end of it. (See sketch B.)

Do not pull on the wires. Instead, grasp the socket casing, turn it and pull it out. This will bring both

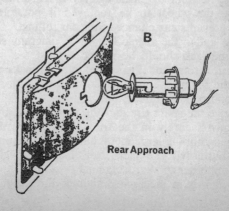

socket and bulb out where you can have room to work. Replace the bulb as stated earlier.

The ignition should be turned off while you are doing all of this.

Bulbs are available at some service stations and at all auto dealerships. They cost 55 to 60 cents.

107 / How to change a flat tire

The best advice on changing a flat tire is: Get someone else to do it if you can.

If you must do it yourself, here are the basic steps:

Park the car on as firm and level a surface as possible.

Turn your emergency flasher lights on or set out flares if you are on a street or a highway shoulder. Put the car in park if it has an automatic transmission; in reverse if it has a stick shift. Also set the emergency brake. Turn the motor off.

Put some kind of block against the tire diagonally opposite the wheel to be removed if possible. This further prevents any chance of the car rolling.

Look under the trunk lid for a diagram showing where the jack should be placed against the bumper. This varies from model to model. Not all jacks even go under the bumper. But most do; and we'll work from that premise in this discussion.

Remove the spare tire and the jack. These are often held down securely in the trunk with a threaded rod and a wing nut—a large metal nut that looks something like a butterfly. The jack itself may be held down with yet another smaller wing nut.

The jack is in pieces—sometimes three, sometimes

four. These are the base, the combination handle and lug wrench, the main body of the jack and, sometimes, the tongue that fits under the bumper. On some jacks, the tongue is not detached.

See sketch for the way in which the pieces fit together.

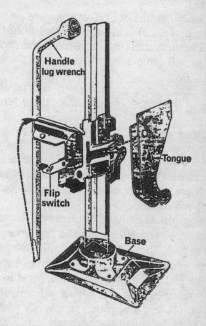

Look on the body of the jack, near where the handle inserts, for a flip switch. This tells the jack whether to go up or down.

Position the jack in front of the bumper and run the tongue of the jack up snug under the edge of the bumper. Flip the direction switch to "up" and hold the jack in place. Insert the jack handle and pump it just until the jack is firmly positioned.

Do not actually start lifting the car yet. That comes later.

Before raising the car, take the hub cap or wheel

cover off the flat tire. The wheel cover usually pries off just like the lid on a can of paint.

Use the tapered end of the jack handle or a large screwdriver to pry. Repair manuals say to loosen the wheel cover at the point opposite the tire's air valve. But don't be a purist. Pry any old place you can to get started.

After removing the wheel cover, you will see the studs (threaded rods) and lug nuts that hold the wheel in place. The nuts must be removed. One end of your jack handle will have a roundish socket on it for this purpose.

Slip the socket over each lug nut and turn counter-clockwise to loosen. Usually. But there are exceptions.

Some auto makers, before 1970, reversed the stud threads on the left hand side of the car (for reasons too long to explain). On these, the lugs must be turned clockwise to be loosened. If you have a car like this, there should be an "L" marked on the end of each left-hand stud.

Some lugs are very hard to remove. If your arms aren't strong enough, try giving the lug wrench a good shove with your foot. A gadget called a spanner—a lug wrench in the form of a cross—gives better leverage than the jack-handle type and is a good investment.

Put the removed lug nuts in a safe place, like in the hub cap. (If you lose them, remember you can take one from each of the other wheels on a short-term basis.)

Now go ahead and raise the car with the jack—but only until the flat tire is barely off the ground. No higher.

Pull off the old wheel. Fit the spare one on over the protruding studs.

Replace the lug nuts by hand, tightening them only as far as you can with your fingers.

Now lower the car. To do this, flip the switch on the jack body to the down position. Then pump the handle just as you did to raise the car. Raise and lower the handle as far as it will go each time.

One last chore. After the car is on the ground, tighten the lug nuts on the new tire firmly with the socket end of the jack handle.

Stow the wheel cover, flat tire and jack assembly in the trunk and drive to the nearest service station. Ask them to replace the wheel cover and secure all the loose equipment in the trunk.

108 / How to check car oil

Learning to check the oil in your own car can be a handy thing, with gas stations closed so often and busy when they are open.

There is a rod called a dipstick that extends into your car's crank-case or oil pan and is made expressly for measuring the oil level. It has marks on the end of it to indicate whether the oil level is satisfactory or running low.

You can find two dipsticks on your engine if you have an automatic transmission. One dipstick is for oil and the other for transmission fluid.

How do you tell them apart? The one for the transmission is located on the passenger side of the engine way back near the dashboard. The oil dipstick can be located almost anywhere else on the engine—the sides, front or top—anyplace the transmission stick isn't.

Look for a hefty wire handle curved into a loop at the end (see sketch). There isn't anything else that looks like a dipstick, so you shouldn't get confused.

Turn the car engine off before checking your oil and let it sit for two or three minutes while the oil

Dip stick

settles down. In fact, first thing in the morning, before you start the car is the best time to check the oil level. If you check while the motor is running, the oil is sloshing around and you won't get an accurate reading.

Pull the dipstick out of its little slot and wipe it clean. Now reinsert it, making sure you poke it in as far as it will go.

Pull it out once more and note the level of the oil film on the stick. There will be a mark on the stick designating "full." Another mark will indicate the level at which one quart should be added.

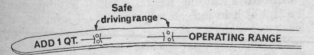

Safe driving range

ADD 1 QT. — OPERATING RANGE

If the oil is at the "add one" mark, one quart should bring it up to "full" again. It's not good for the engine to overfill it with oil. So if your oil level is somewhere between "full" and "add one," let it go until it needs a whole quart.

If there is no oil film at all on the dipstick, you're in trouble and need two quarts or more. (The oil light on your dashboard should also warn you if you get dangerously low like that.)

After checking the oil, put the dipstick back where it belongs, seating it firmly.

109 / How to replenish your car's oil

It is possible to save a third to a half the cost of motor oil by putting it in your car yourself instead of having it done at a gas station.

The auto supply sections of department and discount stores usually carry motor oil—their own brands and standard commerical brands. The price per quart is significantly lower than in a station; and if you buy the oil by the case, it is lower yet.

You can also buy one of those spouts to stick into the top of the can (like the ones used in gas stations) for under a dollar. But a "church key" can opener and a kitchen funnel will do just as well.

Oil is essential to keep your car engine from literally burning itself up. It coats the moving parts in the engine to reduce friction.

Motor oil comes in various "weights" or viscosities. The owner's manual for your car should list the weight recommended for your particular model. If not, check with the person who services your car most often to find out what is used.

Once you have determined by checking the dipstick that the car is low on oil, you will be adding one quart —two quarts in extreme cases.

The hole into which you pour the oil is usually to be found somewhere on the valve cover of the engine.

The valve cover is a long section of metal, rectangular with rounded edges, that runs from the front to the back of the engine (see sketch). Eight-cylinder engines have two valve covers—one on each side of the engine. Six-cylinder engines have only one valve cover.

With an eight-cylinder engine, one of the valve covers is usually hooked with hoses and other paraphernalia to the air cleaner (the round thing that sits up on top of the engine and looks like part of a vacuum cleaner). The other valve cover (the one on the opposite side of the engine) is usually relatively free of encumbrances. Look on this one for the oil cap.

The oil cap is usually a fairly flat cap about the size of a silver dollar with little wings sticking out from it (see sketch). It comes off easily when you give it a half turn counterclockwise.

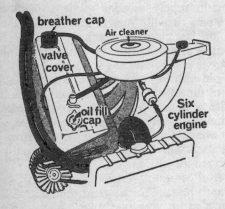

A six-cylinder engine often has the same type of cap toward the front of its single valve cover. If so, that's the opening you want.

But if you don't see such a cap, yours may be the type of engine with a removable "breather cap" for adding oil. The breather cap connects the valve cover with the air cleaner. Some engines have a separate breather cap and oil cap. Some combine the two functions in the breather cap.

The breather cap is round, black and about three inches tall. It sits on top of the valve cover, as shown in the accompanying sketch.

If it doubles as an oil cap, it will probably be closer

to the front of the engine than the one shown in the sketch; and there will be no flat, winged oil cap.

Give it a quarter turn counterclockwise and pull up. If it is stubborn, turn it back and forth a couple of times and put one finger under the hose connection to give added grip as you pull up. Do not, however, pull on the hose itself.

But the best possible piece of advice is this: Pouring oil into the wrong hole could be disastrous. So if your engine does not match any of these descriptions or if there is doubt in your mind about what you are doing, get out of your car and watch the attendant the next time you have the gas station add oil to your engine.

One assumes he will be putting it in the right place. Once you see it done, you'll be able to do the chore yourself from then on.

110 / How to unstick that stubborn choke

In cold or wet weather it's not uncommon to hear a car grind and grind trying to start. The battery seems fine, but the engine just won't catch—it sounds almost like it's flooded.

This condition is often caused by a sticking automatic choke valve. A simple procedure involving a screwdriver will usually get the car started.

If the cause of the sluggish start is something other than the choke, you won't harm the car—and you won't lose anything except about five minutes by trying the screwdriver trick.

The first thing to remember is not to grind the starter forever. If the engine does not start, do not hold the key in the start position for more than about 30 seconds. To do so is to risk overheating the starter.

Now to the choke valve. It is a "butterfly" disc that opens and closes to keep the right blend of fuel and air going to the engine. It can be found under the air cleaner lid.

The air cleaner is a large circular metal thing sitting up on top of the engine. It looks like it could be part of a vacuum cleaner (see sketch A).

Take the top off of it by turning the small wing nut you should find in the middle of the lid (sketch A). The body of the air cleaner surrounds the choke valve mechanism. With the lid removed, you should be able to peer down the center of the air cleaner and see the choke valve—a round or rectangular disc that flips when you poke it (see cutaway sketch B).

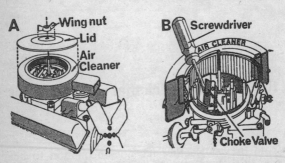

The valve itself is split by a hinge and one side of the disc is usually larger than the other.

Take a screwdriver with a fat handle and a blade no longer than about 6 inches. Insert the blade of it into the choke valve to hold the choke open. If possible, flip the smaller section of the valve upward and insert the screwdriver blade there (see sketch B).

Choosing the small side is a protection against the screwdriver falling through the opening down into the engine. (You use a screwdriver with a fat handle for the same reason.)

Leaving the screwdriver in place, start the car. If

you had been grinding the starter for awhile before inserting the screwdriver, your engine may be flooded. If so, push the accelerator all the way to the floor and hold it there while you try to start the car. You can leave the screwdriver in place for a couple of minutes while the car warms up, too. But, naturally, remove the screwdriver and replace the air cleaner lid before you drive anywhere.

111 / How to start your car on wet days

Damp, misty, or rainy days can be almost as bad as cold days for starting a car. If yours is recalcitrant, there are several tricks to try—one of which is wiping moisture from the distributor cap, coil and spark plug connections.

This is a reasonably simple operation that boils down to one principle: Clean what you can reach with ease. If you can't find it, forget it.

The distributor cap, coil and spark plugs are part of the electrical system of the car. So turn off the ignition.

It doesn't matter if you don't know what coils or spark plugs look like. Key in on the distributor cap. It is located in different places on different cars. But it is easy to spot because it is about the size of a small can of shortening and is the only thing in the engine that looks like an octopus (see sketch).

A main wire comes out from the center of the distributor cap top. It is surrounded by four or six or eight smaller wires. All detach from the cap with a twist and steady pull.

But do not pull on the wire itself. It is held in place

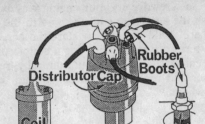

on the cap with a rubber "boot" (see sketch). Grasp each wire by its boot when removing it.

And never remove all the wires at once. You're sure to get them mixed up. Do them one at a time.

Wipe dry the area previously covered by the boot of each wire (also wipe inside the boot). Then replace the wire on the distributor cap.

Now dry the wire connection on the top of the coil. It doesn't matter what the coil is, precisely. All you need to know is that it's a dark metal cylinder that can be found at the opposite end of the center wire running out the top of the distributor cap (see sketch).

The same drying procedure can be followed around the end of each spark plug. To find the spark plugs, go back to the distributor cap again.

Each of the six or eight smaller wires around the perimeter of the cap connects at the opposite end to one spark plug. Remove, wipe and replace each spark plug wire individually. Do not take them all off at once.

Spark plugs are usually reachable on older models and on four and six-cylinder engines. But on some newer eight-cylinder engines, the spark plugs must be approached from underneath the car. In this case, forget them. Wiping just the center wire of the distributor cap and the opposite end of it at the coil will often do the trick.

Preparing your car for summer driving is just as important as readying it for winter.

Water-cooled engines, as the term implies, have water running around the engine block and up front through the radiator (see sketch). Air circulating

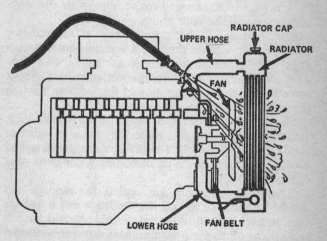

through the honeycomb structure of the radiator dissipates the heat the water has picked up in the engine. The fan (see sketch) helps pull that cooling air though the radiator.

If the belt which drives the fan (and the water pump) is loose or ready to break, you should have it adjusted or replaced. Belts are usually readily visible when you raise the hood. If your car has options like power steering and air conditioning you will see two or three different belts.

Don't worry about which is which. They should ALL be kept in good shape. If the surface of the belt is peeling or covered with little cracks it should be replaced.

Press down on the belt in the middle of its span. It should "give" about half an inch. If it's too tight or too loose, have it adjusted or replaced. A loose belt can sometimes be heard—either a flopping fluttering sound, a continuous tweet or a high squeal.

Needless to say, you should not try any of these tests (except for sounds) while the motor is running.

Check hoses running from the radiator (see sketch) for cracks, swelling around connecting points and leaks or seepage at those same points.

Bugs and dirt caught on the front of the radiator inhibit the flow of air through it and hamper the cooling system. Clean the radiator occasionally with a high-pressure stream of water from the garden hose. Shoot the water from the engine side of the radiator through toward the grillwork of the car (see sketch).

Check the water level in the radiator; but NEVER remove the radiator cap while the motor is still hot from driving. The coolant inside is under pressure and carelessness may send a jet of boiling water onto your face or hands.

Even after the engine has cooled, the radiator cap should be removed in two steps. Give it just a quarter turn at first. A little safety catch inside should keep it from flying off as the pressure hisses down to a normal level. The cap can then be turned further and removed.

The coolant level should come within about an inch of the bottom ring in the neck where the cap was. If only a quart of coolant is needed, you can add plain water. But if a large amount is needed, or if you are having the radiator system drained (at least once a year), antifreeze should always be added with the water to prevent rust in the system.

In replacing the radiator cap, press down firmly while turning to make a good seal. If the cap is solidly back in place, don't get agitated if the radiator overflows the first couple of times you drive after filling the radiator. It is just seeking its own best level.

If it overflows frequently, have a service station check the cap to see if it is maintaining radiator pressure.

Air-cooled engines do not have radiators or fans. They do, however, have belts which should be checked. And it's smart to see whether mud has been thrown and caked onto the bottom of the engine. If so, it will make the engine run hot and should be either hosed off or chipped away with a screwdriver.

Check the tread on your tires by sticking a pencil lead or something else thin into one of the tread grooves. If it measures $\frac{1}{16}$ inch or less, you need new tires.

Find out from your owner's manual or tire warranty how much pressure your type of tire requires for the average load your car carries. (This will change, of course, if you add a load of luggage or a trailer for summer vacation.) Make sure your tires are filled to the correct pressure. Running too hard or too soft can cause tire failure.

Next time you have a few minutes at a service station or garage, have them check fluid levels for the car's rear axle, battery, transmission, power steering and master brake cylinder.

Also have them show you the fluid container for the windshield washer. It is easy to fill, once you know where to find it, and you can carry a little jug of water in the car for emergency refill.

Air conditioners strain a car's cooling system in stop-and-go traffic. To avoid overheating the engine, turn the air conditioning off temporarily or else put the car in neutral during long stops and depress the gas pedal just slightly. This lets you sit still but speeds up the fan, which is pulling air into your cooling system.

Sometimes after becoming quite hot from long driving, an engine will refuse to start up again after a brief stop at a grocery store or restaurant. This is usually because engine temperature has become so high that the fuel is actually percolating. Result is that the engine is flooded.

First raise the hood—it doesn't matter how hot and sunny the day is. The hottest day in recorded history could not approach the temperature under the hood.

Allow a few minutes for the engine to cool. Then follow procedures for a flooded engine. Press the gas pedal all the way to the floor and hold it there while turning the ignition. (This just gives your engine an initial squirt of fuel, not a continuous flow, and allows needed air into the carburetor.)

Before any long trip, have the oil, oil filter and air filter checked. And if the length of the trip will put your car at a mileage total that calls for a tune-up have the tune-up BEFORE the trip rather than after.

113 / How to jump-start your car

There's no question that winter is hard on a car battery. It takes a good deal of power to crank up a cold, stiff engine.

You can and should learn how to jump start your car—in case service stations are closed or busy. Jump starting is done when your battery is low or dead. It is nothing but starting your car off the power of someone else's battery.

You will need three things: a set of jumper cables (available in any auto supply or department store), an acquaintance who will let you hook up to his battery, and a couple of cloth rags.

A sick battery may be indicated whether the car is groaning as it tries to start or is simply making a click or rat-tat-tat noise. To double check, turn your headlights on and ask a friend to stand in front of the car and watch as you try again to start it.

If there is a battery problem, the lights will dim as you try to start. Any clicking or groaning will also be less audible.

Turn the ignition off and raise the car hood. The battery is a rectangular box located at the front and to one side of the engine. It has two cables running off the top of it and a row of little caps across the top. (Some batteries have caps showing; some have a plastic bar cover over the caps.)

Unscrew the battery caps (usually six of them) or pull off the plastic covers and you should see fluid inside the battery right up to the bottom of the six openings. If you can't see, don't use a match or cigarette lighter for help. A battery gives off an explosive gas that can be touched off by even a cigarette. Use a flashlight instead.

Also use a cloth rag in handling the battery and caps. The contents and any film across the top of the battery are acid and will ruin clothes, gloves and discolor skin.

If you can see no fluid in the battery, fill each of the six openings with clear (better yet, distilled) water. This will help the battery recharge itself after the car starts running again.

Replace the battery caps and take a look at the posts (usually located at either end of the row of caps) that the battery cables are fastened to (see sketch). Using

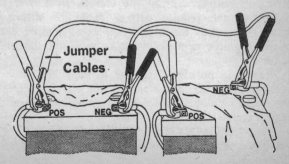

Jumper Cables

NEG
POS   NEG   POS

the cloth rag, grasp the clamps that fit around each post and try to turn them. If they turn easily, they are too loose and need to be tightened. There is a nut and bolt on each clamp for just this purpose. You'll need to dig up a pair of pliers and a wrench.

Now to the actual jump start.

Never jump your car from someone else's battery without asking permission. Ask your friend to bring his car either nose to nose or side to side with your car. Make sure the cars do not touch each other and that both ignitions are then turned off.

Cover the caps of each battery loosely with cloth rags. This cuts down on any explosive fumes circulating around the battery. Some experts say to leave the battery caps in place. Some say to remove the caps and cover the openings with a rag. A veteran garage man, however, says the safest thing is to combine the two methods by leaving the caps on and covering them with a cloth.

Connect the jumper cables. These are 12 to 15 feet long, one red and one black, ending in heavy spring clamps that look like toothy pliers.

One post of every battery is positive; the other negative. The positive post is slightly fatter than the other one and is marked with a plus sign or the letters "POS." The negative post is usually marked with a minus sign or the letters "NEG."

Connect the red (positive) jumper cable to the positive post of your battery and the positive post of the other battery (install the clamps right over the clamps of the regular battery cable, as shown in sketch). Connect the black (negative) jumper cable to the negative posts of your battery and the other battery.

Positive to positive. Negative to negative.

Have your neighbor start his car after the jumper cables are in place and leave it running while you try to start yours.

After your car is running, remove the negative

jumper from your battery and then from the other car's battery. Once that cable is disconnected at both ends, remove the positive cable—first from your car, then from the other.

Do not—repeat, do not—remove both the positive and negative clamps from just one battery, leaving them connected to the other battery. That gives you two "live wires" in your hands and you could easily get a nasty shock.

Now drive to the nearest available place that can check your battery and electrical system to make sure they are operating correctly.

114 / How to replace windshield wipers

Why give yourself a crick in the neck peering between the streaks on your car's windshield?

Windshield wiper blades are simple to change. You can keep a supply on hand. And whenever road oil, salt spray and sun have sent your wiper blades to that big junkyard in the sky, you can replace them yourself.

Two types are among the most common. One is held in place by two small metal arches with red buttons on them (sketch A); the other is attached to

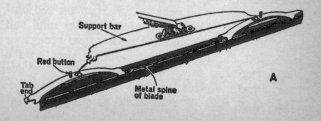

Support bar

Red button

Tab end

Metal spine of blade

A

one long metal arch with no buttons on it (sketch B). Both styles come in varying lengths. So find out what size your car takes before stocking up at a gas station or auto supply store.

We'll take the kind with the red buttons first.

The two small arches disconnect from the straight support bar on the wiper arm But you really only need to remove one of them (it doesn't make any difference which one). On some models you will find a button on only one of the arches; the button might even be black. But don't be alarmed, the procedure is basically the same.

Pick your arch. Press down on that arch's little red button. Pull the arch down and away from the end of the straight support bar while continuing to press the red button (see sketch A). If one span won't turn loose for you, try the other one.

Eack arch grips the spine of the wiper blade with small, turned-under prongs. Slide the old blade lengthwise out of the prongs.

In looking at the new blade, you will see that the spine of it is reinforced with a strip of metal. The prongs on the metal arches fit around the metal reinforcing strip, as shown in sketch A.

Slip the new blade into the arch that is still attached to the wiper arm. Now slip the detached arch over the free end of the new wiper blade. Don't slip the arch on backward. One end of the arched piece has a little turned-down tab that fits over the end of the wiper blade (see sketch A).

Now connect the free arch back to the end of the straight support bar. Just insert the prong on the end of the support bar into the hole next to the red button on the arched piece and press together until you hear a click. (On one-button models, two prongs on the support bar fit into corresponding slots on the arched piece. Just press the prongs into the slots until they click into place.)

The other style of windshield wiper blade without the red buttons) is a bit easier to describe (although both styles are easy to change).

There is only one thing you need to pinch, poke or otherwise mangle—and that is the very end of the wiper blade. You will see that one end has a metal clip that is slightly wider and sticks out a little farther than the other end of the blade.

Squeeze in on the sides of the clip (see sketch B).

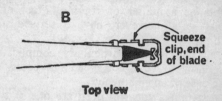

Top view

The edges are sharp, so use a small pair of pliers if you wish. This releases two little notches from the grip of the prongs at the end of the blade arm. Then just slide the blade out (it is held by prongs wrapped around its spine, just as in the other case).

Slide the new blade into place until the prongs at the end of the arm snap over the notches at the end of the new blade. Take it slow and easy or you will push the new blade in too far—past the notches at the end. If you do you may have a hard time getting it out again.

115 / How to replace auto headlights

Some do-it-yourself enthusiasts change their own car headlights as a matter of routine. Most of us less ambitious sorts, however, have a service station or garage do it.

But the job is not particularly complicated. And knowing how to change a headlight could come in handy in case of an emergency.

The first things you will need are one or two spare headlights to carry in the car trunk. You can get them at a service station or dealership for anywhere from $1.50 to $4. There are two kinds of headlights. One is only a high or bright beam. The other is a double-filament light that serves as the lowbeam lamp until you switch it to high beam with the foot button inside the car.

If your car has double headlights, you'll need one of each kind of lamp. The two lights nearest the center of the car (inboard) are high beam only; the two lights nearest the side of the car (outboard) are combination high-low beam. If the car just has single headlights, you need one of the high-low lights. Make sure you get the right size for your particular car.

The other pieces of equipment you will want to carry include a No. 2 Phillips screwdriver (or in some cases the same size flat-blade screwdriver), a can of penetrating or rust dissolving oil (to help loosen screws) and possibly a small wrench or pliers.

The headlight assembly described here in detail is that used in late model General Motors cars. The systems used by Ford and Chrysler are similar.

The first thing you need to do is turn the lights and the motor off. Then remove the bezel. This is just a funny name for the shiny chrome (or painted) frame around the headlight. The fancier the car, the more difficult the bezel is to remove. It may even be combined with a chunk of grillwork. But look for three to four screws on the bezel itself near the edge of the headlight or in that immediate area.

If the screws are several inches away from the headlight, open the car hood and check to see if the screws are supplemented by a nut-and-bolt arrangement on the back side of the grill. This is where the wrench or pliers would be needed. Leave the hood up; you may need it open later anyway.

With the bezel removed, look straight on at the front of the headlight. You will see that it is further held in place by a metal collar or retaining ring around the edge of the light itself.

Around the edge of the retaining ring will be several screws.

Two of the screws on the edge of the retaining ring will have a broader head than the others. These are the adjustment screws or pins and are used to aim the headlight. Don't fool with these adjustment screws. You want them to stay just where they are.

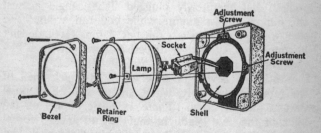

The other screws around the edge of the retaining ring (usually three of them) are smaller. These are the ones you take out to release the headlight. They are sometimes wedged in by corrosion or being tightened too far. If you can't turn them, put a couple drops of penetrating oil on each one, give each one a rap with the screwdriver handle to vibrate the oil behind them as well as possible and then try again after a few minutes.

(On some models, the retaining ring may be held additionally at one side by a spring. If so, it will be apparent that undoing the screws does not release the ring. Slip the edge of the ring out from behind the hook of the spring; or just let it hang there by the spring, if you wish.)

After removing the retaining ring, pull the headlight itself out toward you slowly. You will see that it is attached at the back to an electrical cord. The back side of the light is formed into something like the plug at the end of a lamp cord. The end of the cord coming from behind the grill is formed into a socket.

Pull the headlight out of its socket. This is often easier said than done. Use a screwdriver to gently pry the two apart if you have to. Depending on the length of the cord, you may have to work from the back side of the grill.

To install the new headlight, simply reverse the above procedure. Hook the new light to the electrical socket. Let the newly plugged light dangle against the bumper for a minute while you run around and turn the lights on to test the new lamp. (If if doesn't go on, you may have a defective new light or a wiring problem in the car.)

Nestle the new light snugly into the back shell of the retaining assembly, which should still be in position in the car body. (There are little bumps on the back of the new headlight that fit into small depressions in the back shell. Rotate the headlight back and forth until it is seated well.) Then replace the retaining ring with its screws.

If you are working on a Chrysler product, changing a headlight will be slightly different. The smaller screws on the retaining ring are not supposed to be taken entirely out. Just loosen them. Then turn the front portion of the retaining ring about half an inch and pull out. The ring fits onto its screws with hole-and-slot arrangements.

Ford headlight assemblies are similar to those made by General Motors.

If you aren't sure you have installed the new headlight correctly, have a service station check the job as soon as possible. New headlights should also be checked for aim, even though you have not fooled with the adjustment screws. If the aim is not proper, you can blind oncoming drivers.

116 / How to keep your car finish sparkling clean

Wash; don't wash. Wax; don't wax. Use soap; don't use soap.

Ask ten people the best way to take care of a car and you'll probably get ten different answers. But people in the auto industry who should know what they're talking about do have some guidelines for confused car owners.

If you live out in the country (low pollution) and trade cars every couple of years—of if you wash the car every time it gets dirty—you can probably get by without ever waxing your car.

But in general, say the experts, it is a good idea to protect the finish on your car with a hardy silicone paste wax once every six months. Silicone paste wax is available from auto dealers, gas stations and department stores. The biggest brand selection is usually to be found at the discount, department or auto supply store.

A rumor has somehow persisted that a new car should not be waxed for the first three months or so of its life. This, say the experts, is not true. It's fine to wax it the day after you get it, if you wish.

Most silicone paste waxes go on with a damp rag or a sponge. They are then polished to a high gloss with a dry rag. Do small areas at a time—say, 2 feet by 2 feet.

And one expert says not to let the wax harden and dry after you apply it. He says you gain nothing by doing that and create a harder job for yourself to boot. Put the wax on; rub it in well; then wipe the excess away and polish with a dry rag. Use an old toothbrush to work wax into seams and trim edges to add protection. Wax metal trim if you wish, do not, however, get wax on the windows.

Many auto dealers advertise a super-hard wax finish that you can have applied at the dealership. Industry people say this is essentially the same type of wax you can buy yourself. The only advantage is the mechanical buffer at the garage, which gives a higher gloss than your own elbow grease.

When it comes to washing the car, remember that any soap mild to your hands is mild enough for the car. The best thing to use is a bucket of water and dishwashing detergent mixed to a weak strength. Laundry detergent is too strong.

A mild mixture will not remove a good paste wax—at least not until many washings have come and gone. Yet, it will help dissolve road oil and pollution chemicals. Stronger soap, like laundry detergent, may remove the wax. After a time, strong soap will even discolor the bright metal trim on the car.

You can, if necessary, wash a car right after waxing it. If it's within a couple of days of the wax job, you may want to use plain water. Road oil will probably not have accumulated to the point where you would need detergent.

Do keep road salt washed off the car in the winter. It is very destructive. But don't panic if your car gets salty and the weather is so cold you're afraid the doors will freeze after a wash. There is engineering research indicating that road salt does not eat away at a car if the temperature is below 25 degrees. Between 25 and 40 degrees, however, road salt is at its most destructive.

During bad winter weather, a drive-through car wash is about the only reasonable option. But nothing beats a good careful home driveway job in decent weather.

Actual procedure is to soak the car with water first to soften dirt. Follow with the soap mixture; then rinse well. Always work from the top of the car down. Do the wheels last. Don't wash your car in the blazing sun. Choose shade, early morning or late afternoon. Hot sun has been known to bake leftover soap film right into the paint. It also creates annoying water spots.

Drying can be done with either a chamois or an old towel. Just make sure you rinse the drying cloth often to get rid of any grit that might scratch the paint surface.

117 / Best way to clean a vinyl car top

White vinyl car tops can look pretty crummy after a winter of baked-on dirt and air pollution. Other colors suffer with time, too.

Just a nominal amount of grub doesn't call for anything more troublesome than dishwashing detergent and water (rinsed well afterward). The secret is using a brush for the scrubbing. In fact, you need to use a brush with any cleaning agent on a vinyl top. A sponge won't get down into the little crannies that give vinyl its "skin" texture.

You may want to try some of the special vinyl top cleaners and waxes on the market for a case of criminal neglect.

I tried four different products on two different cars —one with a white top and one with dark brown.

The first cleaner was a spray foam by a very well-known company. (It looks a lot like bathroom tub and tile cleaner when you spray it on.) The directions said to spray the product onto the dry car roof, scrub with a brush, then wipe away with a dry cloth.

It loosened the dirt all right. But wiping with a dry cloth simply smeared leftover dirt and drove it back into the wrinkles of the vinyl. There were grayish streaks and circles on the white top; light brown ones on the dark top. A second application helped. But wiping with a damp sponge helped even more. And the directions said nothing about using water or a damp sponge.

The other half on both car tops was cleaned with a solution that called for water. The directions said to wet the car top, squirt the product onto the vinyl scrub with a brush and rinse well with clear water. (The cleaning agent was an almost clear liquid that foamed up when worked with the brush.)

It did a superb job, leaving both white and dark tops without a trace of dirt or smear.

My conclusion after admittedly limited testing is that any product using water or a water rinse is going to work better than a wipe-away-dry product. Either one may get the vinyl clean. But the dry wipe-off is going to mean about four times the work for you.

Both products supposedly condition the vinyl. Both should also be washed off of the car body if they splatter. They can dull paint and chrome surfaces.

The two other products tested were vinyl waxes or

"dressing" to be used for lasting protection after cleaning.

One was a well-known paste wax with an attached applicator. Directions said to apply the wax with a circular motion, wipe excess away with a clean dry cloth and then buff with a cloth or shoe brush.

The wax went on easily. The wiping and buffing seemed to give a satisfactory finish—a sort of semigloss shine.

But ten minutes out in the sun revealed flaws. The buffing had apparently been uneven. Going over the top two or three more time with a dry cloth was more work than I was willing to do. A run through a nearby car wash heightened the splotchy effect.

The top dressing used on the other half of the roof was a liquid manufactured by the same company that made the liquid cleaner.

Directions said to soak a cloth with the liquid wax, then wipe it onto the car top, buffing after drying. The dressing went on easily and evenly. It dried to a finish that required almost no buffing at all, leaving the vinyl with a high-gloss "wet" look.

A later trip through the car wash seemed to have no effect on the finish.

My choice again, the liquid dressing—for its ease of application and durability.

118 / Spray paint away a car's rust blemishes

A rolling hunk of rust. That's what you feel you're driving when even a few flaky brown spots have broken out like teenage blemishes on your car.

A fairly new, expensive car that you plan to trade

soon should be patched up by a professional. But you can spot treat blotches on an older car—one you plan to keep for awhile but don't want to spend much money on. The job will cost about $5.

The spots you do yourself may never blend perfectly with the surrounding paint. But they'll certainly blend better than the rust spots do.

There are two or three brands of car paint on the market. Some are sprays; some are like bottles of fingernail polish with little brushes in the caps; some brands offer both kinds. They are available at a few auto dealerships and at large, well-stocked auto supply stores.

The paints are labeled according to car make, year and color. The paint I bought, for instance, read, "General Motors, 1970–71 acrylic, Chev. Sandalwood, Pont. Sandalwood, Buick Sandpiper Beige, Olds. Sandalwood." The color was designed to match any of four cars mentioned. It matched mine exactly.

The directions on the spray can said to remove all dirt, rust and grease from the surface to be painted. Then sand with No. 400 (very fine) wet-or-dry sandpaper. Hold can 10 to 12 inches away from the surface and move spray rapidly back and forth. Do not apply single heavy coat. To avoid sags and runs, use sevral light coats.

I agree with the directions but would add a couple of things:

Invest in a can of white polishing compound (at auto supply stores). It is part of the $5 discussed earlier. The compound is a white paste with a very fine grit to it. You'll need it later after painting, but it makes a good cleaner to prepare the surface, too. Directions are on the can.

And don't rely on just the No. 400 sandpaper to smooth the surface. Get a sheet of medium grade to do the initial work, using the 400 as a finishing paper.

The painting directions don't say anything about scraping. But you'll need to. Rust creeps under the edges of the paint. It's ready to flake, even though it may not look that way. So use a putty knife or wire brush to get rid of all the blistered paint around the rust spots.

Next, use the polishing compound to clean the whole area.

Sand with the medium paper to feather the edges of the old paint where it dips down to the rusted surface. You can get away without this step, but the newly painted area will always be uneven and resemble a relief map.

Clean again with the polish if need be. End by using the fine No. 400 sandpaper and wiping away the dust with a brush or dry cloth.

Shield chrome and other decorative pieces in the vicinity with masking tape. Use sheets of newspaper over large areas like nearby sections of contrasting roof.

If you have gone right down to the bare metal in a large area (as big as your hand), it is best to apply a coat of spray primer for metal. It's not so important with small spots about the size of a nickel. Use your own judgment on in-between sizes. Paint supposedly lasts longer with primer under it.

Find yourself a reasonably large piece of cardboard before you start spray painting the small spots. Cut a

hole in the middle of it—about 2 inches in diameter is good.

You need to hold the paint can a good 10 inches away from the car to keep the paint from sagging and running. But this means you cover quite a large area with one shot. Hold the cardboard target an inch or so in front of the car surface and the paint spray will go only through the hole you cut, restricting the coverage area.

Spray the area several times. One or two coats won't cover satisfactorily because each coat is so thin. Use short bursts rather than moving the spray back and forth rapidly. The paint dries very quickly, so you don't need to wait more than about a minute between coats.

Allow the finished paint job to set or cure for a few hours or overnight. You'll find that the edges of the sprayed area are a bit duller than the rest of the body paint. Polish these edges with the white polishing compound until the difference in shine in minimal, then give the whole area a once-over with the compound.

Follow with a good car wax.

The brush-on paint in the little bottle often doesn't carry any directions, but preparation should be essentially the same. It works well on very small nicks or scratches. But the brush tends to give you a rather bumpy, lumpy finished surface compared with the spray.

119 / How to thaw out that frozen car lock

There are days when you'd much rather not go in to work. But the day the locks on your car door freeze is always the day you have to be on time.

Some people still make the mistake of pouring a kettle of boiling water down the side of the car window and the door handle. This is bad for two reasons. For some reason, boiling water freezes again quite rapidly. And you can easily crack the window glass by putting it through such extremes of temperature.

The ice inside a lock is usually not thick. The best and fastest method for melting it is to heat your key with a cigarette lighter, then insert the key into the lock. (Wear gloves to keep from blistering your fingers.) It may not work at first, but repeat the process two or three times and the lock should turn.

Once you get the key into the lock, you can even leave it there and heat the exposed end of it briefly while it is in place. That way, it doesn't cool down between lighter and keyhole.

If you don't have a lighter or matches, another method is rubbing alcohol on the key or squirt a little shot of it into the keyhole. But don't put fire near the lock afterward.

There are products on the market, too, for unsticking and preventing frozen locks. Some are sprays and some are in squirt cans. They are available at lockshops and department stores and sometimes come in handy for another problem with cold car doors. After you unfreeze the lock and depress the latch button, the door often won't close again because the latch mechanism is frozen or stiff with cold.

Try spraying some of this thawing chemical on the moving parts of the latch on the face of the door edge. Also spray it as far into the door as you can through any crevices around the latch mechanism (see sketch).

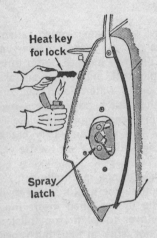

Heat key
for lock

Spray
latch

The only other alternative is closing the door as far as possible and running the car heater long enough to warm the whole door. Or, if the car is parked close enough to the house, put an extension cord on your hair dryer and haul it out to the car to blow on the door and latch for a while.

120 / How to change your car's license plates

The people who thought up using metal nuts and bolts for fastening license plates to cars were all graduates of the Marquis de Sade School of Human Relations.

They were the same people who dreamed up midwinter deadlines in some states for license plate changeovers.

There isn't much to be done about the deadlines, but fasteners have improved over the years.

Most passenger cars built within the past eight years have a small square plastic nut or "sleeve" that snaps into a square hole in the bumper or plate bracket (see Sketch A).

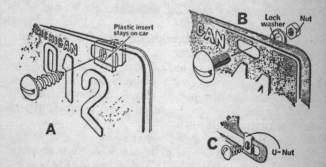

A slot-headed metal screw screws into the plastic nut, which is supposed to remain in place permanently.

There are two beauties to the plastic nut. First of all, it doesn't rust like the old kind used to do. Second, it stays put as you turn the screw. This means you don't need to reach around behind the license plate for any reason.

You approach the whole business straight from the front with a screwdriver. If broken or lost, plastic nuts can be bought for a few cents at auto dealerships.

If you have an older car, you may have one of two other systems. One is a metal bolt and free-spinning nut (see Sketch B). The other is a metal bolt and U-nut (see Sketch C).

A U-nut will not turn as you turn the screw. But a free-spinning nut will—which means you must reach behind the bumper or plate holder and wrestle the nut with an adjustable wrench or pliers. (To loosen, turn the bolt or screw counter-clockwise as you face the license plate. Hold the nut stationary or turn it clockwise.)

A rusted nut and bolt is almost impossible to remove whole. You can try putting a rust dissolver like penetrating oil (from hardware stores) on it. But you have to apply it where the nut joins the bolt; and this sometimes means crawling under the car to see what you are doing.

The alternative is a service station or garage, where they will cut the bolt loose.

Unfortunately, you usually cannot replace the old nut and bolt system with one of the newer plastic sleeves because the plastic gismo requires a specially shaped hole. You can, however, go to a brass nut and bolt, which will not rust.

There is no way to tell what system you have just by looking at the license plate, since both old and new methods use a metal, slot-headed screw. The easiest approach is to just try turning the screw with a screwdriver. If it comes right out, fine. If it doesn't, start looking for a rusted U-nut or a free-spinning nut behind the bumper.

Part VII:

Odds and Ends

121 / Diary eases housekeeping

Remember those emotion-packed early teen years when you kept a faithful diary of every throbbing experience?

Try keeping a diary now (with a more level-headed approach, of course). It can help you run your household almost like a business.

Buy a reasonably large, one-year diary that has whole pages for each day, plus extra memo pages in the back. Then record literally anything of importance that happens during a day.

Note when children or other family members see a doctor, what vaccinations were given, how long the vaccinations last before requiring boosters, etc.

Keep track of service or complaint calls, what time they were made and the person spoken to. It is impressive after the third call to straighten out a bill, to be able to write, "I first spoke to your manager, Mr. Blank at 10 a.m. Thursday, Dec. 14. My second call was two weeks later at . . ."

Record any bills received. Make another entry the day they are paid and mailed. The same for gifts received and thank-you notes sent.

When did the car last have a tune-up?

Note in advance the dates of all school and work vacations.

Keep track of annual store specials, like white sales. When your linens start wearing thin, you can check last year's diary to see how close the next sale is.

Jot down the date any magazine subscriptions or catalog items are first ordered.

It's even handy to note who comes to dinner when, and what is served. When they come again, you won't have to wonder if you're cooking them the same dinner.

Note bank account, credit card, driver's license and Social Security numbers on the diary's memo pages in the back for quick reference (or in case any card is lost).

Memo pages are also good for stockpiling summer vacation activity ideas. Come a rainy day, you won't be wondering what to do with the kids.

Of course, any financial transactions should be noted, whether performed by yourself or your spouse. Examples would be stock purchases, bank account transfers, loans.

Every household is run differently. With experience, you'll develop your own handy uses for a daily diary. The books make nice shower gifts for brides, too.

122 / Types of locks to slow down sly burglars

The totally safe apartment or the totally safe house does not exist. But the right kind of lock can slow a burglar down to the point where entering your home is not worth his effort.

The most common types of locks cost from about $12 to $60 or more. This does not include the cost of installation, which varies widely according to the situation.

A few common locks, with their advantages and disadvantages are:

Mortised spring latch—often provided as standard equipment in apartments. Mortised means it is in-

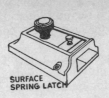

SPRING LATCH

SURFACE SPRING LATCH

serted in the closing edge of the door—like a regular door knob assembly. The latch or bolt is beveled (as in sketch) and is pulled back by the action of the door knob. A plastic credit card slipped into the door crack and pressed against the slant side of the bolt will open the door easily. Protection is minimal.

Surface spring latch—a heavier lock of the same type mounted on the surface of the door, often called a night latch. Most models have the same disadvantage as the mortised spring latch.

Combination spring latch-dead bolt—also seen often in apartments and houses, it looks like a plain spring latch except for the addition of a small bolt (as in sketch) that operates independently. Once the small bolt is depressed, the spring latch portion cannot be pushed in. But if the lock or door is badly fitted, the bolt is not effective and a credit card will open the door. The newest night latches come with this same combination and are somewhat more effective than the mortised type.

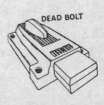

SPRING LATCH DEAD BOLT

DEAD BOLT

Simple dead bolt—any lock where the bolt portion is finished off square or flat. It does not slant or taper like a spring latch. Dead bolts come in various sizes;

some are mortised and some are mounted on the surface of the door and facing. No credit card or thin piece of metal will force them back. But if installed on a flimsy door, even a dead bolt can be "jimmied" by an expert.

Jimmy-proof dead bolt—Perhaps the safest common lock for householders, the bolt locks vertically into a special plate (as in sketch). It cannot be pried

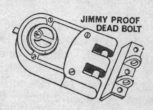

JIMMY PROOF
DEAD BOLT

open if made of good metal. The most expensive have an added feature that protects the lock if the cylinder (the part where the key goes) is pulled out by a burglar.

Single cylinder lock—any lock which operates with a key from the outside and a button or flip switch on the inside. If a door contains a window near the lock or has thin wood panels, a burglar can break the panel, reach inside and flip the lock open. If a burglar enters through a window, he can unlock a single cylinder lock from inside the house and carry anything out through the door.

Double cylinder lock—any lock which operates with a key from either outside or inside the home. It cancels the problems of a single cylinder lock. The only disadvantage is having to use a key coming and going.

Window locks—There are two basic types. One looks like the latch usually seen on wooden windows, but a key lock is part of the assembly. The other is a bolt mechanism that secures the lower sash to the upper sash (or else the window frame) in more than one position. It allows you to open the bottom sash

WINDOW LOCK

a few inches and then lock the window in place (see sketch).

Patio door locks—Patio sliding doors are often double-pane glass. They make a loud exploding noise when broken; so burglars prefer to slide the door if possible. Many patio doors are installed backward— with the sliding member on the outside. This will limit your choice of effective locks. But dead bolt locks are available to fasten the sliding door to the stable one or to the door frame. The safest are operated with a key or padlock.

A few general tips:

Elderly people who find it hard to grasp keys can have a large metal disk or washer soldered to the key as a "handle."

Remember, locks that keep people out can also keep people in during emergencies like fires. If you have double cylinder locks, keep an extra key within reach of children or elderly family members.

Choosing and installing your own locks is risky business if you own valuables. Consult a reputable locksmith.

123 / How to burglar-proof your home

A national magazine once estimated that a burglary occurs in the United States once every 12 seconds. There are all kinds of locks and security gadgets on the market—but common sense rules are just as important as hardware.

Single girls should use their initials (in place of first names) on mail boxes and in the telephone directory.

When moving into an apartment, ask if the locks were changed after the previous tenant moved. They should be.

Look for a place to live where the front and back doors are visible to neighbors.

Doors should have night chains plus a small window or one-way peep hole. Be wary of doors with large glass inserts; burglars can see through and break in quickly.

Check that all hinges are on the indoor side; if hinges are on the outside, an intruder can easily remove the pins.

Keep locks, storm windows or screens on all windows—even upstairs. If you put a metal grating or bars over lower windows, make sure the devices can be removed quickly in case of fire.

Demand good lighting and security measures in apartment building halls, laundry rooms and garages.

A telephone in the master bedroom is another good precaution.

Report to the apartment management or police any

wandering strangers or suspicious activity. Better to risk embarrassment than a break-in.

You can use small engraving tools for marking your Social Security number on valuables for quick identification of any recovered stolen property. Contact your local precinct station to find out whether they participate in such a program.

These are full-page advertisements that no one is at home at your place: Piles of mail and newspapers on the front porch, window shades pulled completely down during the day, an open garage containing no car, an unmowed lawn, unraked leaves, unshoveled walks, no lights at night. A helpful neighbor can solve most of these problems.

Do not leave the door open while working in the yard. Do not hide keys under the door mat, in the mail box or on top of the door frame.

Do not admit repairmen or salesmen without first seeing their credentials or sales permits.

Keep potential weapons such as knives, swords, guns or heavy fireplace equipment out of sight. A cornered thief may turn them against you.

Keep garage doors locked.

Never give your name and address to strangers. Never admit to a stranger on the phone that you are alone.

If you discover a burglary, do not explore the house or apartment. Back out quickly and call police from a neighbor's place.

Do not disturb any possible evidence or fingerprints before police arrive.

If you own a gun, see if it has been taken.

Do prosecute and testify against the burglar if he is caught. Failure to do so will simply free him for more raids.

124 / How to remove household uglies

Painting problems. They seem endless. You wouldn't think a simple wall could play so many dirty tricks.

Recurring spots, mildew, previous coatings can all cause headaches—not to mention backaches. So here are a few hints from a long-time professional in the field:

Spots—Blotches in a new paint job seem to be a particular problem in kitchens, where grease collects on the walls. Often the appearance or reappearance of a spot is followed later by pinpoint bubbles in the paint surface.

One possible cause of this could be a water leak from a nearby pipe or from a bathroom above. If this is the case, nothing short of having the water leak repaired will remedy the situation.

But let's suppose the mark is just a grease spot. Going over a wall with heavy duty detergent before painting doesn't always get it as clean as you might think. Kitchen grease is stubborn and sometimes requires paint thinner or turpentine as a remover.

Once the best possible cleaning job is done, however, one more precaution will keep any remaining grease from spotting your new paint job. That is application of an alcohol based primer-sealer to the wall. This primer-sealer is sometimes called stain kill; and that's exactly what it does. A thin coat of the same thing you plan to use as a finish coat will not do the same job.

Follow the primer-sealer with a coat of enamel undercoat (which is not the same thing as enamel or flat paint), then use the gloss or semigloss enamel that you want. (A "flat" or dull paint is not satisfactory in kitchens because it absorbs grease too readily.)

If you have already painted the whole room and just want to patch an area that keeps spotting, sand the area down and follow the above procedure in the limited space.

Mildew—You will think mildew is just a bit of dirt caught in the paint job until it starts spreading and looking worse with time. Mildew starts in a moist area, but once it takes hold it is quite stubborn and will persist after the moisture problem has disappeared.

Mildew is most commonly found where several layers of wallpaper have been painted over. It takes hold in the glue behind one of the layers of paper and works its way out from there.

The best procedure, although messy, is to remove all the layers of old wallpaper. Then wash the wall with a strong chlorine bleach and water solution to kill the mildew. Follow this with the alcohol based primer-sealer coat mentioned before and then apply the paint you want.

If there is no paper behind your new paint—just plaster—sand the affected area thoroughly, wash with chlorine bleach and water and do the primer-sealer and paint bit. This assumes that there is no chronic problem of a water leak behind that wall.

Previous coats—You can put oil paint over an old coat of latex paint. You can also put latex paint over an old coat of oil paint. Where most people run into trouble is trying to paint over a glossy surface like enamel or varnish or shellac without any special preparation. This is usually not satisfactory, regardless of whether the paint is oil or latex.

The gloss of the old coat of paint must be cut before a new coat will "take." The best method is to sand the old coat—a time-consuming but reliable way. You can also buy paint-on gloss cutters. But if you want to do things the way the professionals do, you will sand.

If you are putting a coat of enamel over a regular, flat finish paint, use a sealer-primer first. Otherwise, you may get an uneven surface where some of the enamel oil has been soaked up by the flat paint beneath.

125 / How to remove surface blemishes from sink

Aging bathtubs and sinks, like ageing people, often display various blotches, blemishes, and dark spots. With sinks and tubs these are usually caused by dripping faucets that leave rust marks and wear away the enamel. In some cases, blows have chipped the surface.

The first thing to do is fix the dripping faucet that's causing the trouble. But after that, you may want to spruce up the sink or tub.

Various cleaning agents can be used to try removing rust stains. Start with a bleach-action powdered cleanser. If that doesn't work, try a paste of cream of tartar and peroxide.

Another possibility is a 5 to 10 percent solution of phosphoric acid and water. This is available at well-stocked drugstores and surgical supply houses. They will probably wish to dilute it for you in the store, since the straight stuff is pretty caustic.

Some people decide to refinish the entire tub surface. This is not a job to be undertaken lightly. But if you decide to try it, the only product readily available to householders for the purpose is epoxy paint.

Epoxy paint is a very tough coating that is supposed to stick well to glass and similar surfaces. But there is no guarantee the paint will cling forever. Ask for a pure, rather than modified, epoxy paint.

Start by scouring the tub thoroughly and rinsing well. Then roughen the enamel surface by rubbing it with coarse, wet-or-dry sandpaper. Use the sandpaper wet to keep dust down. Rinse the tub two or three times. Dry it with a towel. There can be no oil, soap scum or cleanser grains left in it.

If there are chunks out of the enamel or porcelain, fill them with an epoxy putty. (Both the putty and the paint should be available at stores specializing in industrial paints.)

Any pure epoxy product involves mixing two agents which then harden by chemical reaction. Follow the mixing instructions to the letter as they appear on the product label.

Blend the putty with a putty knife on a piece of glass or metal, kneading it a bit with the knife. Then spread it into any cracks or chips in the tub surface. Allow it to harden for the prescribed time; then sand it for a smooth surface.

Clean the surface well again. Then you can paint.

Epoxy paint should not be thinned under normal circumstances. But you will need a special solvent for the clean-up later. Use a medium-grade, pure bristle brush and apply the paint in a moderate thickness. If you make too thick a layer the paint will sag as it dries. Better two thin coats than one thick one.

Two coats will suffice for most tubs or sinks. Concrete basement tubs may need three. Wait as long as the label says between coats. Epoxy paint begins hardening soon after it is mixed. So if you know you will be spreading the job over a couple of days it is better to buy two small batches of paint rather than one large one.

Most hardware stores carry small bottles of white paint advertised as a touch-up for enamel and porcelain. The product is often lacquer based. If you plan on doing a whole tub or sink with epoxy paint, do not use the lacquer paint beforehand. The two products are not compatible.

You can smear around with a damp rag on Venetian blinds for just so long. But you do end up with streaks and there comes a time when support tapes are graying and there's no alternative to a good wash job.

Washing a metal Venetian blind is like battling an aluminum octopus, but perseverance will triumph.

To remove the blinds, pull them up tight with the cord to the top of the window and lock them in that position. Then flip up the metal bands at each end of the top section (see sketch A), and slide the blind out.

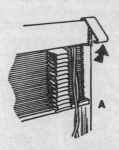

The bands may have been bent or painted over, so use a small screwdriver to save fingernails:

Remove the metal or plastic caps covering the ends of the bottom rail of the blind. This will allow water to drain out after washing.

Mix a strong detergent solution with reasonably hot water in the bathtub; make the solution a bit weaker if the blinds have painted wooden rails.

Hold the blind up over the tub and release the cord, allowing the blind to unfold as fas as it will go. Lower it into the tub and let it soak about 10 minutes. Poke the blind and stir it around occasionally to keep the slats from sticking together.

Then use a brush to go over all surfaces. A brush with a handle will keep your fingers out of the sharp slats as much as possible.

Empty the tub and lift the blind up through the shower spray to rinse. To avoid spraying the whole bathroom, you may want to be in the shower at this point. Roll the blind up loosely and lean it in a corner of the tub to drain.

When you rehang the blind, let it hang fully extended at the window until completely dry. Otherwise the tapes may shrink as they dry.

But before rehanging the blinds, check the cords for signs of fraying or an impending break. Restringing a Venetian blind from scratch is a tedious project and you can save yourself a lot of grief by doing the job before a break occurs. Here's how:

Suspend the full-length blind from some object like the shower curtain rod) with a couple of loops of twine around the ends of the top blind rail.

The new lift cord (the looped one) should be a single piece. Measure twice the length of the blind, once the width and add two yards. The tilt cord at the left hand side is usually about two yards long (or twice the distance the two ends hang when pulled even).

Remove the little metal clip usually found part way

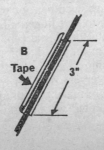

B
Tape
3"

up the looped rope "handle" of the blind. Then cut through the loop of the handle cord so that you have two ends hanging there.

Splice the two ends of the new lift cord to the two ends of the old lift cord by wrapping them with a three-inch piece of masking tape laid lengthwise. (See sketch B.)

The old rope is fastened to the bottom rail of the blind with concealed knots. To get at these knots, pry off the metal clips covering the bottom of the support tapes. (See sketch C.)

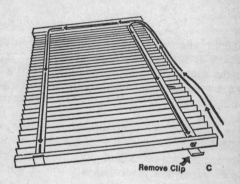

Remove Clip   C

Grasping the old cords near the point where they attach to the bottom rail, pull them gently, gradually drawing the new cord up through the top structure of the blind and down through the slats. Then simply remove the masking tape and fasten the new cord to the bottom rail with knots.

You may get some interference from the trip catch (the toothed thing that keeps the blind at the level you set), but you can keep the catch open with a little finesse (and maybe a bit of tape).

If the masking tape on the cord balks at going through crevices and pulleys, climb onto a stool and peek into the top part of the blind to see what's wrong and help the cord along.

To replace the shorter tilt cord, splice just one end of

the old cord to one end of the new cord and pull it through. The initial tug on the tilt cord will close the blind slats as far as they will go. But you can continue pulling on the cord without wrecking anything.

127 / How to remove candle wax

Candlelight dinners are very romantic—sometimes even essential during power outages.

But the atmosphere loses something when you discover the next morning that candle wax has globbed itself all over your tablecloth, good buffet or mantlepiece.

To remove candle wax from cloth, break as much of the cooled wax off the surface of the cloth as possible.

Place the stained portion of cloth between two pieces of blotter paper and press with a warm, dry iron (see

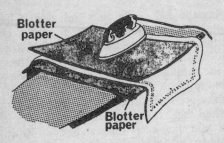

Blotter paper

Blotter paper

sketch). Thick paper toweling can substitute for blotter paper. Move the paper or use fresh pieces often as the wax is absorbed into it.

Another method, if the fabric will stand it, is to pour boiling water through the wax stain, melting it out.

The final traces of wax can often be removed with dry cleaning fluid. If you have used the boiling water treatment, let the fabric dry before applying the fluid.

Most modern furniture has a fairly rugged varnish finish. So candle wax itself should not wreak much havoc. Any damage is more likely to happen while you are trying to get the stuff off.

To make the job easier make sure the wax is as hard as possible. Run an ice cube over it. If it is soft you will just smear it around.

If there is a big pile of wax, you can scrape the worst of it away with a dull knife. But as you approach the surface of the table, it is better to switch instruments.

A popsicle stick (or a tongue depressor, if you happen to be a nurse) is a good choice. The wood is soft enough to minimize any possibility of scratching the table. Those stir sticks given out by paint stores are also useful.

You can make the scraper more effective by sanding the end to a spatula-like edge.

Remove the last traces of wax with a piece of clean cheese cloth and a couple drops of lighter fluid or cleaning fluid. Turn the cloth often and confine your efforts to the stained area.

Follow up with furniture polish or paste wax. Treatment of painted furniture is the same. But if the paint job in in poor condition, there may be no way to avoid damaging it slightly.

That coppertone, side-by-side refrigerator freezer you bought a couple of years ago probably looked pretty jazzy when it first arrived. But now it's got Snow White and her dwarfs on one door and Yogi Bear on the other one—all the result of free, stick-on decals and your six-year-old's enthusiasm.

Or maybe it's the hallway to the bedroom that has two pink snowflakes and a picture of the Flintstones on it.

Decals are among the hardest things in the world to remove. And manufacturers of the stick-on adornments admit as much with mingled embarrassment and pride.

"You see," says a man at one firm, "one of the claims to fame for any decal company is that their product stays on through any kind of abuse. And the longer you leave a decal, the harder it is to remove."

Decals fall into three general types—the partially clear kind that you soak in water first and then apply wet to the surface ("transfers"), the pressure-sensitive paper kind that you apply dry, and pressure-sensitive vinyl decals.

All three are made with a variety of glues and basic materials, according to which company puts them out. So it's almost impossible to come up with a removal method that will work with all of them. But there are a couple of things you can try.

The first step is to soak the decal for some time with water. You can either keep dousing it, or tape a sponge over it with masking tape and keep the sponge wet.

Some decals can then be scraped off with your thumb-nail or a wooden popsicle stick. Don't use anything sharp.

With a paper stick-on decal, you can at least scrape away the picture portion, leaving the glue behind. But water won't do much to a vinyl decal.

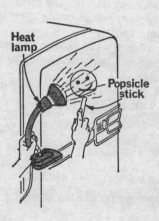

Body shops remove vinyl stick-ons with something like an extra-hot, hand-held hair dryer. The heat softens the adhesive; the vinyl is then peeled away leaving the glue behind. One man who works with one of these gadgets speculates that a home heating lamp, set close to the decal, might do the job.

But there is a percentage of risk in trying this. You could scorch or blister the paint with too much heat. Some decal adhesives become even more stubborn with application of heat. And you could also just melt the vinyl into a plastic mess on the wall or appliance.

If you do get a pressure-sensitive decal off—at least to the point of exposing the glue—the problem is to remove the glue without ruining the paint beneath it.

One possible remover is mineral spirits, available in most paint stores. This will usually not damage anything like an enamel surface and, used sparingly, should not do terrible damage to a good oil-base wall paint.

Another, stronger option is denatured alcohol—sold either as such or as "shellac thinner." Tested on one appliance door, the denatured alcohol did remove leftover glue from a stick-on picture after the front paper portion of the decal had been scraped away.

It did not seem to damage the enamel finish on the appliance. However, before trying it on your own, test an inconspicuous spot.

Denatured alcohol even worked on glossy enamel-painted kitchen walls fairly well (although it left dreadfully clean spots).

But it will definitely remove mat-finish paint, especially latex base.

129 / Easy way to clean copper and brass

Having personally tried to clean a blackened old copper boiler with a toothbrush, salt and vinegar, I have sworn off ever owning anything made of copper.

But copper and brass are both beautiful metals and can be maintained by persons with more patience.

Col. Edward R. Gilbert, chief conservator at Henry Ford Museum and Greenfield Village, has a special brew that he likes for copper, brass and pewter, too.

It's a mild polish designed to clean, yet preserve the patina on fine old pieces. But Gilbert says repeated applications will eventually clean even the grubby and neglected.

The formula is one part distilled water, one part denatured alcohol (also known as shellac thinner in paint stores), one half part concentrated ammonium hydroxide and enough gilder's whiting to form a thin paste.

The museum has access to more chemicals than most people do. Concentrated ammonium hydroxide is similar to, but much stronger than, household ammonia you can buy in the supermarket. It has to be bought in bulk from chemical supply houses.

Gilbert says you can approximate the formula by leaving out the distilled water and using one and one half parts household ammonia in place of the one half part concentrate.

Gilder's whiting is a powdered form of calcium carbonate or chalk. It, too, is hard to find. Since the main cleaning work is done by the ammonia and alcohol, you can probably substitute ground-up chalk or even flour for the gilder's whiting.

Another possibility would be rottenstone, although that would give you a slightly abrasive mixture.

Museum people apply the polish with cotton balls, throwing away each piece of cotton as it becomes blackened. Use what you wish, but do turn up a clean surface now and then. Rubbing with a blackened rag defeats the cleaning purpose.

The polish can also be used with fine steel wool, if you are trying to clean brass or copper that's covered with the crust of ages. But Gilbert won't give steel wool his official endorsement because it can scratch the metal's surface.

Wash the cleaned piece in mild detergent to remove traces of the polish; rinse with clear water; buff dry. Handle any display pieces with cheap cotton gloves to avoid leaving perspiration salts on the surface.

Some people spray copper and brass with lacquer after cleaning. Gilbert thinks this is a bad idea, though. There is usually one little spot that isn't covered.

Oxidation begins there and spreads. When it comes time to clean again, you have to remove the lacquer as well as the oxidation.

You can remove lacquer from a new copper or

brass item with lacquer thinner from the paint store. It won't ruin the metal finish.

As mentioned, the polish formula works well on pewter. But old pewter usually can't be shined enough to look like new. You don't want it to look new anyway.

And make sure to avoid serving food in very old pewter. Some pieces contain a high quantity of lead (a very dull finish is one indicator). Acid foods like those containing orange juice or tomato juice will form a poison on the lead. (Pewter bought in bridal stores these days contains little if any lead.)

130 / How to strip paint from wood floors

Why anyone would paint over a good hardwood floor is a mystery. But it is done often. If you move into or live now in a house with painted floors and want to get back down to the natural wood, you've got a real job in store.

It will be dirty, dusty knee-bruising work. But if you feel the result is worth it, keep a few pointers in mind:

You will, at some point, need to sand the floor. But if there are several layers of paint over the wood, it is best to strip the paint off chemically first. Trying to sand thick paint away will only gum up the sanding machine and frustrate you.

There are various preparations for stripping paint from floors. Some are relatively fast and expensive. Others are cheap and more work. Go to a good paint store and discuss the project with the salesman.

You choice of remover will be at least partly influenced by how many square feet you must cover. The square footage equals the length of the floor times its width.

Sanders can be rented. The type used for the large open spaces of the floor is usually a drum or belt sander. Belts or strips of sandpaper in different grades come with the sander. You'll want coarse, medium and fine grades. Tell the rental store man how many square feet to your floor, and have him show you how to change the sandpaper strips in the machine.

Rent a small disc (hand held) sander for doing the edges of the floor. Get three grades of paper for this, too.

Before sanding anything, search the entire floor for nails that stick up a fraction above the boards. Countersink any of these. (That means use a nail punch or another nail to drive the head of the offending nail down below the board surface.) Any protruding heads will rip up the sandpaper belt.

Close doors leading from the room. Open windows. Carefully pry up the quarter round molding around the edge of the room. Wear soft-soled shoes to keep from marring the floor.

The big floor sander is sort of like a small lawn mower, in that you walk behind it. And it can tear

Move in one
direction
with the grain

the floor up almost as much as a lawn mower would if you don't keep moving.

Start the sander with the machine tipped back a bit, then ease it down onto the floor when you're ready to start moving. Once you start moving, don't stop. Keep your pace even and sand with the grain of the floorboards. If you let the sander sit in one place, it will keep eating down into the floor. A few stops and the floor will look like a choppy lake.

Walk the length of the room. Then, instead of trying to turn around, simply walk backward with the sander—over the same strip, if it needs more sanding, or over the next few boards. Change to fresh sandpaper when one belt stops doing a good job. Also empty the dust bag when it gets about a third full.

The floor sander will leave about a 4-inch border around the edge of the room. This is where the hand-held disc sander comes in. (Also where the sore knees come in.) Even the disc sander won't reach completely into corners. You'll probably have to sand those by hand.

Vacuum the floor before you switch from coarse to medium paper. Vacuum again before sanding with fine grade.

What you do to the floor after sanding is entirely up to you and your paint store man. You can seal, fill, stain or not stain; or pick from final finishes, including shellac, varnish, polyurethane, penetrating finish and so on.

131 / The ups and downs of fixing limp shades

Someday a small child will get rolled up in a berserk window shade as it goes snapping and flapping wildly up out of reach. When that happens, of course, shades will be banned by an irate public.

But until then, they must be dealt with.

How does that plain-looking wooden roller know enough to send the shade up and down with a tug from the home owner?

The answer is—it isn't plain. It has a spring hidden inside.

When you pull the shade down, you wind the spring tighter—and vice versa.

One end of the shade roller has a little round pin sticking out from it. This pin does nothing but sit there in the supporting bracket, holding the shade in place. At the other end of the roller is a flat rotating pin, which fits a vertical slot in its supporting bracket. This pin is attached to the spring and does all the work.

The gismo that keeps the shade at the level you want and also lets you raise it) is a pawl and ratchet assembly in the same end of the roller as the flat pin (see sketch). The pawl and ratchet may be covered by a removable cap.

If a shade won't hold position after it's pulled down or is difficult to raise because it catches constantly on the way up, the pawl probably needs to be cleaned.

Remove the shade from its brackets, flat-pin end

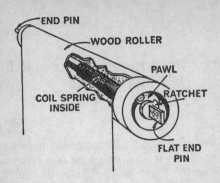

first, clean the pawl and ratchet thoroughly with a brush. (While fooling with pawl and ratchet you will undoubtedly release the spring tension. But just roll the shade tightly by hand, put it back in the brackets and adjust the tension from there.)

If the shade takes you along with it when you raise it, the spring is too tight and the tension needs to be adjusted.

To do this, raise the shade as high as it will go. Gently remove it from its brackets and unroll the shade by hand to about half the length of the window. Replace the partially unrolled shade in the brackets and check the tension. If still too tight, repeat the process. (The pawl and ratchet are supposed to behave themselves and stay locked in position during this process.)

If spring tension is too loose, the procedure is reversed: Pull the shade about two-thirds of the way down, remove it from the brackets and roll it up tightly by hand (see sketch). Replace the rolled-up shade in the brackets and test the tension. Repeat if necessary.

If it is impossible to create any tension at all, the spring may be broken and the shade should be replaced.

If a shade rolls up and down unevenly or wobbles

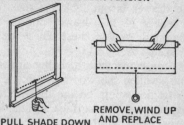

TO INCREASE ROLLER TENSION:

PULL SHADE DOWN   REMOVE, WIND UP AND REPLACE

a lot, the little round pin (the one that doesn't do anything) on the end of the roller may be bent. Straighten it with pliers and clean it with a small piece of sandpaper or steel wool.

NOTE: As with everything else, some manufacturers make their window shade rollers differently. These instructions cover those most commonly found in homes.

132 / Unsticking sticky drawers

Humid weather sometimes causes dresser drawers to stick. Nearly everyone has special little tricks for getting around this problem but here are a few hints on doing the job right.

Jiggling the drawer while pulling will usually remove it eventually. If this doesn't work, take out the drawers above and below the offending one (or in an extreme case, remove the back of the bureau) to look for obstructions.

Once the drawer is out look for signs of wear on the runner edges of the drawer and in the runner tracks inside the dresser or chest. These are the trouble spots. (See sketch A.)

The most common cause of balky drawers is moisture that has swollen the wood.

Sand the friction spots on the drawer runners with fine sandpaper until the surface is smooth and the drawer works well. Sand a little at a time, trying the drawer between sessions. If there are rough spots in the runner tracks in the chest, sand those smooth too.

Remove all traces of dust after sanding. The dust is another source of friction.

At this point, some people suggest shellacking the

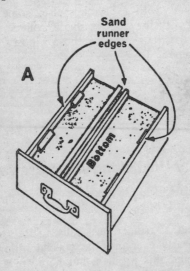

runner surfaces and the tracks. But several knowledgeable woodworkers say no. Shellack can sometimes become tacky or sticky; then you're right back where you started.

Instead, simply rub the runners and tracks with paraffin or an old candle. If you insist on using a bar of soap, use it dry. A dampened piece of soap adds more moisture to the wood.

There are silicone lubricating sprays on the market designed expressly for wood. They do an excellent

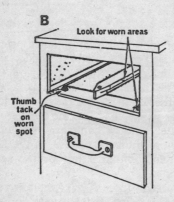

job (you'll pull the drawers clear out the first time you try it) but are rather expensive. The sprays do, however, last a long time.

Runner tracks in an old dresser sometimes get worn down so badly that the drawer, when closed, sits off center—either so high or so low that it actually exposes part of the drawer opening.

If caught in time, this situation can often be remedied by pushing thumb tacks into the bottom of the running tracks in the dresser. (See sketch B.)

The tacks not only build up the surface of the groove, but also protect it from further wear. The rounded heads of the tacks make a good running surface if pushed in straight.

The most common cause of jammed windows is a previous paint job that sealed the windows closed.

Be careful in prying at the sash or you will damage the wood. The best thing to use is a thin-bladed putty knife inserted between the sash and the window frame (as in sketch). Tap the handle of the putty knife moderately with a hammer, working your way around the entire frame. Don't forget the middle span where the top and bottom sashes meet (where the lock is usually located).

If this doesn't loosen the window sufficiently, there may be sticking paint spots on the outside

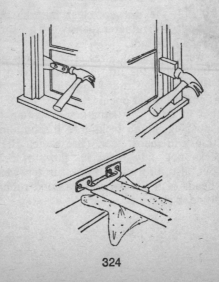

of the window or even in the channel. A ground-level window can be attacked with a putty knife from outdoors. But higher windows pose a problem. Try using a block of wood and a hammer to jar the window sash and break the paint seal. Wrap the end of the wood block with a piece of towel to avoid ruining the finish on the sash. Tap the end of the block smartly with a hammer. But don't get too carried away; you don't want to crack the glass by mistake.

After doing everything you can to loosen the window, try again to raise it. You can save yourself some back strain by using the principle of leverage. Prop a board under the handle on the window (as in sketch) and press down gradually on the end of the board. Be sure to pad the window sill with a towel to protect its finish.

Use common sense. If the window doesn't move after reasonable pressure, stop pushing. You can wreck the window sill or pop the handle off of the window sash by pushing too hard.

If you have not painted since the last time the window was opened, the sash or frame may simply be swollen with moisture. Pounding and prying won't help and may damage the wood. The best thing to do in this case is just live with the situation until a dry, windy day comes along.

Then open the window and coat the sliding channels with soap, paraffin or spray silicone lubricant. Don't use petroleum jelly; it collects dirt.

One last thought. Make sure you have removed any pieces of stick-on weather stripping around the edges of the window. These strips can sometimes keep the window from moving, depending on where you have placed them.

134 / How to fix stuck fireplace screen

Warm weather is a good time to do some repairs on that pesky fireplace screen that won't slide anymore.

Some screens are free-standing, some are built-in, some mesh panels are pulled to the center by hand, some operate with a pull chain like draperies. Glass screens are something else again and won't be treated here.

The screens that seem the most troublesome are those with pull chains. Nothing serious really. Just annoying.

Chains sometimes get tangled or clogged with carbon and oil deposits. The remedy is to take the whole screen down and give it a good, over-all cleaning.

Fireplace screen styles vary from maker to maker, but the instructions here should apply, with some modification, to most types.

Free-standing screens (those with a complete rectangular frame and little legs in front) are often not attached to the fireplace at all.

Built-in screens are usually flush with the face of the fireplace and have only a top bar instead of a full frame.

Most built-ins are attached with bolts to the "ceiling" of the fireplace cavity. Get down on the floor and look up behind the screen for a metal brace held to the brick of the fireplace with a bolt—one at each end of the screen. Unscrew the bolt with a wrench or screwdriver and slide the screen and its metal braces forward.

Carry the screen outside and prepare for a messy job. First step is to brush and wipe the entire length of the pull chain with cleaning fluid. Then lubricate it with spray silicone, graphite or light machine oil.

The accompanying sketch shows the pattern that most chains follow—a single length that runs through

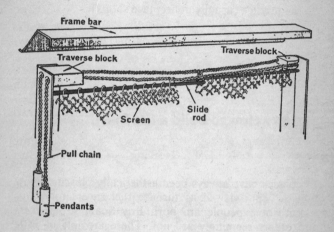

two traverse blocks (small braces), one at each end of the frame bar.

Each sliding mesh panel has a small wire circle at its top inside corner. This circle clips through one link in the pull chain (see sketch). The rest of the mesh panel is supported with wire loops over a support bar. Wipe the support bar with cleaning fluid.

You can replace a broken pull chain for about 25 cents a foot. The new chain should be 2½ times the length of the frame.

It's even easier to unclip the pendants at the end of the pull chain and just throw the chain away. Then fasten the pendants to the top inside corners of the mesh panels and operate the panels by hand.

You can rejuvenate mesh panels, unless they are warped and twisted. Put the screen on the ground and clean the panels with a stiff brush and a mild detergent solution.

Rinse with clear water and hang the screen in the sun to dry quickly. (If it's a rainy day, blow it with a hair dryer.)

Now spray the mesh with special paint that resists high temperature. Black, copper and brass sprays are on the market (usually at fireplace shops).

135 / How to build a fire in a fireplace

Fireplaces have always been esthetically pleasing. Now they're being viewed as furnace fuel savers too.

But some people are born Boy Scout fire makers and others seemingly are not. There are lots of little things to know about making a good wood fire. But only two principles are absolutely essential.

• A fire needs adequate air or ventilation in order to burn.

• A fire must have something to burn *up* to. It won't burn sideways.

This means you need three logs to make a fireplace blaze. But that comes later. The first step is to make sure the damper in the fireplace is open.

The damper is the little trap door in the chimney or flue that controls the flow of air up the flue. Some dampers are operated by turning a handle on the face of the fireplace. But most dampers are operated with pull chains, rods and-or other assorted mechanisms usually found immediately up from and inside the fireplace opening.

You don't need to get a face full looking up the

chimney to check the damper. Use a mirror instead. Holding it near the back of the fireplace you should be able to see a glimmer of daylight if the damper is open and no birds have established residence in the chimney.

Now check the bottom of the fireplace. Ideally, there should be some ashes in the bottom, but you'll have to gauge the correct amount by guess and by gosh. There should be enough to help hold the heat of the fire and keep the paper and kindling where you want it. But there should not be so many ashes that they crowd up against the fire and restrict the flow of air.

Build your fire well back in the fireplace. Too far to the front often means a room full of smoke.

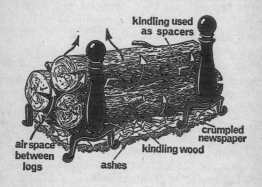

air space between logs / ashes / kindling wood / crumpled newspaper / kindling used as spacers

Some fireplaces contain a metal basket affair; others have andirons across which the logs are supposed to rest. Begin by placing a layer of wadded or twisted newspaper either in the basket or between the andirons.

Top the twisted paper with a layer of kindling. A mixed handful of wood ranging from ¼ inch to 1 inch in diameter is good. The idea is to put together things that burn at different rates so that everything doesn't go out at once.

On top of the paper and kindling place two medium logs. Don't snug the logs up against each other. Leave a couple inches of air between them.

The finishing touch is a final medium log on top of the two base logs. Without this top one, the two base logs will never burn the way you want them to because there is nothing to draw the fire up past them.

Turn the top log so that its bumps and knobs keep it from making airtight contact with the two bottom logs. If necessary, use a few pieces of kindling to prop the logs apart and allow for air circulation.

One last step. Twist a large sheet of newspaper into a torch. Light it and hold it inside the fireplace up toward the damper for a few seconds. This is to warm the air in the flue and start it moving upward. Unless you warm the air and get it moving, the newly lit fire will not burn properly and may smoke the room.

Now light the fire and enjoy.

A few extra comments are in order.

Do not use green wood. Always buy aged or cured firewood or, if you cut your own, let it sit for a year. Green wood not only doesn't burn well, it will mess up your damper and flue with a sticky substance in the smoke.

The average fireplace does not need—nor can it really handle—anything larger than a three log fire.

Always close the damper when the fireplace is not in use. Otherwise your home will lose heat through the flue.

136 / Some fire extinguisher facts

Every time the broiler flares up with grease from a steak, you think to yourself that you really ought to get a fire extinguisher.

What kind, what size, what chemical?

Fire departments aren't all that crazy about home fire extinguishers. But their objections center not so much on the devices as on the people who use them. People try to put out fires themselves before calling the fire department. (They should operate the other way around.)

There are lots of different kinds and styles in extinguishers, with more coming out on the market all the time. Here are some general guidelines to clear away the smoke:

Fires are split into four classifications, uniform across the country. Class A is burning wood, paper, cloth and other common rubbish. Class B is fire on top of liquids like gasoline, grease or oil. Class C is fire in a live electrical cord or circuit. Class D is burning metal, a type of fire rarely encountered by homeowners.

Never buy a fire extinguisher that lacks an Underwriters Laboratory (UL) label. As part of the UL label, you will see a rating code that reads something like 5B:C.

Translation: This extinguisher will handle five "units" of Class B fire and is also suitable for Class C fires. Don't worry about what a "unit" of fire is. It's just a testing term used by laboratories.

Just remember that for a kitchen, you should have at least a 4B:C extinguisher. A 5B:C is even better.

The normal Class A extinguisher is filled only with water under pressure. It works fine on Class A fires but cannot be used on Class B or Class C. (Water just spreads a grease fire out, making it worse. With an electrical fire, you run the risk of shock when you use water.)

Class B extinguishers are usually also rated for Class C fires. They are normally filled with either dry chemical or with carbon dioxide (CO_2) gas.

Plain "dry chemical" is basically baking soda under pressure. It is more effective than carbon dioxide (so comes in a smaller container), but leaves a powder that has to be cleaned up.

Carbon dioxide is less effective, but leaves no traces at all. It just disperses into the air after smothering the fire.

Neither plain dry chemical nor carbon dioxide extinguishers can be used on a Class A rubbish fire. They just blow it around.

There is such a thing as an all-purpose dry chemical extinguisher rated for all three fires—Classes A, B and C. An all-purpose dry is usually a bit more expensive though. And it's quite messy. The chemical is slightly sticky, and it gets even stickier as it strikes the heat. In addition, it cannot handle a deep-seated Class A fire because it does not penetrate as well as water does. (A typical UL rating for one of these might be 2A:4B:C.)

Know how to operate your fire extinguisher. Read the instructions right at the store. If you don't understand them, ask the salesman or take the device to your fire department and request an explanation.

One typical construction features a pin that must be pulled to release the extinguisher's handle. The instructions never say where the pin is.

It usually is a metal ring (like the pin on a hand grenade) held to the handle mechanism with a thin string of plastic or wire. The string is supposed to break as you yank the pin out (see sketch).

Don't panic and grip the extinguisher handle too hard while trying to pull the pin. You'll bind the pin in there for good.

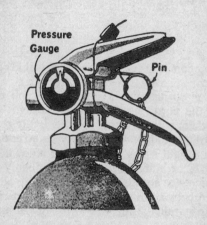

Also know how to check the pressure on your extinguisher. Many dry chemical types have a small pressure gauge located near the handle see sketch). Carbon dioxide extinguishers are usually weighed to determine their status. Look for a live weight and dead weight chart on the side of the device. You can use your home scales to weigh.

Obeserving common sense safety rules will keep Christmas merry.

Check all strings of Christmas lights and extension cords. If the cords show the slightest signs of wear, reinforce them with electrician's tape. Badly cracked or frayed cords should, of course, be replaced entirely.

Plug in a light string; tighten each bulb; then shake the string. If the bulbs flicker, there's probably a broken wire. Replace the string.

There are two kinds of light strings—parallel and series. In a parallel string, two wires run in and out of

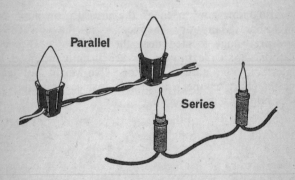

each bulb socket and each bulb functions independently. So if one bulb or socket is defective, it will be easy to spot.

In a series string, only one wire runs to and from

each bulb socket. And if one bulb is faulty, the whole string will fail to work.

If one bulb will not light, replace it. If it still won't light, look inside the bulb socket for signs of corroding. You can try scraping the inside of the socket clean with a screwdriver. But be sure to unplug the light string first. Replace any loose fittings or cracked plugs.

Do not plug Christmas lights into an already loaded circuit. Figure out how many watts each string of lights represents.

Indoor Christmas bulbs are usually seven watts each (so a string of twenty lights would represent 140 watts). Heavier outdoor lights are usually 10 watts each. Wattage is minimal for the tiny "Italian" lights, now popular.

Remember the fuse or circuit breaker controlling the Christmas tree outlet probably has other things on it like floor lamps and radios.

A 15-ampere fuse should carry no more than 1400 total watts. A 20-ampere fuse should carry no more than 1800 watts.

Outdoor lights should be just that—special oudoor lights with heavy duty, weather-proof sockets.

Outdoor connections between light strings and extension cords should be wrapped with plastic or tape to keep out moisture. If running an extension cord through a window, do not close the window on the cord. The window edge, especially if metal, can cut through the cord insulation exposing bare wire.

Cut a board to fill the space of the window opening; then drill a hole through the board for the cord. Drive nails or install bolt latches to secure the upper and lower window sashes against prowlers. (With a board inserted in the window you will not be able to lock it in the usual manner. The idea is to block movement of the sashes in some way.)

Do not put electric lights on a metal tree. Overlooked breaks in the wire insulation could bring "hot" wire in contact with the tree, resulting in a fire or shock.

Cut the base of a green tree at an angle, exposing as much of the trunk as possible to water. Water the tree regularly to keep it as moist as possible. Also keep the tree away from radiators and other heat sources.

138 / How to wrap a box securely for mailing

Every year, countless packages end up in "heartbreak corner" at the post office, unclaimed and unsent because of insufficient wrapping and labeling.

Individual postal clerks have the responsibility of deciding whether a particular package is sturdy and well wrapped enough to make it safely through the mail. They can and do refuse to accept flimsy packages, especially if the parcel is insured. So, here are a few recommendations from the postal service to help you avoid such a turnback.

Anything that can be damaged by mashing or puncturing should be packed in a plastic, wooden or sturdy corrugated cardboard box with generous cushioning around the item. Since many retail store boxes are rather lightweight, you'll probably have to search out supermarket boxes for at least some of your packages.

These often are without tops, but it is simple to cut such a box down and create new top flaps. Get a box considerably deeper or taller than the height of the item you're wrapping. You want to allow for at least 2 inches of cushioning top, bottom and all sides of the item. The sides of the box will also have to be folded over to form the new top.

Measure the height of the item to be packed and add at least 4 inches for the cushioning that will go under and over it. Make a pencil mark all the way around the box at that height (line A in the sketch). This will be your fold mark.

Now measure the width of the box opening (as shown in sketch) and divide by two. If, for instance,

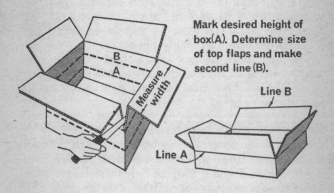

Mark desired height of box(A). Determine size of top flaps and make second line (B).

Line B

Measure width

Line A

the box opening is 20 inches, make another pencil mark all the way around the box 10 inches above the first pencil mark (line B in sketch).

Cut straight down each corner of the box just to line A. Then cut all the way around the box following line B. Fold each side along line A, and you have a box custom sized to fit whatever you're mailing.

Wadded newspapers are all right for cushioning material; but shredded newspaper is even better. It settles into all the nooks and crannies much better than whole sheets. It's important to support all interior surfaces of the box with cushioning to avoid weak spots.

Cushioning material tends to settle during mailing. So mound it up a bit higher than the opening of the box before securing the box flaps.

Do not use ordinary cellophane tape to secure the flaps. It breaks or turns loose too easily under pressure. Use some kind of tape that is reinforced with fiber. The postal system recommends nylon tape, that milky white kind that drives you crazy when you try to open a package.

Most people wrap a packed box in brown paper as a finishing step. But the post office actually prefers an unwrapped box. The wrapping paper sometimes tears away, taking the address with it.

So if you must paper a box, rig a back-up system by putting a slip of paper with the address inside the box before you seal it. Or write the address on the outside of the carton before wrapping it in paper.

The final touch on any carton should be a double wrap of string or cord around the length and width of the box. It is not required, but is strongly recommended as protection against the box coming open, should the tape give way. If a parcel is insured, the postal clerk will almost certainly insist on string.

No alcoholic beverages can be sent through the mail. If discovered, they will be confiscated. Highly flammable objects are also forbidden. If there is any doubt about the acceptability of an item, call the post office first to check.

139 / Reduce the moisture on that storm window

It is said that horses sweat, men perspire and women "glow."

What windows do is anybody's guess. But they do sometimes get drippy on the inside.

The moisture is condensation and is usually caused by a combination of factors: high indoor humidity, warm indoor temperature and cold outdoor temperature. When warm air hits a cold surface (in this case the glass), moisture always forms.

Storm windows help the situation because of their insulating properties. The storm window absorbs the main shock of the outside cold air. Then comes a pocket of air between windows. Then comes the main indoor window, which stays just cool instead of cold.

But occasionally, you will get condensation on an inside window even though storm windows are in place. This may be because the storm windows are loosely fitted and have warped, allowing too much cold air to flow past the storms and onto the interior windows.

Try caulking the edges of the storm windows or installing stick-on weather stripping. It should cut down the flow of cold air and reduce the condensation on your interior window.

There's another problem, encountered almost as

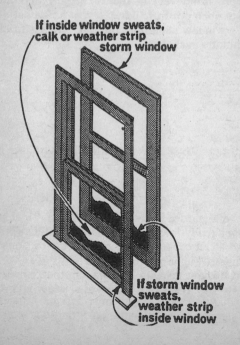

If inside window sweats, calk or weather strip storm window

If storm window sweats, weather strip inside window

often: Condensation may be appearing on the inside surface of your storm windows rather than household windows.

Again, the problem hinges on one of the windows being the wrong temperature. But in this case, the storms are probably tight enough.

It's your interior window that's leaking air. It is allowing too much heat from the house through to the storm window, creating another warm-air-cold-surface situation.

Install stick-on, removable weatherstripping along the edges of your interior window and condensation on the storm window should diminish.

Other tips to reduce condensation are:

Reduce operating time for humidifying devices in the home. Be sure attic ventilation louvers are open. Run bathroom and kitchen vent fans longer and more often.

If there is no vent in the kitchen, try not to boil liquids in open pots; use lids. No vent in the bathroom? Lower a window slightly at the top. Air out the house a few minutes each day.

140 / How to keep slippery rugs in place

It's a well-guarded secret that the song "Inchworm" was never really intended for the film "Hans Christian Anderson." It was written as an ode to someone's creeping area rug used atop a carpet.

What do you do with an area rug that buckles and inches its way from one end of the underlying carpet to the other?

One solution is to literally nail the thing down with

carpet tacks or small nails driven through the top rug, the carpet and into the wooden floor.

This will not necessarily damage the carpet, since the pile can be fluffed later to cover the little tack holes.

But it can't be done with an expensive area rug. The action of walking on the smaller rug will put enough stress on the tacks to eventually enlarge the holes in the top rug.

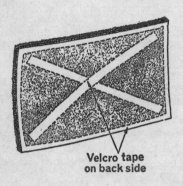

Velcro tape
on back side

The best alternative is Velcro tape—that prickly tape often used in sewing in place of snaps or buttons. Velcro doesn't cling to all types of carpet. So test a strip of it first.

If it clings fairly well, sew (or have a store sew) wide strips of the tape around the perimeter and across the middle of the area rug.

You can also glue the Velcro tape in place. But be careful. Too much glue can spill out around the edges of the tape and, if it remains tacky, stick to the carpet beneath.

A thin layer of nonskid padding bonded to the back of an area rug can also help sometimes. But bonded padding is not recommended for hand woven Oriental rugs. In such cases you may be able to simply lay the padding down between rug and carpet without fastening it.

If the under carpeting is in bad shape and you don't care what happens to it, try to find some giant snaps. Some automobile carpeting is fastened this way.

Fasten half of the snaps to the carpet with carpet tacks or small nails. Then stitch the top half of the snap to the bottom of the area rug.

Index

Learn to live with somebody... yourself.